The Family
Badin High Girls Soccer

Dirk Q. Allen

Design by Dale Schierholt
Dana Point, California

Cover photo: Terri Adams
Badin senior goaltender Michelle Hessling gives sophomore teammate
Malia Berkely a ride after the Rams won the 2013 Ohio Division girls
state soccer championship, downing Gates Mills Hawken 3-2 after a
penalty kick shootout at Columbus Crew Stadium on Nov. 8.

First published by Dog Ear Publishing
4010 W. 86th Street, Suite H
Indianapolis, IN 46268
www.dogearpublishing.net

ISBN: 978-145753-365-5

This paper is printed on acid free paper.
Printed in the United States of America

Pain is temporary ...
Victory is forever

The Badin High School girls soccer motto, 2013

Congratulations to the Badin High School girls soccer program and its ongoing dedication to excellence. In the 19 seasons covered by this book – 1995 through 2013 – the Rams have been to the state championship game eight times and captured titles in 2005 and 2013. That's a record of success that is well worth writing about!

"Coming together is a beginning, staying together is progress, and working together is success." – Henry Ford
2005 Badin High School girls soccer motto

"We played because we were talented, and we won because we became sisters."
Sammi Burton '07

Thank you to the JournalNews of Butler County, Ohio, for permission to reprint game stories from all eight state championship games in the final chapter of this book.

Thank you to Dale Schierholt – a graduate of Taft High School in Hamilton and Miami University in Oxford, now of Dana Point, Calif. – for another tremendous job making this book look good. It's starting to become habit forming!

Thank you, once again, to Megan Weddle and the talented staff at Dog Ear Publishing in Indianapolis, Ind., for handling all of the publication details.

Sophomore Taylor Smith leaps into the arms of teammate Malia Berkely following Badin's 2013 Division III state championship win, 3-2 in a penalty kick shootout over Gates Mills Hawken at Columbus Crew Stadium.
Photo by Terri Adams.

Contents

2013 Badin High School
Girls Soccer Roster

Head coach: Todd Berkely
Assistant coaches: Ken Murrell and Jeff Pohlman

00 – Nicole Visse	5-6 Fr.	G	St. John Dry Ridge
1 – Michelle Hessling	5-4 Sr.	G	Sacred Heart
2 – Brianna Scowden	5-5 Jr.	Def.	Sacred Heart
3 – Lydia Braun	5-4 Soph.	Mid.	Sacred Heart
4 – Morgan Langhammer	5-6 Jr.	Mid.	Lakota Plains
5 – Taylor Smith	5-4 Soph	Def.	Colerain Middle
6 – Madi Kah	5-8 Jr.	For.	Fairfield Middle
8 – Rachel Riley	5-10 Soph.	Mid.	St. John Dry Ridge
9 – Holly Reed	5-5 Sr.	Mid.	Lakota Plains
10 – Kate Bach	5-5 Jr.	Def.	St. Peter in Chains
11 – Annika Pater	5-8 Jr.	For.	St. Peter in Chains
12 – Maggie Adams	5-8 Sr.	Mid.	St. Peter in Chains
13 – Malia Berkely	5-7 Soph.	For.	Lakota Liberty
14 – Emily Henson	5-6 Jr.	Mid.	Lakota Plains
15 – Shelby Lamping	5-6 Soph.	Def.	Fairfield Middle
16 – Sam Lehker	5-1 Fr.	Mid.	Sacred Heart
17 – Amy Seither	5-2 Sr.	Mid.	Sacred Heart
18 – Gabby Geigle	5-7 Soph.	Def.	St. Peter in Chains
19 – Lindsey Brinck	5-7 Fr.	Mid.	Lakota Liberty
20 – Ali Kalberer	5-3 Soph.	Mid.	St. Ann
21 – Katie Pohlman	5-6 Soph.	Mid.	St. Peter in Chains
22 – Sabrina Bernardo	5-8 Fr.	For.	St. John Dry Ridge

Also, up from the reserve team for the tournament:
Sophomore Morgan Deitschel (Sacred Heart), sophomore Gaby Ems (Mother Teresa), sophomore Jessica Stein (St. Ann) and freshman Maddie Smith (Queen of Peace)

Maybe it started with Morgan Langhammer. Ok, that's not quite right because when it comes to Badin High School girls' soccer, "it" – high-profile success -- had begun years before and never really ended. The Rams were a premier small school program in Southwest Ohio with perfectly legitimate state title aspirations year-in and year-out.

But when Langhammer decided in the spring of 2011 that she would attend Badin, that was the first domino to fall, the first tumbler to click, the first ripple in a critical chain of events for the BHS girls soccer program. Langhammer's decision started a chain reaction that ended with the Division III state championship trophy presentation just after 2:30 p.m. on Friday, Nov. 8, 2013, at Crew Stadium in Columbus.

Terry Kah, whose daughter Madi subsequently starred for the Rams, puts the key date more accurately as the first Tuesday after the first Monday in November of 2010 … in this case, Nov. 2, Election Day, when a tax levy for the Lakota Local School District went down to defeat. With that setback, and the pending program cuts in their public district, the Langhammer family started thinking about Badin.

"Lakota had some spending problems, and basically the only thing I'm good at is soccer and the honors program," Langhammer recalled, "and both were in jeopardy at Lakota."

Still, Langhammer wasn't sure that she would be Badin-bound.

"I told my parents that I would take a look at Badin," she said. "They brought me to Open House and I was still in my soccer uniform (from a Sunday club game as an 8th grader). I was hot and tired and I didn't want to go to Open House that day.

"I was like, 'I'll go to Open House, but I'm not going to go to Badin!'" she added. "Then I looked around and I really liked it."

She liked it enough that she started encouraging her club soccer teammate and fellow 8th grader Madi Kah to join her at Badin. In fact, when Kah and her parents came to Badin for a tour in late spring, Langhammer took the morning off school to join them for the visit and lobby Madi to come wear Badin green.

"Madelyn and Morgan had played every game together their whole life," said Terry Kah, perhaps the only person in the world who refers to his daughter by her given name. "We're talking literally thousands of games. But Madelyn was excited to go to Fairfield and play for (girls soccer head coach) Heather Fischer."

Kah's older sister, Mallorie, had played volleyball for Fairfield High and was headed to Ball State University on a D-I volleyball scholarship. Terry Kah – the last name is pronounced Kay -- was well known in the community as the former general manager of WMOH radio, the AM radio outlet for local sports.

But two things had happened. Heather Fischer was no longer the girls soccer coach at Fairfield, and at an organizational meeting, new head coach Patrick O'Leary indicated that incoming freshmen did not need to attend varsity soccer tryouts.

"Madelyn said, 'I don't know if I could make the (varsity) team, but I think I should be given the chance,'" Terry Kah said of his daughter's reaction. "So she asked if she could go take a look at Badin. It wasn't just about soccer – we knew about Badin's reputation as an excellent school. It's been a wonderful situation for Madelyn."

"I was going to Fairfield, but they had changed coaches," Madi said. "Morgan was talking about how excited she was about going to Badin. So I decided to take a look, and I'm glad I did."

A year later, it was Langhammer and Kah together who not-so-subtly encouraged their club soccer teammate, one-year younger Lakota 8th grader Malia Berkely, to join them at Badin as well. They kept putting Badin Open House signs in her front yard!

If Malia does not enroll at Badin, it's hard to think that her father, Todd Berkely, would have had any interest in taking over the Badin girls' soccer program in the summer of 2013, when an unexpected head coaching vacancy occurred.

"When Morgan Langhammer determined that she would go to Badin – I give all the credit to that for state in 2013," Terry Kah says flatly.

Badin had won a previous girls soccer state title, in 2005. But that was a team that went wire-to-wire, opening the season ranked No. 1 in the state and ending the season with a thrilling 2-1 overtime Division II state championship triumph over Doylestown Chippewa.

This 2013 group did not even have a head coach as of May 2013.

All they really knew is that their current head coach was leaving the program. Yet all of them – Langhammer, Kah, Berkely and their remarkable teammates – were part of a memorable championship run just a few scant months later.

Todd Berkely is an excellent coach. But he is also relentlessly positive, and that was exactly what this talented group of girls needed. They needed someone to believe in them, so that they could believe in themselves.

When you're down 2-0 at halftime of the state title game, in a game where any and every goal is like gold, plenty of doubt could creep in. But these Rams were not doubters – they were believers. They believed in themselves and each other. They were winners, and they won. In fact, that's a statement that could be applied to the Badin girls soccer program for quite a few years now. They were winners, and they won. This is their story.

2013

Maggie Adams headed to the penalty kick line. It had come to this. After 23 games, after 30 minutes of overtime in the 2013 Division III Ohio girls' soccer state championship affair at Columbus Crew Stadium, it had come to this. Penalty kicks. Penalty kicks would decide the title between Badin and Gates Mills Hawken.

The score was 2-2 after Badin had made a dramatic recovery from a 2-0 halftime deficit, deadlocking the game with just more than six minutes remaining and keeping Hawken from scoring again for the final 87 minutes of regulation and OT.

In other words, after trailing 2-0, the Rams had played shutout soccer for what amounted to more than a full high school game to keep themselves in it.

No one necessarily expected Adams to be making that long opening walk. The senior co-captain was a solid midfielder, but she wasn't a scorer – and wouldn't you send your scorers to the line? Even her father, former Hamilton Taft basketball standout Tom Adams, was taken by surprise. He saw the pre-kick huddle, and figured his daughter was just trying to fire up her teammates.

"There's no strategy about penalty kicks," first-year Badin head coach Todd Berkely said. "The only strategy is, put it in the back of the net. It's all about technique, and Maggie's technique was fantastic."

Berkely had been thinking about penalty kicks for a couple of weeks.

"As you continue on in the tournament, the quality of the field keeps narrowing," he said. "The difference between the teams becomes less and less. We beat Fenwick in double overtime in the state semifinals. It only makes sense to think that the next game might go to penalty kicks."

Berkely knew full well that penalty kicks were not about the team's top scorers … they were about who felt comfortable enough to take them … and make them.

"It's all about getting your mind right," he said. "At one practice we simply asked the girls, OK, who wants to take a penalty kick? Who might be OK with taking a penalty kick? And who absolutely did not want to take a penalty kick? That narrowed the list."

In a penalty kick shootout, each team selects five players to kick in a rotation. If the score is still tied after the first five shooters, it goes to sudden death PKs – at which point the first team to score while the other team fails is the winner.

"We always wanted to practice penalty kicks, because they're fun to do," said sophomore Malia Berkely, the coach's daughter and, much to the ongoing delight of Badin soccer fans, an elite national player. "So now here we were, and the coach said, 'all right, who wants to take 'em?'"

Six girls were in the immediate mix … and four hands quickly went up – Adams, Berkely, junior Kate Bach and, interestingly enough, senior goalkeeper Michelle Hessling. Berkely looked at sophomore Gabby Geigle and put her in the initial rotation. Junior Brianna Scowden would be the first to kick in sudden death, if it came down to that.

"Then we had to decide what order," Malia Berkely said. "Maggie, being a great captain, she said she would go first. She knew we were all nervous. She had kept us calm all year, especially in that moment.

"She told us just to take a deep breath, that we would be fine, that we could do this," she added.

"I thought I would be a nervous wreck, but I had confidence that I'd make it," Adams said. "I was shaking, but I wasn't as nervous as I thought I'd be.

"On penalty kicks, you always do the same routine every time," she said. "I would look left and kick right. I would never look at the goalie at all. As I was walking to take the penalty kick, all I could think of was my mom because I knew she was having a panic attack."

Hawken had taken the first shot in the penalty kick portion, and their senior star Katherine Zalar, en route to Miami University, had already put the Hawks on top 1-0. It was her third goal of the afternoon.

"I have a lot of respect for that girl," BHS coach Berkely said of Zalar. "She was a classy player. She left quite an impression on me."

Badin's Hessling was disappointed.

"I barely got a hand on that first shot," she said. "That would have been the one that bothered me the most. I wanted some revenge on that girl. I knew where she was going. I got a hand on it, but I couldn't stop it."

Now, Adams was in the spotlight, 12 yards away, several thousand fans in rapt attention in the middle of a crisp early November afternoon.

"I said, when you make your shot, don't be too cocky about it," Hessling had advised her teammates in the pre-kick huddle. "And if you miss your shot, come back with your head held high."

Adams did not miss. She pounded it into the upper right corner, well clear of Hawken goaltender Hannah O'Day. She could breathe again. Her mother, Sharon, could breathe again. Badin fans could breathe again.

"A beautiful ball," Hessling marveled. "Almost unstoppable by any goalie."

It was 1-1 in penalty kicks. The Rams had lost two previous state title games on PKs. They were not planning to lose another one.

1995

When Badin High School defeated Finneytown 4-0 to open the 1995 girls soccer season, it was a nice win to kick off the campaign. At the time, no one would suspect that victory represented the opening salvo in two decades of high-profile success for the Rams.

Over the next 19 years, Badin would play for the Ohio state championship eight times, win it twice, reach the Sweet 16 via district title triumphs 11 times, and generally have fun playing great soccer.

Badin High School had opened in the fall of 1966, the merger of an all-boys Catholic high school, Hamilton Catholic, and an all-girls Catholic high school, Notre Dame. Hamilton is the county seat of Butler County in Southwest Ohio, a city of some 60,000 located about 45 minutes in either direction between Cincinnati and Dayton.

Badin is named in honor of Father Stephen T. Badin, the first priest ordained in the United States, known as the "Johnny Appleseed" of Catholicism in the Ohio Valley. His travels brought him to what is now Kentucky in 1793, at the age of 25, and his missionary efforts during the next 60 years took him throughout Ohio, Indiana, Michigan, Kentucky and Tennessee. The fact that he had a parish on Front Street in Hamilton late in life made him a logical choice for the new high school's namesake.

Badin passed away in 1853 and is buried at the University of Notre Dame. He is French, so his name, according to Badin's first principal, Father Francis Miller, was probably pronounced "Ba-dehn", with a hard French accent on the second syllable. But students were not going to attend "Ba-dehn" High School, Miller said. Neither were they going to attend "Bad-in" High School, so that would-be comedians could refer to it as a "bad" school.

So the founders deliberately called the new school on New London Road, on Hamilton's west side a bit more than a mile up from the Great Miami River, "Bay-din" ... even though at Notre Dame, it is pronounced "Bad-in", which confuses Badin High grads for a little while until they decide to, as one grad explained, "just go with it."

Enrollment has ebbed and flowed at Badin over the years, with as many as 1,100 students in the co-ed building in the early 1970s to as few as 450 students in 2011. The number stood at 520 and growing for 2013-14, with students coming from all over Butler County, northern Cincinnati and even southeast Indiana, nearly 25 zip codes represented in the school.

Badin girls soccer debuted in 1983 and was competitive right from the start under head coach Barb Fritz.

"It was a good program, that's the bottom line," nodded Sally Kocher, who oversaw girls sports at BHS for some four decades before her retirement at the conclusion of the 2013 school year. "We seem to attract good players because they want to play in a good program."

There were enough teams in the state that the Ohio High School Athletic Association added a girls soccer tournament to its annual championship calendar in 1985. Ohio boys had been playing a state soccer tournament since 1976 and split into two divisions in 1981.

One division in the girls ranks was a problem for a smaller school like Badin. Southwest Ohio is a hotbed for soccer in the Midwest – Cincinnati and St. Louis are two cities known for substantial soccer talent – and Badin had a hard time getting past talented big public schools like Fairfield and Lakota, where BHS soccer players suggested that they cut more athletes than Badin had try out.

In fact, Badin had never played for a district championship and a berth in the Sweet 16 in girls soccer when the state added a second tournament division for the sport in 1995. But that was one facet of a three-pronged confluence of events that helped catapult Badin into the headlines of the Ohio girls prep soccer ranks -- the second tournament division, a determined new coach, and a serendipitous influx of young talent who were all about success.

Craig Manahan, who had been an assistant for the Rams the previous year, stepped up as the head coach in 1995, and he was the right man to tackle the job. Though he was just five years out of high school, Manahan knew what he was doing, and did it well.

"Craig was very good for our team," said Stacey Kuhl, the Rams' captain and the only senior in the program that year. "He pushed us in a way we hadn't been pushed before, and he saw promise in our young players. He knew when to run a practice that mentally let us be kids and how to communicate with us about the next step and how to overcome it. We were a team with a united focus."

"Craig Manahan was young, but he was very mature," Kocher said. "He took charge – he was a take-charge kind of guy. He did very well, obviously."

Today, Manahan is the director of the Warren County Soccer Association, and in computer sales. Then, he was Badin's head coach for only four seasons. But what memorable seasons they were.

"I learned as much from those girls over the years as they learned from me," Manahan said. "I have never met a group of girls so hungry to give their all to something. It made me a better coach every day. You couldn't show up to practice with those girls and not give 100 percent."

Stacey Kuhl had thrown down the gauntlet early. Maybe she meant it, maybe it was a challenge, maybe it was just a throw-away line. Who knows at that age? Before the team's first scrimmage, she told her teammates that they had to go all the way and win state; they didn't have any other choice.

"As a kid, it must have been blind faith," recalled Kuhl, who said her teammates just laughed at the suggestion. "But that faith had a strong desire, and I know where that came from. Soccer had always been my life, but playing basketball the prior three years taught me about discipline and focus. Hard work wasn't enough. It had to be pointed.

"I remember losing a tournament game in basketball, and (assistant coach) Matt Thompson looked at us and said never forget that feeling of losing and going home. Never forget how the seniors must feel, unfinished. It was that feeling that made it impossible to lose in soccer my senior year. I wanted to go to state because I just didn't want to stop playing. The team was 'my girls', my family, my life. I couldn't imagine the magic ending."

Manahan had plenty of young talent at his disposal.

Sophomore Aimee Hurst was quick and capable and had been one of the leading scorers on the team as a freshman. Sophomore Megan McKnight was strong and relentless and would go on to be a Division I soccer All-American at the University of Dayton. Sophomore Lisa Sutton was tall and athletic and would later be named the conference Player of the Year for the College of Mount St. Joseph.

Freshman Shannon Kuhl, Stacey's younger sister, would subsequently be the leading scorer and an Academic All-American at the University of Dayton, after being co-valedictorian in the Class of 1999 at Badin.

Freshmen Shannon Roberto and Emily Giuliano would play Division I soccer at the University of North Carolina/Charlotte. Freshman Christina Hinkel was fast and skilled and, like the others, a four-year starter for the Rams.

Manahan, to his credit, knew what to do with all of that talent. "You have to give credit to the parents – those students were blessed with absolutely fantastic parents," Manahan said. "They were role models for their children, and they were role models for me as well. I really looked up to them as parents and as people," he said, alluding to people like Joe and Peggy Hurst, Kim and Karen McKnight, Ted and Diane Sutton, Tony and Peggy Roberto and Cathy Kuhl "at the risk of leaving some out."

Manahan also gave a nod to various club coaches who had readied the players for high school, "coaches like Steve Brown, Pat Myron and Randy Hurley were critical in teaching them the right foundation of skills at a young age to make them so successful later on."

Paying it forward, Manahan's varsity assistant, Jill Carter, started a club team that prepared a host of players who subsequently became the linchpins of Badin's soccer success a decade later, players like Kristina Anderson, Janie Jeffcoat, Ashley Roberto, Jenny Rosen and Lindsey Smith, players who became household names for Badin girls soccer in the mid-2000s.

Carter is now Dr. Jill Manahan, married to Craig and a successful family practitioner in Cincinnati. Manahan said he was blessed to have her as a "fiery assistant who would help drive the girls past their comfort zone and give them a solid female role model to look up to."

"We were really fortunate to have a coaching staff that cared about what we were doing off the field as much as what we were doing on the field," McKnight said. "You realize later how much they did to promote us to the next level. They played an important role in helping many of us achieve our dreams of playing soccer in college."

Manahan's first strategic step toward Badin girls soccer success was to make Hurst his goalkeeper. Hurst was a tremendous athlete, with great hands and quickness. She did not like playing goalie – in fact, she turned down a subsequent D-I scholarship opportunity to Western Michigan University, so much did she not like playing in goal – but she was a consummate team player, and if this was what the team needed, she was there.

"They needed someone in goal and Aimee was willing to do it," said her father, Joe, a 1971 Badin grad and an assistant coach on the club powerhouse, the Fairfield Fox, that had brought a number of those girls along. "The girls had grown up playing together and they really put their heart and soul into the game. It was neat watching their success."

"Aimee Hurst loved to play in the field, but she gave it up to become the best keeper I knew," said Stacey Kuhl. "We swore there were balls in the back of the net that her long arms pulled back before the referee could see them cross the line. She was amazing, and although any state run does not appear to be a sacrifice, she certainly sacrificed for our team."

Over the next three years, Manahan would frequently pull Hurst out of the goal during lopsided games and put her into the field, because that's where she wanted to play. Today, that might be unthinkable – to risk injury to the goalie of a state-caliber team.

Looking back on it, Manahan said, "As a matter of fact, I still would have put her out on the field, probably even *more* than I did back then. I understand that it's serious, and maybe I'm looking at today it from the perspective of my own kids. But at the end of the day, they were still kids, and needed to have fun. She didn't truly enjoy playing in the goal, even though she was very good at it."

When the Rams knocked off Roger Bacon, 2-0, in the 1995 district finals, it put them in the state Sweet 16 for the first time ever and now suddenly people were talking about girls soccer at Badin High School.

That unexpected surge in the BHS girls soccer program was being played out in front of a backdrop of Badin as a girls basketball powerhouse. The Rams had never won a girls state championship in any sport, but they were knocking at the door of a Division II state basketball title.

Badin girls basketball had reached the regionals ... the Sweet 16 ... in 1990, 1992, 1993 and 1994. In 1992 and '93, they were in the Elite 8. That 1993 team, in fact, had put together a perfect 20-0 regular season and was ranked No. 1 in Ohio, finishing 25-1 after bowing by one agonizing point in overtime to defending state champion Urbana in the Division II regional finals.

While Manahan was in his first season directing the girls soccer program, the girls basketball program had a new head coach as well. Dan Purcell, who'd had solid success with his prep alma mater, Talawanda High in Oxford, during six years from 1986-92, had been named head coach for the 1995-96 season, and his expectations were high.

"There was a lot of cooperation between the soccer and basketball programs as far as putting together summer workout dates that would not conflict with each other," Purcell said.

"When the soccer team got on a roll in the tournament, particularly that first year, that put us a little behind in basketball," Purcell said. "We had a lot of good basketball players on the soccer field. But you couldn't help but be impressed with the soccer success.

"I was disappointed for them that they didn't win a soccer championship," he added. "Obviously the girls were disappointed, too. But they never let that soccer disappointment carry over onto the basketball court.

"There are a lot of things that are similar from soccer to basketball, things like quickness and footwork," Purcell said. "The girls would move from one sport to the other without missing a beat. They weren't just excellent athletes -- they were winners, too."

Aimee Hurst was not just an outstanding goalie in soccer, but she was a terrific small forward in basketball as well. Joe Hurst told Purcell that he had the makings of a state champion on the hardwood.

"I just wondered if he realized how hard winning a state championship would be," Purcell said. "So many things have to go right."

Things went right for the Rams. Soccer players like Aimee Hurst, Megan McKnight, Lisa Sutton, Kerri Fiehrer, Shannon Kuhl, Christina Hinkel and others played key roles in maintaining the prominence of the girls basketball program.

The basketball Rams reached the Elite 8 in 1996 and 1997, then fought their way to the state championship Holy Grail in 1998, downing Dover 50-31 in the finals at Ohio State's St. John Arena. It was Badin's first girls state title. They finished as the state runner-up in 2000 and again in 2004, and in Purcell's 13 years as head girls basketball coach, went to the Sweet 16 nine times. Invariably, soccer players were valuable members of that success.

In 1995, those soccer players were just starting to flex their muscles and get some attention on the field.

"It wasn't an easy season," said Stacey Kuhl, who anchored the defense in front of Hurst as the sweeper. "I remember the lights at Garfield Stadium being turned off while I was still sitting in the goal, talking to Coach Manahan about the team, about why we didn't win, about how we could be better, about everything soccer. It was my whole life."

Manahan called Kuhl "one of my favorite players of all time. She is one of the most positive and determined leaders that I have ever met.

"One of the things we always did at practice was juggling, which is just a good way to improve basic touches on the soccer ball. Each practice Stacey would come up to me and say, 'Hey coach, I got so-and-so juggles in a row!' I would pick up the ball, juggle one or two more than the number that she got. She would frown for a second, and inevitably the next day she would come back and say that she had beaten that number.

"Some players would just accept that they couldn't do more, but not Stacey. She rose to each and every challenge that was put in front of her. She was the leader of that team her senior year, and we spent countless hours discussing the team and what it took to get to the state finals.

"To the younger players at the time, they just went out and played each game, not really understanding how great an achievement they were accomplishing. Stacey understood," Manahan said.

Manahan realized that to play in the big games, his team had to be physically and mentally stronger.

"We played a game in practice called WWF," Shannon Kuhl said. "There was a soccer ball involved, but basically we wrestled each other in a confined box, two at a time, while the rest of the team cheered. Craig did that to toughen us up."

Stacey gave credit to junior Erin Chafin, "who would use our warm-up time to knock us off the ball, telling us she was getting us ready for the Roger Bacon girls who were physical. If it wasn't for her, my sister would not have scored the winning goal in the district final. Shannon was hit in the back of the head while doing a head ball, and her head just focused on the ball and it went into the back of the net."

"Those girls, starting freshman year and going all the way through, were honestly and truly my best friends," Shannon Kuhl said. "We were like family. We had such a special bond on and off the field.

"I didn't know at the time how special and unique that was. I didn't know that most teams didn't have that – that they fought for playing time and held grudges," she added. "I never felt that at Badin. First string or second, we cheered each other on and wanted everyone to succeed for the good of the entire team. We had so much fun! It was like our own special club."

Badin had gone 10-5-1, but lost three of its last four regular season games before heading into '95 tournament play. That late stumble didn't distract the Rams from the task at hand.

Freshmen were playing a huge role – Amy Allen scored the lone goal in what Stacey Kuhl recalled as "a mud pit and pouring rain" to oust Kings 1-0 in the regional semifinals, then classmate Sarah Gaynor did the honors in a 1-0 triumph over Clermont Northeastern in the regional finals.

"I loved playing soccer, I just loved it," Megan McKnight said. "Craig wanted us to have fun and that was the biggest part of it. All he ever said to us was 'Just go out there and have fun', because we were talented, but at first we were so young. We just played with so much heart – that's how we were good, that's how we went to state.

"We had so much fun that first year because we were riding this huge wave of emotion and all this publicity and we really didn't know what to do with it," she said. "We were just having a good time."

That good time was taking Badin to the state semifinals – and its first, but certainly not last, tournament throw-down against Kettering Alter.

"Freshman year was so exciting," Christina Hinkel said. "We were like, 'State? What's that?'"

"No one expected us to be there and we just had so many people coming to our games, reporters coming to our practices every day," Aimee Hurst said. "We got so much publicity and it was just so neat because we had such a young team. We were just like, 'Gosh!'"

"We had a ton of players who had played for good club teams, and they were used to winning," Lisa Sutton said. "During the season, it wasn't like it was our goal to get to state, it was just to have fun and do well. So getting to state was not like something we'd ever planned or imagined. We worked hard – but not nearly as hard as we did (the next two years) when we really realized we had what it took to get to the top."

The high school soccer championships in Ohio are not like volleyball or basketball or baseball or softball, where teams typically play back-to-back dates at the same venue in the semifinals and finals. The soccer semifinals are at each end of the state, and then the winners come together a few days later for the weekend finals in Columbus.

Badin's first-ever date in the state soccer semifinals was at nearby North College Hill High, and the Rams did not disappoint their followers. In fact, the Rams have never disappointed their girls soccer followers in the state semifinals. The stadium site has changed, but the outcome has not – a perfect 8-0 record in the semis for Badin over the years.

On this night in early November 1995, it was a 2-0 blanking of Kettering Alter behind second half goals from Hinkel and Sutton, Amy Allen and Emily Gersbach notching assists.

"I remember we were just kind of screaming on the bus and we went out for warmups and Craig said, 'Time out!'" Stacey Kuhl said. "He just told us about Alter's all-state players and how good they were. He brought us back down to earth a little bit. He told us that we weren't the best players, that we had to play as a team.

"That year started something – it started a belief in those girls," Kuhl added. "Craig taught us to believe in each other so much that you could have put anyone out on the field for us and we knew they were going to do well. There was not one weak link on the whole team."

Shannon Kuhl recalled Stacey telling the seven freshman players on the team before the season that the Rams were "going to 'State'. And stupidly, I say that in the very nicest of terms, we believed her! We believed everything she told us and it worked out exactly how she said!"

Indeed, the Rams were state-bound, preparing to play a veteran Columbus St. Francis DeSales team that had lost just one game and had a familiar face in goal – talented 6-foot-1 sophomore Mindy Hammond, who had backstopped a summer club squad that had derailed a Fairfield select team populated with numerous Badin players in the State Cup finals.

Badin was hoping to exact a measure of revenge – but in utterly frustrating and bizarre circumstances, couldn't make it happen.

Both teams showed up at Westerville High in suburban Columbus for the title tilt, originally scheduled for Saturday, Nov. 11, but there was no game to be played on this day. It was postponed. A wintry mix of rain, sleet and snow had left the field covered with water. John Dickerson, assistant commissioner for the OHSAA, pronounced the field unplayable.

It was déjà vu all over again for DeSales, 19-1-2, which had driven two hours north to face Chagrin Falls in Medina in the state semifinals earlier that week. They'd shown up, only to find out that Chagrin Falls couldn't make it because of the weather.

"I think it was a blessing we didn't play that day, because we were all so nervous," Stacey Kuhl said. "We were sitting on the bus and we couldn't move. Usually we were partying all the way to the games, but that day we were just so tense. We were trying to have fun, but we were just going crazy in our minds.

"I remember we stopped at a gas station to get some candy, and it was hailing out, and we just didn't want to play under those conditions. Our emotions were so high and our feelings were running wild – this was the state finals, we had no idea what to expect.

"So when it got called off, we got back on the bus and it was just like a huge weight had been lifted off our shoulders," Kuhl added. "We just took a deep breath and we all just kind of relaxed and started gabbing. We were talking about how badly we'd been treating our parents lately because we were so stressed out, it was seriously like a bundle of nerves in every household."

Two days later, Monday night, Badin was at it again – and as far as Badin players were concerned, the field conditions were no better than they had been on Saturday.

"We took that two-hour drive, we probably get there 90 minutes or less before the game, we're half asleep – you don't think about that stuff being hard on you, but here's DeSales, they're probably 20 minutes from home, they're well rested," Lisa Sutton said. "And the field was terrible. It was muddy, rainy, icy, sleety; it had snowed. The conditions for that game were absolutely terrible. It kind of stinks to have to play that kind of (important) game under those conditions."

But play they did – and while the Badin girls came up as 2nd best in the end, they still hold their heads up high – understandably so -- over this particular game.

No one scored, and though DeSales controlled the action, they could not put the ball in the net. It was 0-0 at halftime. It was 0-0 at the end of regulation … and again in overtime … and again after the second overtime. No one scored.

"We were undefeated and unscored upon, all the way through the state tournament, through the state finals, through the overtimes as well," Shannon Kuhl pointed out. Badin played seven tournament games in 1995, and goaltender Aimee Hurst and her defensive mates never allowed a goal.

"Aimee hated playing in the goal – she called it 'her dungeon'," Kuhl added. "But she was so good at it and did it every game for us. She was like a brick wall!"

And so the match had gone to penalty kicks, the five player rotation … with sudden death penalty kicks for good measure if no winner had been established.

No winner was established.

"When it comes to shootouts, it comes to luck," Manahan said simply. As many soccer aficionados point out, soccer is a team game … but penalty kicks turn it into an individual sport. Alas, the game must end somehow.

On this night, it did not end in the regular penalty kick rotation. It was 2-2 early, after Shannon Kuhl and Megan McKnight matched opening PK makes by DeSales' Melissa Fox and Elise Berry.

"That was just a tremendous amount of pressure," McKnight said. "That was the longest walk I have ever walked in my entire life. From midfield to the penalty spot could have been the longest walk ever."

With DeSales on top 3-2, the Stallions could have won it outright. But Hurst stepped up big to block the shot by Julie Fox, and now Badin had the opportunity to force a sudden death shootout if the Rams could score on their fifth kick.

That kick rested on the foot, and the mental self-confidence, of senior captain Stacey Kuhl.

"When we set the order of penalty kicks, I told Craig I wanted to go last," she said. "He said, 'Are you sure you can handle that?' And I said I wouldn't put that pressure on anyone else on the team – but I want it."

She pounded it home, and the match was tied.

"I still don't feel like we lost that game," Kuhl said. "You never play 100 minutes of scoreless soccer, then lose in the overtime shootout and all of the sudden you're told you're second place in the whole state. That just doesn't happen."

Somewhere in Badin's vast amount of athletic hardware, there is a second place trophy from Division II Ohio girls soccer in 1995.

Now it was sudden death (the term "sudden victory" has never quite caught on, has it?) and DeSales' Mindy Hammond – who would later sign to play basketball at the University of Cincinnati – pulled off one of those clutch "doubles" that earn goalkeepers well deserved accolades.

She went from goalie to shooter, and pounded a laser into the left corner of Badin's net. Then, settling herself, she went back between the pipes … and just got her fingertips on the tying effort by Badin junior Erin Kraft. It deflected wide.

"I thought it was going in, but it bounced out luckily," Hammond said of Kraft's attempt.

DeSales was the 1995 D-II state champion.

"Losing in a shootout is the worst way to lose," said Lisa Sutton, who'd had her PK saved by Hammond in the round of five. "You replay that and you just think, 'Why couldn't we have put a goal in before?' Penalty shots – everyone says that's the easiest shot to make, yet everyone says that's the hardest one to make, too. There's so much pressure and so much tension on the shot."

"It's so exciting as a parent, watching your kid get to state, watching all of the girls you have coached over the years come up and do so well," Joe Hurst said. "Especially that first championship game, that first game was unbelievable. It was cold and snowy … the Hammond girl was a great player. That's my all-time favorite soccer game."

The Rams were devastated – but in fact, they were the first team to play in a girls state championship game for Badin.

"My senior year of soccer was everything I wanted it to be," Stacey Kuhl said. "It was the longest season possible. I loved every member of the team, and those are not just words.

"When I look back, losing in the state final was not devastating. Ending the season is what tore my heart at the seams," she added. "We experienced bliss, and I did not want that to end. I recall in a fog some of the newspaper articles and quotes. I have them stashed away. I know we had a lot of attention paid to us.

"But what I recall most are the lockerroom talks, praying to God during the National Anthem and promising to play with everything He gave me to keep the ball out of our net if He would just help one of us put the ball in theirs. I remember watching the minutes turn into seconds on the scoreboard and diving into my sister's arms after the games. I remember people coming to watch soccer who had never been to a game.

"And I remember sliding in the mud, feeling the cold air on my bare legs, just living in those moments where my heaven consisted of a green haven between four white lines," Kuhl said.

If someone found that state runner-up trophy, it might have a slight scratch on it, or a nick where the figurine stands on top.

"We got home at 2 or 3 in the morning, and I had been entrusted to take the trophy into school the next morning," Kuhl recalled. "I took it out of my trunk, and our driveway is on a slant, so it fell over and broke. I was like, I don't even care. They were able to get it fixed, so it was no big deal. But that loss was so depleting, of energy, of emotions, of everything."

That loss was also motivation for the following season, when

Badin would have nearly its entire team back – Stacey Kuhl had been the only senior – and once again have the opportunity to make some serious noise in the tournament.

"That next year, everyone had matured one more level, we were getting bigger, we weren't always the smallest team out there anymore," Sutton said. "We did a really good job that season. Practice picked up a lot and things got more serious. Getting back to state was really our goal that year."

Aimee Hurst had felt the same way.

"No one thought we'd be here. I didn't think we'd be here," she told the JournalNews after the 1995 championship game. "It's a good feeling to be here, but now it's not so good. We'll come back next year and we'll win it all."

Sutton stepped in at sweeper for the departed Kuhl – who was now playing for Xavier University -- and joined with Shannon Roberto and Emily Giuliano as an excellent defensive trio. Taking care of business at the scoring end of the field were senior Gina Andriacco, sophomore Shannon Kuhl and freshman Kerri Fiehrer.

Fiehrer, also an excellent basketball player, would go on to start every basketball game during a four-year Division I career at the University of Troy (Ala.).

It all added up to a 10-2-3 regular season, and when the Rams dominated Mariemont by a whopping 40-9 in shots, that added up to a 3-0 victory in the regional championship game at Amelia and another trip to the state semifinals.

"To get this far again is really great," Sutton said. "It's hard to do this twice in a row, especially in our situation. We're the top dogs now, and everybody's gunning for us."

The Andriacco sisters, senior Gina and freshman Lindsay, scored in the first half to make it 2-0, and when Shannon Kuhl put one away early in the second half, the Rams were home free.

"I think winning the regional title is exciting within itself," Kuhl said. "But state is what we really want. That's what we've been thinking about this season."

Manahan said he wasn't taking a "championship or bust" mentality in the postseason.

"I can't put that pressure on 'em," he said. "Don't get me wrong – I want to win the state title. But what I really want is their best."

They'd need that in the state semifinals against the No. 1-ranked Division II team in the state, unbeaten and untied Bellbrook, 21-0-0.

"On paper, if you look at the poll and their record, we are the underdog," Manahan said. "But if you look at Badin and the teams we've played … I don't feel like an underdog. … We know Bellbrook is (unbeaten), but we feel like we're a better team, the best team in the state."

Manahan had put his finger on one thing that made Badin a force to be reckoned with in many sports – the schedule. Playing in a skilled Catholic school league got the Rams ready. Playing a number of Division I teams, and then playing in the Division II tournament, helped prepare the Rams for post-season success. In some situations, the regular season was almost a shakedown cruise for the tournament. Yes, Badin always wanted to have a strong season … but it also wanted to be set for the post-season.

"There's never been a girls team at Badin to win a state championship," Manahan said. "We want that state title. (The girls have) worked hard and they deserve it."

Bellbrook wasn't going to get in the way. Battle-tested by the much tougher Girls Greater Cincinnati League schedule, Badin dominated the game en route to a 4-0 state semifinal verdict at North College Hill.

"We knew if we wanted to be No. 1, this is the team we had to beat," Sutton said. "For us to make (the state finals) two years in a row is something you dream of."

Sutton helped make those dreams a reality, scoring two goals for Badin on headers off corner kicks. The sweeper was typically brought up front for those plays, and teams ignored her size (5-foot-10) at their peril. Her goal at 28:26 of the first half gave Badin the lead, and her goal with 2:24 remaining in the game finished off the win.

Two other first half goals by the Rams had taken Bellbrook out of the game. Erin Chafin tallied on an assist from Amy Allen to make it 2-0, and it was 3-0 at the half when Megan McKnight marked on a free kick following a Bellbrook handball.

"We were controlling the ball, controlling the tempo," Manahan said. "Bellbrook may have a good team, but we came out in both halves and never gave them a chance."

It put the Rams back in the state finals at a new site against a new team. Badin was set to play Chagrin Falls at Scioto High in Dublin, another Columbus suburb. Chagrin Falls had dethroned last year's state champions, Columbus DeSales, in a semifinal shootout – and thus avenged its own setback to DeSales in the 1995 state semifinals.

"Every day I look at the banner at school that says 'state finalist'," Aimee Hurst said. "I'm not going to stop until it says 'state championship'. ... No one wants the state title like we do."

Hurst noted that the Rams get long-sleeved soccer warm-up shirts every year. "This year they say, 'This is the team. Now is the time'."

She looked back at the sudden death shootout setback from 1995 and added, "I felt horrible. I felt like it was my fault. I was scared to face my friends because of what they'd think of me."

"I just remember the overtime. I wish we could have kept playing until someone scored," Shannon Roberto said. "That was awful. I don't ever want to feel that again."

"We rode a wave of emotions to the (1995) state final," Manahan said. "We knew we were good enough just to be there, and that was very satisfying. But we haven't forgotten what it was like to lose. Just being in this game brings back those memories.

"We don't want second place," he added. "We know what second place is like. ... The only way to get rid of (last year's) feelings is to win the state final and replace those bad feelings."

Chagrin Falls looked like a mirror image of the Badin squad from a year ago – with just three seniors, making its first appearance at state, and having been unscored upon in the tournament. The Tigers were 20-1-2 overall and had dominated opponents all year – outscoring them 130-13 overall, 51-1 in the post-season.

"That last game (in 1995) was enough motivation for this year," Hurst told the JournalNews. "I don't think there's any team in the state that can beat us this time."

Unfortunately for the Rams, there was one team: Chagrin Falls, in a game that still leaves a bitter aftertaste in the mouths of Badin players.

"Chagrined" read the headline in the JournalNews after the Rams absorbed a 1-0 defeat, the Tigers scoring a breakaway goal late in the first half, while junior All-Ohio goalkeeper Katie Carson kept Badin off of her doorstep all afternoon.

"After the game, we just sat there and cried," senior Gina Andriacco told the JN. "Then we saw them cheering, and we cried again, because that was supposed to be us celebrating."

"We should have beat them 8-0," McKnight said. "There's no way. They got across midfield once and somehow put the ball in the net. That is by far the most frustrating game. The hardest thing about it is, if we score first, it's 8-0."

Badin outshot Chagrin Falls 10-1 in the first half, and it was a McKnight attempt with 23 minutes remaining in the half that still stings.

Her direct kick from the left side hit the left post, spun all the way down the goal line, hit the right post, then bounced free. With Badin players momentarily frozen by what they expected to be a goal, the Tigers cleared the ball away.

According to McKnight, there is film that shows the ball crossing the line on its spin between the posts, but the referees missed it. "I'm still mad," she lamented. "Granted, someone should have been there to put it away, but they weren't."

"What can you say? We dominated for 38 minutes, they had one shot in the first half, they scored and we didn't," Manahan said. "I'm feeling frustration, disappointment. We were the better team here today. To work this hard and come up with second place again, it's hard."

With 1:33 left in the first half, Chagrin Falls took advantage of a Badin defensive breakdown to score. The Rams were pushing up offensively when Chagrin chipped the ball up the sideline and created a two-on-one break.

Hurst was caught in no-man's land when Jenny Freshman, on the right side, sent a crossfield pass to Trish Kruse by the left post. Kruse scored easily – and the Tigers made that lone goal stand up for the rest of the game.

"We needed to be prepared," for when the Rams mounted an attack, Manahan said. "We weren't ready for them to come down the field and score. We were in shock."

"That was the year we should have done it," Lisa Sutton said. "We should have killed that team. There was a lot of tension between our teammates during that game. People got really frustrated with each other. It doesn't help when you're behind. Everybody kind of pushed back a gear instead of going up."

"It happened again," a downcast Hurst said afterwards. "I think everybody played with all their heart. We just didn't get it done."

The Rams would run into Chagrin Falls again, not on the soccer field, not even as competitors. But when Badin was playing for the Division II state championship in girls basketball in March of 1998, with soccer girls like Hurst, McKnight and Sutton leading the way on the hardwood, there was Chagrin Falls, playing for the Division III crown, leaving the practice gym at Capital University just as Badin was walking in.

Both teams captured titles that weekend, and Chagrin Falls head coach Frank Phillips called the Tigers "blessed" to have senior Katie Carson on their side – during her high school career, she made nine, count 'em, nine trips to state in various sports. A year earlier, her prowess in goal had helped push the Tigers over the top.

But as far as Badin is concerned, it was one of those games where the better team definitely did not win. The Rams, 15-3-3, had allowed just eight goals all year – but one goal too many in the championship game.

Yet the reality was that Badin had every reason to anticipate another big run through the tournament in the fall of 1997. The names were virtually the same – Aimee Hurst in goal, Lisa Sutton, Emily Giuliano and Shannon Roberto spearheading the defense; Shannon Kuhl, Megan McKnight and Kerri Fiehrer on the attack.

"Let the pretending end and the contending begin" is the way the JournalNews reported it after Badin won its third straight regional title, 3-1, over McNicholas at Amelia High.

"They were really good," Joe Hurst said of the Rams. "They had to be to get to state three times. They played a lot of strong teams, and they kept winning.

"The girls were great athletes – they could have played any sport. You name it, they could have played it and been good at it," he added. "They had a lot of expectations, but they lived up to them. When they went on the field, they expected to win. They had no doubts. And if they lost, they'd shake hands and say, 'We'll get 'em next time.'"

"Those teams in the mid-1990s – as a unit they were so cohesive," Sally Kocher said. "If one player had a bad game, it didn't matter because someone else was there to pick up the slack."

The '97 girls had knocked off a Murderer's Row of top teams in Greater Cincinnati to finish the regular season 12-1-3, then rolled through the first five games of the tournament outscoring foes 20-1, that McNick goal the lone postseason tally allowed to date.

Shannon Kuhl scored twice in the first 11 minutes of the verdict over McNicholas, then a textbook header by Kerri Fiehrer, off a free kick by Emily Giuliano, made it 3-0 at the half. Game over.

"Team unity is a very big strength of ours," Manahan said. "We're a team all the way around, and it comes from the leadership of our seniors. Our unity has had a chance to mature and grow."

Those five seniors included Hurst, McKnight, Sutton, Emily Gersbach and Jenny Fiehrer. Sutton was named the Player of the Year in the Grey Division of the GGCL.

"We've made it to state two years in a row and now we're on our way back and that's quite an accomplishment," McKnight said. "I'll always be proud of what we've had, and we've accomplished some really great things and gotten everywhere we've wanted to be.

"But we haven't quite finished it yet," she said.

For the second time in three years, it would be Badin vs. Kettering Alter in the state semifinals at North College Hill. Badin and Alter would soon face off in annual Catholic league battles, but they weren't there yet. The powerful Alter contingent was 19-2-0 and featured one of the top players in the state, junior Missy Gregg, who'd scored 40 goals on the year.

She hadn't gotten one in the first game of the year, when Badin downed the Knights, 1-0. And she wouldn't get one this time, either, in a 2-0 Ram victory that BHS players refer to as the Night the Rams Turned Out the Lights on the Knights.

"That's my favorite memory from that year – it's just ingrained in my mind," Shannon Kuhl said with a knowing smile.

Badin parents had slipped into Badin and put signs all over the school saying, "Turn Out the Lights on the Knights!" They didn't expect it to really happen … but with Alter attacking hard in the first half, the lights at NCH suddenly went out for 17 minutes.

"They were pounding us," Kuhl recalled. "And then the lights mysteriously went out. We were able to huddle up and decide that Fate had us in her hands!"

Kuhl subsequently played college soccer at the University of Dayton with a number of Alter players who were on the field that evening. "They became some of my closest friends and teammates at UD," Kuhl said, "and they certainly believed there was foul play at that game!"

McKnight enjoys similar friendships. "I didn't realize it at the time, and to this day it still makes me laugh," she said, "but I was playing alongside and against some of my future college teammates – even roommates! Who knew this sport would bring such lasting friendships? Some of them started at the age of 10 and are still going strong. I was so fortunate to play with some amazingly talented ladies who I am still proud to call friends."

Alter outshot Badin 29-12 for the contest, and Hurst was forced to make 16 saves. The BHS defense was up to the task, though, as the Rams played their way into a third straight state championship game.

"They seemed to be in our end most of both halves," Manahan said. "I just thought we did what we do best, and that's play good defense. At this level of play, defense is what wins championships. … Our defense played a great game tonight."

Almost immediately after the power came back on in the first half, a McKnight pass found freshman Angela Vilkoski splitting a pair of defenders for a breakaway goal. That made it 1-0 at halftime, and the Rams got another opportunity early in the second half on a tripping call. Giuliano came up to take the free kick, and ripped it into the top of the net.

Though Alter pelted Hurst with shot after shot, nothing found its way into the net. The Rams prevailed 2-0 ... and earned a third straight bid for the championship ring. There was no foul play with the lights – just great Badin defense on the field.

That championship bid would come against a familiar foe – Columbus DeSales, unbeaten, No. 1 in the state with a 22-0-0 record for new head coach Eric Ekis. Senior Mindy Hammond, who was making her swan song in the nets for the Stallions, had turned in another dominant season. She'd registered 19 shutouts and allowed just two goals on the year.

"(Alter) only had three losses this season, one by DeSales and two by us," Manahan noted on the eve of the game. "We think we've got a solid game plan, and if our defense plays as tough as they have all season, we've got a shot."

For Badin, Hurst had pitched 18 shutouts and opponents had scored just seven goals on the Rams all year. For her career, Hurst would start 20 tournament games in goal. Opponents scored exactly six goals in those games.

The Rams were the decided underdog in the 1997 title game, but that did not deter them. They had won 49 games over the previous three seasons, and they thought maybe No. 50 should earn them a long-denied state championship.

Playing with a gritty determination, Badin controlled the first half. A big crowd had followed the Rams to the title site at Dublin Scioto High, and they sensed a championship in the chilly November air.

Sweeper Lisa Sutton sensed it to the extent that she wouldn't come out of the game for a knee injury.

"I went in for a (slide) tackle with another girl and we both hit the ball at the same time. I heard something pop and I was like, 'OK, this didn't happen,'" Sutton said. "I knew I had to get up, but I was in so much pain. People were like, 'You're OK. Get up. Walk it off. You're not hurt.' That's the way the team was. We cared for each other's health, but we always thought we could play.

"And the whole time I was saying to Aimee, 'I can't! I can't!' And she said, OK, then go down (injured). But I couldn't do that either, because if a coach came onto the field, I'd have to go out of the game. You don't know what to do."

So Sutton stayed on the field, though just about every time she moved, she felt a sharp pain in her right knee.

"I was scared, but I didn't think it would be anything serious. I thought it was just a bruise," she added. At halftime, Sutton's family encouraged her cousin, Julee Foley, to go down from the stands and take a look at her. Foley was an athletic trainer and a former three-sport standout at Fairfield High who spent her entire career seeing her first name misspelled by the media.

"She plays soccer and she's just like me – she knew I wouldn't come off the field," Sutton said. "She said, 'I know her. It's not going to do any good to go down there and tell her what's wrong with her. She's not going to stop playing.'

"So she stayed in the stands, because she knew that's what I wanted. That's exactly what I would have done, probably, too. I finished out the game," Sutton said … and found out the next day that she had played most of the title tilt on a partially torn MCL.

With 14:38 left in the opening half, the opportunity Badin was searching for presented itself. Shannon Kuhl, attempting to get a shot off in the goal box, was knocked down – and the official quickly whistled a penalty kick.

"It was such a hard game – you could feel the intensity," Kuhl said. "Right there, I had the ball in the box and I knew I was going to score. I was wide open – and then I got taken out on the play."

If the Rams could get the lead, with the momentum and the adrenaline, maybe their defense could do the rest. Kuhl was the Rams' leading scorer for the season, with 19 goals, and Manahan called for her to take the penalty kick.

"You never get that kind of moment in your life, but it's the kind of moment you dream about. You know it's going to be the most incredible feeling," she said of the opportunity to put her school on top in the state championship game. "When it's a penalty kick, you know you're going to make it. You don't care who takes it. … Usually I was nervous on penalty kicks, but that time I was so ready."

Unfortunately, it's not a pleasant memory.

"I was just waiting for the referee to blow the whistle. And the shot went where I wanted it to go. When I think of the whole thing happening, though, it was like it was in slow motion – and then she (Hammond) came over and stopped it. It went from the best feeling to the worst feeling, all in a split second. It was like my heart fell out.

I could have started bawling right there," Kuhl said.

There was no lead. Hammond stoned the shot, DeSales cleared the ball, and Badin did not pose much of a threat from there.

Though it was 0-0 at half, and Badin's crowd was in full throat, DeSales had weathered the storm. Danielle Slupski scored on a header for the Stallions less than three minutes into the second half, then added another goal a dozen minutes later, and that was plenty.

"I was standing at midfield when we got that penalty kick, and I turned to Aimee (Hurst) and I was like, 'This is going to be ours!' This was the turning point in our story," Sutton said. "I had a lot of confidence. And then we didn't score and I was like, 'Oh, no, this is another year, this can't be happening to us again!'"

McKnight gave the boisterous Ram fans a clenched fist salute as the squad came off the field at halftime, but DeSales took control after intermission.

"They came out a lot harder in the second half," McKnight said. "We kind of got back on our heels in the first couple of minutes. We still played hard after they scored, but they just had two great shots."

"They were definitely the best team we've faced all season," Hammond said of Badin. "I really feel for that team. They've been here three years in a row and haven't been able to get it done."

"Three years in a row – I don't have a whole lot to say," Manahan told the media after the 2-0 championship setback. "They're a great team … and we're a great team. It was a great final. What else can you say?"

"It was really frustrating," McKnight said. "We all had a real hard time dealing with that, me especially. I just felt like, 'God, what does it take to win?'"

"When they put those two goals in, I was like, 'Oh, geez, this is not fair,'" Sutton said. "We had a great season, it was my senior year, but it wasn't good enough. It definitely was the biggest disappointment. It was like, three years in row, we've worked so hard, but we've gotten so little out of all our hard work."

"It hurt, but I was kind of used to it," conceded Hurst. "Sad to say that, but I was. This hurt more because it was my senior year and I could never go back. But there wasn't a doubt in my mind that we could win it in basketball. That kind of pulled me through the soccer hurt, just knowing that."

"That was the longest bus ride home," McKnight said. "I think I sat with my head in the seat in front of me, just sitting there for two hours. I couldn't even talk to anybody because I was so frustrated.

I just thought about every play in the game, what we should have done. Why this, why that, what should I have done?

"But when I look back on it, I'm very proud of what we did. It's a very positive feeling," McKnight added. "I played with some of my best friends in the world. We had some great times. We played some great games, won so many games we weren't supposed to win. ... It's a heckuvan accomplishment to get there three times in a row. I just wish we'd have won one of them."

"You always think, 'What if?'" said Shannon Kuhl, nearly inconsolable after the game, surrounded by family. "You can't help but feel that you let the whole team down. That (penalty kick) is one thing in my life I wish I could do over – as long as I didn't have to remember it that way."

Yet time, more than 15 years, has a way of softening the memories, of softening the sadness.

"Overall, it was a magical time," Kuhl remarked recently. "Getting to play every day with my best friends, meeting with unexpected but hard-worked-for success, and having the support and recognition of our school and our community.

"Back then I don't think we ever realized how big it really was or would become – we were just a bunch of goofs!" she laughed. "All of our antics -- before practices and before and after the games. We were not at all serious. Or at least we acted crazy to keep ourselves from becoming too serious and freaking out because we always felt the pressure to win and hated to lose so badly.

"Even today, whenever I run into a teammate, you can still feel the bond and the Badin pride – I can't explain it," Kuhl added. "Of course, there's also the dagger of despair that we got close so many times without finishing off the title. We wanted so badly to be the team to be the first (to win a girls state championship at Badin). We were good enough. What happened?"

Not only did the Rams suffer three consecutive state championship losses, but in what must be the most exasperating memory for the Rams of '95, '96 and '97, in three state title tilts, three great teams never scored a goal. Not one. Only in the penalty kick phase of the 1995 championship did Badin put the ball into the net.

In the trunk of his car, for three straight years, Joe Hurst carried a Badin state championship banner. It stayed there, sight unseen. Sometimes he wonders if he had inadvertently jinxed the girls.

"More than 15 years later, my memories are of all the good, forgetting the bad," Stacey Kuhl said. "Now, I look back on that young girl who learned so much more that (1995) season than she expected. I see God in everything. I see Him in the friendships. I see Him in the sacrifice players made to something bigger than themselves, the sacrifice parents made to us kids who were 'on the edge' and balancing late nights, soccer and school. I see Him in the community's support.

"It may sound very, very silly," she added. "But learning to love so many people for who they are, not who we want them to be, and battling with them to accomplish something bigger than we expected to accomplish. It wasn't ever about winning or losing. It wasn't about being the first state champions. It was about heart, and it was my first experience with His greatness."

"Those four years of playing soccer with the name 'Badin' written across our chests prepared me for the future more than I realized at the moment," Megan McKnight said. "Sure we learned teamwork; we learned to take direction, criticism, and praise from coaches, teammates, even opponents. We think in the moment that we know how to work hard, that we know what pushing ourselves really means – however, that was only a beginning.

"I credit our Badin playing days to where we really began to develop into leaders, not just in the sense of sport, but in all aspects of life," she added. "Now with balancing work, family, children, friends and more, I feel that the Badin experiences help to remind us that we can handle all that life has to offer."

McKnight was stunned, too, to think about the fact that it was two decades ago when she first went to try out for Badin soccer, looking forward to her freshman year of high school after graduating from St. Peter in Chains School in Hamilton.

"It seems impossible that the year was 1994!" she laughed. "As I reflect on those years, I smile as a rush of memories come to mind. I remember two-a-days, hot training sessions, long fitness runs along the bike path. I remember feeling like pre-season was going to last forever – how quickly you realize that time passes faster than you can blink.

"I remember how much I loved our home field, our goofy pre-game rituals, celebrating after goals, and how much we laughed," McKnight said. "Those are precious memories, things that came to pass in the coming days and next four years that I could not have even dreamed of at the time. And most importantly, I feel so blessed to have played with such awesome teammates."

"Looking back on it, I'm proud of being able to impact so many girls in a positive way, and I am proud of what we achieved," Craig Manahan said.

"You know the problem with the word champion? Too many people define it by winning trophies," he added. "Anyone who met the girls that I had the privilege of coaching at Badin, and who spent any time with them, knew they were champions – in every sense of the word.

"Stacey Kuhl once wrote to me, 'A state championship would have been nice, it would have spared a lot of tears, but it would have been one day in history, in our pasts. Moreover the trip and the journey were so much more fun and important than the end result.' I can't agree more," Manahan said, "… though I would have taken a state title, of course!"

Author's note: Many of the details and quotes in this chapter are excerpted from Chapter 15 of the book "Good Tears", published by the author in 2000, regarding the Badin High girls basketball program's march to the 1998 Division II state championship.

Pained by defeat, Badin's Christina Hinkel reacts as the Rams lose the 1996 state championship game to Chagrin Falls. Photo courtesy of the JournalNews, Hamilton.

Badin standouts Megan McKnight '98, Shannon Kuhl '99 and Reba Sedlacek '02 were subsequently All-Americans for the University of Dayton. Here, they are one day away from UD winning the Atlantic-10 conference championship in Richmond, Va. Photo contributed by Shannon Kuhl.

Don't drop her! Members of Badin's 2000 state runner-up squad, rear from left, Megan Collins, Ashley Timmer, Megan Filipek, Sarah Graf, Amanda Margello and Steph Streit hold up an obviously injured Betsy Browe. Photo courtesy of Beth Filipek.

Three girls who played a key role in Badin's 2005 Division II state championship included, from left, Abby Milillo, Heather Rains and Kristina Anderson. This picture was taken while they were in college, Milillo and Anderson of Ball State and Rains of Akron. Photo by Gail Milillo.

2013

Malia Berkely headed for the penalty kick line. She was not in a hurry. Gates Mills Hawken goaltender Hannah O'Day could wait for her.

Badin fans were hoping that Berkely, the team's leading scorer and marquee player, was pretty much automatic. Not that there is anything even remotely automatic about a penalty kick. But Hawken was on top in the penalty kick phase of the 2013 Division III state championship game, 2-1 at this point. Junior Marley Magruder had knocked one inside the lower left corner, and the Hawks, who were shooting first, had "held serve."

"I didn't put up too much effort on their second kick," Badin goalie Michelle Hessling said. "I don't know why. It doesn't look very good on tape."

Now it was up to Berkely to deadlock matters, and the daughter of first-year Badin head coach Todd Berkely had been turning heads for two years as a member of the Rams.

"Badin soccer is probably the most enjoyable soccer I've ever played," Malia said. "The girls are great and the atmosphere is so much fun. You have the whole 'Ramily' thing in the school, but it's even closer among the teams. It's a great experience and a fun time. … I love every minute of it."

Berkely would be named first-team all-Ohio and a finalist for the Gatorade Ohio Player of the Year award. Yet while playing soccer at a top level, Berkely was not a diva or someone who would walk around the Badin hallways acting like she was "all that." She was a quiet, down-to-earth sophomore who would occasionally disappear from view for a few days to play on a U.S. National teen team through the Olympic Development Program. It was, after all, a good excuse to be gone.

"Malia got a poster of (U.S. national great) Mia Hamm and that was it," Todd Berkely recalled. "Instead of curtains in her room, she has a huge flag of Mia Hamm. She sees it every day, and that's kind of the motivator."

"I always wanted to be the next Mia Hamm," Berkely agreed. "I grew up with soccer; it's always been in my heart. I've always been willing to work hard and strive for it."

"I couldn't be more proud of everything she has accomplished," said Malia's mother, Nicole. "When she was three, she was terrified of the ball. The coach had to carry her around the field. It's been quite a transformation."

Head coach Steve Tabar was more than happy to have Berkely show up as a freshman for the 2012 season. "She's obviously a very special player who doesn't come around very often," he said. "Madi Kah is very good, and when she told me, 'There's a player coming who's better than me' that really said something."

When her husband Todd was named head coach in the summer of 2013, Nicole Berkely cautioned her daughter.

"She knew she had expectations," Nicole said. "I told her there was no slacking off. She was going to be scrutinized and she had to be a leader for everybody else. She had been the leading scorer as a freshman, but she had not been a leader. Now it was time to lead. That was challenging for her at first."

Malia – called Milly by her friends – had graduated from Liberty Junior School in the Lakota Local School District, but did not consider attending Lakota East High. Todd Berkely is a 1985 graduate of Moeller High School, an all-boys Catholic school in the eastern suburbs of Cincinnati, so the family thought Catholic high school would be the right place for Malia.

"We did some research and came up with a list of four or five schools," Todd said. "St. Ursula was up there, but it was too far away. I liked Fenwick … but as soon as Malia walked into Badin, she said, 'I want to go here.' The iPad initiative was huge. The small, family environment – that's what sold her.

"I'm still to this day amazed that the Badin reputation is not all smoke and mirrors," he added. "It really is a family atmosphere. When I relay that to people, they give me a skeptical look – until I explain it to them."

Malia was also being wooed by some of her teammates from a 3 v 3 soccer squad that was referred to as the Magnificent M's – Madi Kah and Morgan Langhammer. The group played club ball together, and had won a 3 v 3 national championship at Kings Island at the age of 11.

Friends and family, as it were, led Berkely to enroll at Badin.

"It seemed like the right fit for me," she said. "As a freshman, it was really intimidating. You always hear about how freshman are treated differently, but it wasn't that way at all. Everyone was really nice."

Asked what makes an elite soccer player, Malia said, "practice, a lot of hard work, and belief in yourself."

"She did everything everyone else did, and then some," Todd Berkely said. "The key is the 'then some.' She took ownership of her efforts very early. Most of the time she was doing it on her own. We had soccer balls flying through the living room and everywhere else."

Berkely was particularly pleased with his daughter's growth from freshman to sophomore year on the soccer field for Badin. As a freshman she had scored 17 goals and had six assists. As a sophomore, she had 19 goals and 19 assists.

"She tripled her assists and made everyone else on the team dangerous," he said. "Teams could no longer just mark her and be satisfied. She's a dynamic player, but she's also humble and modest. She can play with reckless abandon, or switch to calm, controlled play. She's very committed."

The 19th goal had come with 20 minutes remaining in the state title game, when Berkely hit a bending laser just inside the left post from 20 yards out. Badin, trailing 2-0 at the time and on life support with the clock ticking away, was suddenly rejuvenated. Morgan Langhammer had tied it in spectacular fashion with barely six minutes left … and now the Rams would win or lose on penalty kicks.

Malia Berkely was at the PK mark, 12 yards out.

"I was sooooo nervous," she admitted.

She had preferred not to lead off Badin's penalty kick rotation, and that was fine with Todd Berkely, who expected his daughter to make her kick and had held her back in the event he needed to "restore order." Nothing was in disorder for the Rams, though, as senior co-captain Maggie Adams had opened the Badin PK effort with authority.

Now it was Berkely ... who powdered it into the lower right corner ... setting off the Badin student section chant of "USA! USA!"

"When I made my shot and everyone started chanting 'USA! USA', I felt like the happiest person ever," Berkely said. "Every time you make a penalty kick, it's so exciting because you're that much closer to winning."

Berkely's 20th goal of the season had put Badin into a 2-2 penalty kick deadlock. The drama was just beginning.

2000

Reba. Just the first name. That's the only one you need. Say it around veterans of the Badin girls soccer community, and they know exactly who you are talking about. No last name necessary.

Reba Sedlacek was a tremendous soccer player for the Rams – and she was also a tremendous "presence" at the school on New London Road. Not the kind of girl who seeks attention, but the kind who earned attention because of her skill and personality. She could score the game-winning goal one night, and come in the next day ready to put on glitter and circus makeup to help encourage 8th graders to join the Badin family – and not be at all embarrassed to do so.

Sedlacek was the Player of the Year in the Girls Greater Cincinnati League for three years running, yet also earned the Archbishop Leibold graduation medal at Badin in 2002 for her "outstanding service to the school and the community." She cried on her way up to receive the medal, because being a part of Badin had meant that much to her.

And she was the ringleader of a team that returned the Badin girls soccer program to the spotlight, powering its way to the 2000 state finals her junior year in a surprising and impressive run to what was Badin's first trip to Columbus Crew Stadium.

"Shannon Kuhl was my idol!" Sedlacek said. "I had always wanted to be just like her. I remember watching her in club play and being mesmerized."

Sedlacek was a student at St. Bartholomew School in Finneytown, which did not have much of a feeder connection to Badin. Her mother, Anne, had gone to Ursuline Academy, and St. Bart's (since renamed for John Paul II) was primarily a feeder school of Roger Bacon in Cincinnati.

But it was Kuhl … and Badin's trip to the 1997 state championship game, its third straight … that had Sedlacek's attention.

"That state run solidified my choice of Badin," Sedlacek recalled.

"I remember going to all of the games and hoping that could be me someday. Badin offered everything that gave me the potential to thrive – solid education, small community feel and a stellar soccer program rooted in success."

"Reba was so much fun to watch play," said Sally Kocher, Badin's longtime athletic director. Of course, she only called her by her first name – and knew that anyone taking notes would have no doubt who she was referring to. "It's hard sometimes to judge intensity, but her intensity on the field was just amazing to watch."

By the time Badin battled its way to the state finals in 2000, Sedlacek and many of her teammates had played for three varsity head coaches.

Craig Manahan stayed on for the 1998 season, the Rams' bid for a fourth straight trip to the state finals coming up short in a 2-1 setback to Roger Bacon in the district championship game. RB -- en route to the state semifinals in '98 and '99 -- probably figured it owed Badin at least one, having lost seven consecutive games to the Rams, including three straight district final contests.

It was a loss that left a sour taste in Badin's mouth. Playing in front of a full house at Fairfield Soccer Stadium, Badin trailed 1-0 at the half when the Spartans scored with three seconds remaining following what Manahan felt was a questionable free kick opportunity.

Sedlacek accounted for Badin's lone goal, cutting the margin to 2-1 with 34 minutes left off a corner kick. But the Rams' would-be tying goal by sophomore Angela Vilkoski was negated by an offsides call, which had Badin fans howling.

"I know some people will think I'm crazy," Manahan said after the game, "but we ended up 12-4-4 and, in my mind, I consider that a successful season.

"I am just real disappointed for the seniors," he added. "They have been to the state finals three straight years and don't get to go back their senior year. It's real tough for them."

A year later, Dan Cullen directed the Rams to an 8-6-4 mark that ended with a 3-0 loss to Wyoming in the sectionals at North College Hill. Badin had beaten Wyoming 4-3 during the regular season after trailing 2-0, but when Wyoming tallied just 37 seconds into the match, it was the start of a long and fruitless evening for BHS. The Rams hit the post three times, but nothing found its way into the back of the net.

"We had a young team, an interesting mix of youth and seniors," Cullen told the JournalNews after the match, "and we have tremendous potential for the future."

Cullen was right about the potential, but he was not there for that future, giving way to Katy Brennan, a 1993 Badin grad who had been an assistant in '99 and now took over the Ram fortunes in 2000.

"The thing about Badin is, everybody is ready to play," Brennan said. "You get that devotion, that passion for the sport."

Brennan had played for Badin at the time there was just one division in the girls state tournament, so the Rams did not advance out of the sectional. But she remembered her playing days fondly.

"There is so much pride, history and success in the program," Brennan said. "I remember playing in the rain as a freshman, having been brought up for the tournament and being really pumped up. Our final game (as a senior in 1992) was a whole ball of emotion. We have a rich history."

Now, it was up to her to help extend that tradition.

"It was a question of getting them prepared," she said, complimenting her coaching colleagues Rick Keyes and Erin Alexander for helping make that happen. "At the time, I felt so young. I've learned a lot since then."

While Sedlacek was the headliner, the 2000 Rams were blessed with a solid corps of talent.

Angela Vilkoski – her father, Vince, was a familiar voice as the public address announcer for girls soccer – was back for her senior year, and a strong offensive threat. She would go on to study education at Miami University and play for a college club team that made the national finals. When she returned to Badin to teach science as the married Angela Breetz for the 2013-14 school year, she was just in time to follow another powerhouse squad to state.

Juniors Megan Collins and Sarah Graf would go on to play Division I soccer at Morehead State University, and anchored an excellent defense. Sophomore Lauren Gersbach would be good enough to walk-on at Butler University, and at her BHS graduation in 2003, she earned the Stephen T. Badin medal as the most outstanding member of the class "by every measure."

Junior Steph Streit was a 5-foot-2 dynamo in goal, never afraid to get dirty – she was also the catcher on the Badin softball team. As a freshman at Miami University, she tested into one of a handful of medical school slots reserved in advance for Miami grads at the University of Cincinnati. Then she went into the Air Force ROTC program, which earned her a commission as a captain with deferred duty and paid for all of her medical school training. For the 2014-15 year, she was named the general surgery administrative chief resident at her hospital in Charleston, S.C. Brains and skill.

"For me, Badin soccer started in 1996," Streit said. "Megan Collins and I would go watch all the games that we could convince our parents to take us to. I idolized Aimee Hurst. Megan Collins adored Megan McKnight. Those girls were like celebrities to us. We watched them cruise into the state finals each year, and we cried with them when they fell short each time. We would always talk about what would happen when we had the chance."

"I would just run up and down the hallways for what feels like a million times thinking how cool it will be one day when, not if, I became a Badin Ram," said Collins, whose father, Tom, was the highly-regarded principal of the school when she was a child, and whose mother, Kay, remains the popular chair of the science department. "Being a part of Badin from an early age, you learn to be proud of the school and the accomplishments of the students and wear Badin gear with your head held high.

"I remember the three years in a row when the girls soccer team made the state tournament," Collins added, "and I sat there in anticipation, hoping for a win, yet each time they fell short. I was so honored just to be there and I was anxious to get to high school, knowing one day that could be me!"

Streit laughed that she didn't really think about being short for a goalkeeper.

"I had been my team's goalkeeper since I was 12, when my club team's keeper didn't show up for a summer tournament," she said. "At 12, being 5-foot-2 wasn't so short. Little did I know that I was done growing.

"I didn't actually know that I was short until I started to play varsity as a junior. People kept asking me, 'Aren't you a little short to be a keeper?' I kept replying in the negative until one day I realized that they were right. I couldn't do anything about my height, though, all I could do was work harder."

Streit had already had a taste of varsity tournament play, one that she never forgot.

"My freshman year, we played a team that wore yellow jerseys in the first game of the tournament," she said. "We were heavily favored and went on to win handily. But the referee sent our keeper, Caitlin Wolf, off the field at the start of the game because her jersey was bright yellow, too.

"Coach Manahan sent me onto the field to start the game," she added. "I played the first 1:46 until the ball went out of bounds the first time. Caitlin then went back on and I jogged off the field, elated. Craig said, 'Relax, Steph, it was only a minute.' I replied, 'But it was the best minute of my life!'"

"Steph was phenomenal; she was amazing," Katy Brennan said. "She may have been just 5-foot-2, but she was a monster back there. She was a strong leader and she loved playing the position. The goalie is probably the hardest position to fill. Steph more than filled it – she was very good, and she enjoyed it."

Sedlacek was motivated at least in part by a devotion to her handicapped older sister, Tracy, who was born 30 months before Reba with one arm, one lung, one kidney, difficulty walking, and minimal hearing in one ear. They shared the same room at home, and if Reba was playing somewhere, Tracy was probably there as well.

"Reba is extremely capable in everything she does, and at the other end of the spectrum, Tracy needs help getting dressed and cleaned up," their mother, Anne, said in a memorable column by Tom Archdeacon in the Dayton Daily News written while Sedlacek was an All-American soccer player at the University of Dayton. "But they are the best of buds. And each of them makes the other better. It's kind of like God knew what he was doing after all."

"With all this (talk) about what I do for Tracy," Reba told Archdeacon, "really, she does more for me. Any day I ever thought my life was bad, I just had to look across the room at her in the next bed and I got things back into focus. Nothing stopped her. And it's not like that just for me, but with everyone. Even my teammates ... once you meet my sister, you never forget her and what she can do."

"There are so many things I can say about Reba, and they're all positive," Brennan said. "She was such a positive person, and a huge leader. She loved playing soccer so much.

"Her family was so positive, too, they really encouraged her," Brennan added. "Reba wants to be a motivator for people. She did not want to be put up on a pedestal, she just wanted to play soccer. She was very focused, very bright and very athletic."

"That was a special, special year," Sedlacek recalled of the 2000 season. "To be honest, we didn't have the most talent, but we had a true *team*. A group of girls who loved each other and worked hard every day.

"Class didn't matter," she added. "Seniors, juniors, sophomores – we were all united as friends and teammates. We spent what seemed like every waking second together, laughing and laughing and laughing some more."

Sedlacek fondly recalled the pre-game team meals, the hair braiding, and the team car caravans to Garfield Soccer Stadium on Fair Avenue in Hamilton.

"Our music was blaring, we hung out the car windows and screamed at the top of our lungs," she laughed. "The freedom and exhilaration of those moments, I will never forget. And Garfield was the best soccer stadium around. The grass was plush and green. Perfectly cut, with no divots. There was nothing better than those cool, crisp nights under the lights."

Alas, the Hamilton City Schools subsequently built an elementary school on top of Garfield Stadium, then ran out of building levy funds before it could deliver an expected soccer stadium complex at the new Freshman School. Badin would play at Hamilton High's football field, Virgil Schwarm Stadium, but Garfield was always a pleasant memory.

"We genuinely liked each other, and our play reflected that," Vilkoski said. "What we thrived on was pure team chemistry. There was no 'I' in our team ... ever! I'm 100 percent convinced that is what got us to state. Anything you did on the field was for your teammates and the good of the team, period. And that mindset was never announced as our team mantra. Everybody just knew it and played like it."

"As a Badin soccer player, I learned what it meant to be a family on and off the field with my teammates," Sarah Graf said. "The bonds that I made with the girls were as rewarding as wearing the Badin uniform and winning any game.

"We worked hard, played hard, and we had fun!" she added. "The reward was not only winning the games, but also turning a physical and competitive sport into as much fun as we could."

"Those were some of the best days of my life," said Collins, admitting she had tears in her eyes just thinking about them. "It still brings chills to my body and so many emotions. It's crazy to look back and think that I don't remember a whole lot about each game. I just remember the feelings I had inside every time I walked on the field and was around my teammates.

"We had an unexplained bond that I don't think any of us to this day can describe," she continued. "And it wasn't just the girls in my graduating class. It was everyone on the field, on the bench, and the coaches. We all meshed together and understood each other. I still deeply believe that our respect for each other and the bond that we all shared is the reason we made it to Columbus Crew Stadium."

But while Badin beat Wyoming 3-1 to earn a bit of revenge to open the 2000 regular season, there was little about the campaign that would have suggested a run to state. In fact, the Rams lost four of their last five games and took a 6-5-4 record into the opening round of the Division II tournament.

"There was some turmoil," conceded Brennan. "It came to the point where we needed to either get together and win or be done with it. We had a pre-tournament pow-wow at Joyce Park. I told them it was a matter of them trusting me and the coaching staff. This was the tournament and we had to be the best that we could be."

Brennan pointed to Angela Vilkoski as one who led the way to success.

"Angela's senior leadership played a key role as to why the team got over the hump," she said. "She stepped up and said, 'This is my last year, we want to be successful, let's move ahead.' She had their attention."

"Just like every team and season, there are tough times and obstacles," Vilkoski said. "But they didn't define us. It was just all the more motivation to stick it out together, and it paid off."

Badin had tied Summit Country Day 1-1 in the regular season, but in the sectional finals, the Rams pounded SCD 6-0. They downed always capable Mariemont 4-1 in the district finals, and ousted Indian Hill – another team they had deadlocked in the regular season -- 3-1 to reach the state semifinals. When you're beating quality Cincinnati Hills League teams like Mariemont and Indian Hill to advance, you're clearly on top of your game.

"Once we got to the tournament, we were unstoppable," Sedlacek said. "We pulled together and started picking teams off one at a time. When we beat Indian Hill, one of our biggest Division II rivals, and with a few of my club teammates on the team, that was sweet!"

"When the tournament came around, we were firing on all cylinders," Streit said. "Everything clicked. We loved each other. We fought for each other. We never gave up.

"I can still remember a few clutch saves that I had," she added. "One in particular was a last-minute diving stop against Mariemont. I showed up at school the next day with a black eye. I completely missed the fact that I got kicked in the head by (teammate) Amanda Margello during another save/collision!"

Badin was back in the state semifinals for the first time since 1997, facing Springfield Greenon at Winton Woods Soccer Stadium, the old Greenhills High School field.

Stunningly, it was no contest. The Rams powered their way into the Division II finals with an 11-1 demolition of a Greenon squad that came in 17-3-1 and had given up 11 goals in its previous 18 games combined.

Common opponent scores would have favored Badin – for instance, Badin downed Bellbrook 2-0, which had beaten Greenon 4-2; and the Rams tied and defeated Indian Hill, which scored a 1-0 tally over Greenon -- but obviously not to that extent. The game was like a UFO – it couldn't be explained.

"That was a blast," said Sedlacek, who counted three goals for the evening. "We just kept scoring and scoring. The celebration and feeling afterward was second to none. We did it! We earned a trip to play at Columbus Crew Stadium for the Division II state championship! The bus ride home was filled with loud singing, laughing and ear-to-ear smiles. We wanted the ring and we were ready to go get it!"

Sophomore Steph Caudill had added three goals for the Rams, who were on top 3-0 in the first nine minutes of the game and led 7-0 at the half. Jill Broermann, Megan Filipek, Lauren Gersbach, Annie Hinkel and Amanda Margello also tallied for BHS.

"I don't know what happened in the state semifinals," Brennan said. "I would love to say that our girls just exploded. We were on such a roll.

"But I don't know what sort of competition Greenon had played to get there," she said. "Up to that point in the tournament, our games had not been easy. Now this is the state semifinals – it was a combination of things. They were outmanned and we were playing well.

"Scoring 11 goals, letting that happen, that's not one of my finest coaching moments," Brennan said, since generally schools were expected to back off before they got to double digits. "But it was the state semifinals, and you can't tell your girls not to play.

"But a win like that – it certainly didn't prepare us to play in the state finals," she added.

Badin had enjoyed the thrill of victory in the state semifinals ... and now, once again, it would taste the agony of defeat in the finals. Badin was finally playing at Columbus Crew Stadium, but unbeaten Cuyahoga Falls Walsh Jesuit (21-0-1) made it a long day for the Rams, 4-1.

"I had no idea how overmatched we would be," said Sedlacek. "We got blown out. We really got dominated all over the field. They were an incredible team with an unparalleled amount of talent. But we did our best and fought hard the entire game. We never gave up or put our heads down."

Walsh Jesuit scored on its first two shots of the game and led 2-0 with just four minutes gone. The score was 4-0 when Badin finally got on the board as senior Ann Menke knocked home a rebound with 4:58 remaining. It was a victory of sorts -- the first goal Badin had scored in four state championship appearances.

"They had a lot of skill and everything clicked for them," Brennan said. "Some of their goals, there was just no stopping them. I was happy that we were able to score. The season didn't end like we wanted it to, but the girls had great chemistry. They were very determined."

"I was nervous, but so excited!" Graf recalled. "I couldn't believe I was about to walk onto the Columbus Crew field as a Badin player with teammates that were my best friends as well. It was a feeling that could never be replaced.

"I myself try to forget about the game as much as possible, because I was marking the fastest and best player from the opposing team. She beat me several times," Graf added. "But not once did anyone make me feel like I blew the game, although I felt I had."

"We played our hearts out that day," Collins said. "We walked into the stadium with our heads held high, proudly wearing Badin green and even though we didn't leave with a 'W', we still walked out with our heads held high with so much pride and joy."

"We were overmatched in every way in the state finals," Streit said. "They were the better team. In the moment, I was devastated. I was so embarrassed to have spent what felt like my entire life working and waiting for my chance to finally bring home Badin's first girls state soccer championship, only to come up so very, very short.

"After the wounds healed, though, I was so incredibly grateful to have had the opportunity and to have made those friendships," she said. "Badin soccer will always hold a special place in my memories."

"We still joke about it to this day – the state championship game didn't turn out to be much of a game," Vilkoski said. "They took it to us pretty good. They were, by far, the more superior team on the field and deserved the state title.

"Was I heartbroken? Yes. Were there tears? Of course. But on the bus ride home, the smiles returned just like they should when you know you're a part of something special," she added.

The bus ride home still looms large to Sarah Graf, who subsequently was an assistant coach at Badin.

"Most bus rides home after a loss would be miserable, but not that one," she said. "We had the best time celebrating our accomplishments and making it that far. That was when I realized I was on the best team around."

2013

Gabby Geigle – given name Gabrielle – had been a hustling freshman to build around as Badin High began the road back to state during the 2012 season. Now, she was feeling that recovery squarely on her shoulders as she walked to the penalty kick line in the 2013 Ohio Division III state championship game.

Gates Mills Hawken, kicking first in the five player rotation, led 3-2 in PKs, as senior Mackenzie Lesnick had put one into the upper left side of the goal, just eluding a diving try by Badin goalie Michelle Hessling.

"It was in all the way," Hessling said, though observers thought she'd barely missed it. "I dived, the dive looked good, but I don't think any goalie could have stopped that one."

Now, the shoe was on Geigle's foot.

"I didn't know who was going to take the kicks," when two 15-minute sudden death overtime periods ended in a 2-2 deadlock, Geigle said, "so I just sort of stood there, and then they asked me to take one. I said, 'maybe I can do this.'"

Senior co-captains Maggie Adams and Michelle Hessling were in the PK rotation, with sophomore Malia Berkely and junior Kate Bach. Adams said she would go first, and Bach said she would go last. But the other kicker in the rotation had come down to sophomore defender Geigle or her junior running mate Brianna Scowden. Geigle, who teammates said "never missed" in penalty kick practice, was singled out for the rotation. If it went to sudden death, Scowden would be first up for Badin.

Geigle came by her soccer skill honestly. Her father, Joe, had been a two-time NAIA All-American goalkeeper at Tiffin University in north-central Ohio. Her older brother, Grant, had been an all-league player for Badin who was now playing for Cincinnati State.

No one was surprised, then, when Gabby showed up as a freshman in 2012 and immediately earned a starting berth as an inside defender for the varsity.

"Starting as a freshman, that was awesome," she said. "It was really cool to be a freshman on varsity. I was playing with girls who had been there before. The seniors liked this little freshman … that was great!"

The 2012 Rams put together a strong 11-2-3 regular season record, but went out early in the tournament. A year later, under new head coach Todd Berkely, they had played as long as they could possibly play in the post-season. The championship game couldn't go any longer than penalty kicks.

"It's a ton of fun playing for Badin," Geigle said. "We click really well together. I love how close we are as a team. You just feel like you can tell them anything."

Geigle, one of the fastest players on the team, had been switched from inside to outside defender in the Rams' four-deep system.

"That didn't go so well for me at first," Geigle said. "(Coach Berkely) kept putting me at outside backer, when I was an inside back. Why did he do that? I just said, 'I don't know how to play here.'"

Berkely wanted to take advantage of Geigle's speed and toughness on the outside.

"She's hard-nosed and stubborn on defense, and fast so she can be a part of your attack," said Berkely, whose offense included both of his outside defenders pushing up to be part of the attack. "She's very coachable. If you need the job done, call on Gabby. She eats nails and spits rust."

"He wanted me to make more runs," Geigle nodded. "It all came together, and I understood exactly why he wanted me out there. I wasn't thrilled with it. I sucked it up because I needed to suck it up."

Geigle had already been right in the middle of the critical scoring play of the game … the scoring play that enabled Badin to play on to penalty kicks.

With the Time Warner television commentators frequently pointing out that Geigle could be open in space on the outside … the ball had come to her, on the outside, open in space, with some 6-1/2 minutes remaining in regulation.

"I was dead," Geigle said. "Exhausted. The field was huge. We were all so tired. I tried to make a run, but my legs weren't working very well. I got the ball and played it in …"

She popped a textbook ball into the six-yard area, where Morgan

Langhammer was racing right to left. It could not have been more perfect. Langhammer slide-tapped it home, and the Rams had come from a 2-0 halftime deficit to tie the game in the final 20 minutes.

"Morgan was right on it! I was really excited," Geigle said. "I didn't know to react. I've never been in a game that big before. It was the most stressful game I've ever been in … but also the greatest. I just ran up to Morgan and said, 'I love you!'"

Now, with the score 3-2 in favor of Hawken on penalty kicks, there was more stress on Geigle. She was trying to keep negative thoughts from creeping in.

"When I was about 13, playing for my club team, my coach asked me to take a penalty kick," she said later. "It still haunts me. I went up and nailed it way over the goal. That miss still sticks with me."

Joe Geigle and his wife, Gina, were feeling the stress as well.

"It was a fun run; they were such a fun team to watch," he said. "As a parent, at the time, the stress just kills you. But in retrospect, it was fun to watch."

Gabby Geigle headed to the line.

"Now, I'm actually in the penalty kick situation, and I'm freaking out," she said. "I was scared out of my mind. At the same time, I knew I could make it. I tried to stay positive, but I didn't know what was going to happen. It's stressful to kick … but it's equally stressful to stand there and watch others kick.

"I set the ball down, and stared at the goal," she said. "It looks so big, but I didn't know if I could make it. I knew I was going to hit it on the ground, so I didn't look at the goalie. I just looked at the ball and the ground."

Geigle never misses in practice. She didn't miss here, either. Lower right, never a doubt.

"After I made it, I was so excited and happy and going crazy in my mind," she said. "But I just ran back to our team like, 'I've got this.'"

It was 3-3 in penalty kicks. It was still anybody's game.

2004

Ten years later, head coach Keith Harring is still unhappy about the game that ended Badin's 2004 girls soccer campaign. The Rams, ranked No. 3 in the state, were ousted by Kettering Alter on penalty kicks in the Division II district finals, concluding the season at 12-3-3.

"That's still one of the toughest losses I've ever had," said Harring, who was finishing his third year at the BHS helm. "That really bothered me for a long time. That team could have gone on – we had depth and we were starting to roll."

While Badin has had a reputation for playing physical soccer over the years, Alter set the bar high with physical play that night. Badin freshman Tori Mathews went down in the first half with what was thought to be a broken collarbone, and sophomore Kristina Anderson was knocked out in the second half with a concussion.

"I was so upset and disappointed with the physical nature of that game," Harring said. "There was so much after-the-ball contact, almost like hockey checks. It took me several weeks to get over that one."

Though Badin out-shot Alter 24-10 in the contest at Garfield Stadium, it was a scoreless deadlock heading into the penalty kick session.

Mathews and Anderson would have been in the Badin penalty kick rotation, but were unavailable. Then the Knight goaltender put the psychological whammy on the Rams when she set up directly next to the right post. She dared the Rams to go left. When Badin misfired on its first PK effort, Alter capitalized. They converted all five of their attempts, and advanced.

"That was tough for us because we'd never seen anything like that before," Harring said of the Alter goaltender's strategy. "Our players were hitting that left post time and again in practice. We just couldn't do it in the game."

Harring has a more personal reason for being disappointed. His daughter, Gwen, was getting married that weekend. "I was not as excited as I should have been for her wedding, because I was still so upset over that game!" he lamented.

Harring had stepped into the Badin girls ranks for the 2002 season, following the departure of Katy Brennan. Brennan had told the press at Crew Stadium after the 2000 state championship setback, "I'm looking forward to being back here next year," but it didn't happen.

The Rams returned a strong senior nucleus in 2001, led by Reba Sedlacek and Steph Streit, but stumbled through a 5-8-3 regular season, then went out in the district semifinals to Indian Hill, 1-0.

"I blame myself for that," Brennan said. "We had beaten Indian Hill a couple of times (in the 2000 regionals as well as in the 2001 regular season), so I thought we'd be OK in their bracket. That was one of the not-so-great coaching moves I made. Indian Hill felt like we were coming after them."

"We struggled that year," Sedlacek said. "But even through the defeats, I still maintained wonderful friendships, experiences and memories that I carry with me. ... Even today, my Badin soccer teammates are some of my best friends. A group of us still gets together for a girls night, once a month, even after all of these years. We have special bonds and time will never tear that down."

Megan Collins was on two teams that went to state – girls basketball as a sophomore in March of 2000 and girls soccer as a junior in November of that year.

"Each time we fell short, but each time I felt like I was on top of the world," Collins said. "These are memories that I hold close to my heart and I will never forget. Not just because of the sport, but because of the people I shared the experiences with."

Katy Brennan also looked back on them as "fun years. A lot of good memories.

"When you're in the middle of it, you're so stressed. When you look back on it, you wonder why you were so stressed," she said. "You should have had more fun with it. It was a good time."

Harring, in his mid-50s when he assumed direction of the Badin girls soccer program, had an extensive coaching background. He had been a longtime area high school administrator – principal at Waynesville and Springboro, assistant principal at Lakota and Princeton -- who retired from the public school ranks and answered an ad to teach science at Badin for the 2001-02 school year.

He spent that season as an assistant in the boys soccer ranks, then moved over to the girls head coaching position when it opened up for the 2002 campaign. He was excited with what he saw in the BHS girls soccer program.

"I thought this group could be really good," he nodded. "They needed some consistency, some stability. I said I'd take the job for five years. I thought I could get the program going really well."

"To have a coach with that much experience was pretty much a dream come true," said Athletic Director Sally Kocher, who also thought that having a head coach "in the building" was a big plus. "He was always on top of everything. You never had to worry about anything.

"Keith was very passionate about what he did, and that passion was contagious," she added.

A Connecticut native, Harring was a graduate of what Butler County residents always refer to as that "other" Miami ... the University of Miami (Fla.). He and his wife, Pam, had migrated to the Midwest when Harring attended Ball State University in Muncie, Ind., to earn an advanced degree in radio and television.

Harring had coached baseball, soccer and even hockey over the years, guiding first Findlay and then Centerville high schools to state hockey crowns. His club coaching efforts included numerous titles through the strong Fairfield Optimist Soccer Club (FOSC) ... and his daughter, Mandy, had played on a Fairfield High squad that reached the state semifinals in 1992, losing to Centerville 4-1 in a miserable downpour at Sycamore High.

"The girls loved playing for Badin, they just loved it," said Harring, whose eight years as head coach would produce five district championships, two state runner-up finishes and the 2005 Division II state title. "There's just this feeling when you play for Badin. I've always said that. Even though it's not a 'town' school, it's a community."

Harring understood what it would take to be successful.

"You have to have talent," Harring said, "and Badin definitely had talent. You have to get the girls to believe in themselves and work together. I used a lot of psychology to get the girls to believe. We did a lot of things as far as bonding to get the girls united."

The Rams were competitive in Harring's first two seasons as he built the program for the long haul.

The first season, 2002, ended with a record of 8-9-2 following a district final loss to Wyoming. That game turned on a penalty kick with three minutes left in the first half. Actually, two penalty kicks – because as Rams goalie Heather Maus stuffed the first shot, the referee whistled that Badin had been guilty of a violation on the play, and gave Wyoming a second try at the PK. The Cowboys converted this one en route to a 2-1 verdict.

"I don't know how you can make that call," mused Harring, whose first team graduated 11 seniors. "We should have won that game."

Year two, 2003, was an 8-8-3 effort that ended with a 3-1 setback to Middletown Fenwick in the district semifinals at Garfield Stadium. The two teams had deadlocked at 1-1 in the regular season, and Badin was the better seed in the tournament. But Fenwick was undefeated at 13-0-4 coming in, and dominated on the road. It was a hard way to end the year for the Rams.

"That was a tough loss," nodded Harring, though the Rams only had two seniors on that team and were looking forward to making a splash in 2004. "Fenwick really came to play that night."

Harring said he felt that one key to the Badin program was its depth.

"You need depth, and we had it," he said. "I felt like Badin could develop a lot of good players. I had been a hockey coach, and in hockey you're constantly changing lines. That's what we could do at Badin. I played a lot of kids. There were a lot of kids who could play."

Harring and Badin had also benefited from a key hire when Harring brought local club coach Brian Smallwood onto the staff for the 2004 season. Smallwood had directed a well-known Kolping club powerhouse, the Zigs, who had a number of girls playing for Badin.

"I had coached Brian's daughter, Cammie, in the FOSC some years earlier," Harring recalled. "I ran into him while I was at Badin and he was at Kolping. I asked him, 'Have you ever thought about coaching high school soccer?'

"He was a big plus because he knew so much about those players who were coming into the program," Harring added. "He knew stuff that he would use to get their attention. He did a nice job for us."

Smallwood was a significant part of Badin's success from 2004 through 2007. He would subsequently take over the Hamilton High girls program for the 2010 season, and remains the head coach of the Big Blue.

"Tradition is the one word that comes to mind," said Smallwood about Badin girls soccer.

"I've coached for 20 years and those four years were the toughest I've ever had to coach," he said. "Talent is tough to coach. It forces you to be better prepared. You want to do well for the players because you have a team and a community counting on you."

Smallwood, whose mind is like a steel trap when it comes to remembering games and situations, recalled the end of the 2004 district championship loss to Kettering Alter.

"The girls were going through the medal line and getting their district runner-up medals," he said. "Heather Rains got her medal, turned and walked away."

Rains, a junior, had been the opening Badin PK kicker who was stopped by the Knights that evening.

"Halfway back to the team, Heather took her medal off and held it in her hand," Smallwood said. "After that, every player took their medal off. Heather was a leader, and she was basically saying, 'Remember this for next year. We're not playing for second place medals.' That moment was pretty cool."

Badin girls soccer had high aspirations. They'd ended the season ranked No. 3 in the state. That was good ... but not good enough.

2005

Heather Rains plucked the ball out of the back of the Badin net and sprinted for the center line. The senior co-captain was not happy. The Rams were dominating a 2005 pre-season set of scrimmages in Strongsville, but a defensive lapse had cost a goal.

Rains jammed the ball down at midfield and waited for the referee to blow his whistle. Ten seconds later, she had scored at the other end. Then, she grabbed the ball out of the opposing net, and once again brought it back to the center line.

"That's how long it takes!" Rains shouted at her teammates in the story recounted by assistant coach Brian Smallwood. "You have to stay focused at all times!"

Head coach Keith Harring, unprompted, recalled the very same incident.

"We won state because of Heather Rains," Harring said of the Rams' magical 2005 season. "I'll never forget her. She was a tremendous player. I knew we'd win it that year. I really trusted Heather. She is one of my favorite players ever."

Rains, always smiling, has the kind of personality that makes instant friends of complete strangers. Married to fellow Badin grad Chad Smith, she is a physician's assistant with a young daughter and fond memories of a soccer career that included four years at the University of Akron, where she was co-captain as a senior.

"No matter how much I have accomplished and experienced," she said, "one of my most favorite memories is winning the 2005 girls soccer state championship. That is a memory that I will never forget and will cherish my whole life. I was blessed to have a fairy tale ending to my high school career. There is one team that ends their season with a smile, and we were that team."

"It was Heather's team without a doubt that championship year," said Steve Milillo, a 1973 Badin grad who is in the school's athletic Hall of Fame. His daughter, Abby, was a key part of that title squad as well. "Heather took the championship team on her shoulders and carried them right along."

It was a team with its own lofty expectations, stung by the penalty kick loss to Kettering Alter in the 2004 district finals. Others, obviously, had high expectations for the Rams as well – they were ranked No. 1 in Division II in the state as the season approached.

"The players were excited about being ranked No. 1, but it was a lot of pressure," Smallwood said.

"That team will have a bond for life," Rains said. "From the very first pre-season tournament, we had one goal in mind – win state. I knew as senior captain that it was going to take talent, hard work, discipline, leadership and a little bit of luck. Luckily, that team had it all.

"We also had something that can't be taught – team camaraderie," she added. "The girls on that team worked hard for one another, listened to one another, looked out for one another, looked up to one another. We have a bond that can't ever be broken."

The Rams were serious about their success. After dominating in the pre-season, they opened the first half of the regular season with a 7-0-1 mark, with a powerful front line of senior Heather Rains, junior Sammi Burton and sophomore Abby Milillo leading the attack.

Burton was an outstanding player who had put a scare into the Rams by nearly deciding not to play. Smallwood, alerted by Sammi's mother, Cathy, that Sammi's interest was waning, had given Burton a call.

"I told her I was not going to try to talk her into staying," he recalled. "I just told her that things were starting to happen on a Tuesday in late June, and she needed to make a decision by then. She called me on the Thursday before that and said she was going to play."

Burton was a Division I-caliber college talent who opted not to play after high school, concentrating on her academics at Ohio State. She was a casualty of the non-stop, year-around soccer expectations … but when she did play, she was quite a player.

"I think about that a lot," Burton said when asked about college soccer nearly a decade later. "I had played so long, and my knees were bad. But yeah, I do think about it."

"Heather Rains and Sammi Burton – they were unstoppable," Harring said. "They were competitive with each other, but over time they learned to play together very well. They clicked so well together, especially from where they had come from initially."

Rains was tremendous in traffic with her back to the goal, and Burton had a big leg that could score from anywhere. Together, they were double trouble.

Smallwood's call to Burton underscored the great coaching tandem that Harring and Smallwood were over those four seasons from 2004 through 2007.

"I think that's a consistent theme of Badin – a consistent and unified coaching staff," Steve Mililo said. "Nobody cared more about the girls and about being prepared than Keith Harring. And Brian Smallwood had been around a long time – he was a brilliant soccer guy. That twosome was a great blend.

"They got a lot out of the kids," Mililo added. "The players' names changed every year, but they were like interchangeable parts. Keith and Brian really built the program."

"Keith gave me a lot of liberty," said Smallwood, who handled conditioning and the in-game substitutions. "If he needed anything, he'd walk up to me and say he wanted this to happen. I'd either say OK or suggest why it wasn't such a good idea."

The coaches felt so strongly about the leadership of Rains and the unity of the team that one day against local rival Ross High, they simply didn't go into the lockerroom at the break.

"We were always very technical at halftime about what we needed to do, but we wanted to pick a game and let the girls lead themselves," Smallwood recalled. "We were playing very lethargic against Ross, so we just told Heather Rains that we weren't coming in at halftime, that we didn't have a darn thing to say to them.

"Heather came back out for the second half, said the lineup's been set and we went from there," in what ended up as a 3-0 win over Ross. "She had strong composure."

Other BHS players also appreciated the efforts of former Badin coaches Craig Manahan and his wife, the former Jill Carter, from their club days with the FOSC Fairfield Fever.

"I remember being a ball girl in the 7th and 8th grade with some of my teammates from the Fever," said junior midfielder Lindsey Smith. "We were in such amazement watching the Badin girls and we knew we wanted to be as fast, strong, confident, and talented as they were.

"We were so lucky to have the Manahans as our club coaches," Smith said. "They were more than just coaches, they were like having a second set of parents. The love and care they had for us was a big part of why we all became so close as teammates and how we became a unit on the field. They molded us into star players at a very young age.

"Our footskills, speed, passion, endurance, love for the game, confidence, pride and whatever else makes you a star soccer athlete all came from them," Smith added, noting that many of the Fever players attended the Manahan wedding. "I could never thank them enough."

Abby Milillo graduated from the University of Tennessee with a master's degree in sports psychology in May of 2014, after playing D-I college soccer at Ball State, and concedes that perhaps her assessment of Badin girls soccer has something to do with her schooling.

But, like so many others, she said it came down to one word: cohesion.

"We had a family-like cohesiveness," Milillo said. "Yes, we had a strong core group of very skilled soccer players, and received superior coaching. But Coach Harring and Coach Smallwood also did a great job at facilitating a collaborative environment. I recall them guiding, rather than leading, us to the cooperative achievement of our group goals.

"They really empowered us," she added. "That resulted in a high level of motivation, inclusion and purpose for the players. We spent so much time off the field, all three years, developing a collaborative unit."

When the Rams collaborated to win their last three games, knocking off McAuley, Mother of Mercy, and Indian Hill – a trio of strong opponents -- they were headed into the post-season with a record of 11-3-2 and plenty of momentum.

Brian Smallwood remembered a bus ride back to school after one of the three setbacks.

"I was not a bus rider, but on this day, I happened to be on the bus," he said. "We're getting near school, Keith Harring gets up, has the lights turned on, and gives the team their marching orders.

"The lights go back off, we're almost to school, and suddenly the girls started singing the Badin fight song, loudly. It was pretty cool. It said something to me about the girls."

Singing the fight song, win or lose, continues to be a long-standing tradition among Badin girls athletic teams as the bus approaches the school.

"The girls played together," Steve Milillo emphasized. "That's the thing I think of – team unity, leadership and togetherness. The coaching staff really fueled that. It really exemplified those groups.

"There was no individual who took precedent," he added. "Somebody different stepped up each time. There was no jealousy; they really cheered for each other. At times, they played teams that were more talented. But there was no quit in those girls."

Sophomore Emily Flum was someone who stepped up as the season went on – no more so, ultimately, than in the state championship game.

"The biggest thing about the program is that it always pushed us to be better soccer players as well as to be a better person," she said. "The coaches always encouraged us to be the best that we could be. They were always there for us and pushed us to make ourselves better.

"As a whole, we just enjoyed being around each other and most of all loved playing soccer together," she added. "We all loved the sport of soccer and it made it that much better when you played with people who had the same passion for the game that you did. It didn't hurt that we were all friends."

When Sammi Burton scored twice from long range, Badin had knocked off a capable Valley View contingent 2-0 in the sectional finals, junior goalkeeper Jenny Rosen turning in her ninth shutout of the season.

Waiting in the wings: Kettering Alter, which had bounced Badin from the tournament a year ago and handed the Rams their last loss of this season, 1-0 in Game 13. In fact, in what was now his fourth season at the helm, Keith Harring had yet to beat the Knights, his record standing at 0-4-1 against them.

Ken Murrell, a longtime friend of Harring's, was working at Wright Patterson Air Force Base in suburban Dayton, and would frequently scout upcoming Badin opponents.

"Keith had asked me to go scout a Cincinnati school, and I told him, no, I believe I'll go scout Kettering Alter again," said Murrell, who expected Alter to be in the Rams' way and in fact scouted them three times for Harring that season.

Murrell had a master's degree from the University of Southern California, and was a flight test engineer at Wright Patterson. His son, Matt, had played for a Fairfield High baseball team that won the state championship in 1991.

"I loved scouting," Murrell said. "I'd give Keith engineering diagrams, and he'd pass them along to the girls. Keith was always very well prepared. He'd work hard to create mis-matches on the other team's lesser players. We always felt like Badin had the right people to hold the other teams down."

Like Badin, Alter had won 11 games coming into the contest – but the Knights had lost eight times. The burning question for the Rams, obviously, was could the team manage to get past this Alter nemesis … or would it be, "Wait 'til next year!" once more?

"I was not nervous going into that Alter game, and I was pretty vocal about that," Smallwood said.

While district championship games are played at neutral sites these days, that was still not the case in 2005 – so Badin got another shot at Alter at Garfield, now known as Hamilton Soccer Stadium, the site of the penalty kick loss in 2004.

Same site … different outcome, with Badin on top 2-1 on a thrilling Sammi Burton tally with 5:08 remaining in the second overtime. The game was headed for penalty kicks again, but the Rams wouldn't let it get there.

"Sammi Burton launched the ball into the goal, then disappeared," read Rick Cassano's lead to the JournalNews article the next morning.

"The ball was loose, I decided to take a shot, and then I was on the bottom of the dog pile," Burton told him. "Scoring that goal was the biggest weight off my shoulders. It was finally over."

"This was a big, big game," Harring said that night. "It's really exciting for the players and the school. The kids wanted to play Alter. They were hustling like crazy to win this game."

Badin had taken an early lead when sophomore Tori Mathews scored on a header off of a corner kick by junior Kristina Anderson, but Alter tied things at 1-all with a tally off a free kick in the final minute of the half.

Then, the two teams settled into a stalemate that looked like it might run out the clock.

Smallwood recalled a tableau of senior co-captain Kelsey Fontaine, who rarely played, having an overtime "chat" with her teammates.

"She had the girls in a half-circle and she was really lighting them up," he said. "She said we are NOT going to lose this game. She said she hadn't sat on the bench, come to all the practices and barely gotten into any games to lose at this point.

"After that, we didn't need to give any rah-rah speech," Smallwood added, enjoying the memory.

Badin had taken control of the second overtime period, but Alter had managed to stem the tide until Burton got off the game-winner from mid-range in front of the goal.

"This team has been together for a long time," Harring said. "It's neat as a coach to just step back and see the kids do what they need to do. When you watch these girls, you see a team that's united.

"We have so much depth, and every kid contributes," he added. "We're like a tree. All the roots and branches are part of the tree, just like every kid is a part of this team."

"I don't know if there's anybody out there that can beat them," Alter coach Jason Balogh remarked. "It's going to take an extraordinary effort to do it. This might have been the state championship game."

Burton, who helped keep the Rams alive in '05, called her favorite soccer memories "the small moments."

"It was collectively holding my breath with these girls, my teammates, while clutching each others' hands during shootouts," she said. "Girls who hailed from completely different backgrounds, cliques, socio-economic statuses, boyfriends or interests. But who dated who or, 'OMG, she wore *what* this weekend?' didn't matter the second the whistle blew and the game was on."

"The kids feel better getting rid of that Alter hex," Harring remarked. "We've had kind of a mental block against Alter."

Indeed, Madeira got to feel the hard edge of Badin's collective relief in the regional semifinals. There was no letdown for the Rams in the wake of that 'whew!' win over Alter. Instead, a rejuvenated Badin squad rolled into the regional finals with a 5-1 trouncing of Madeira, then slipped past Springfield Northwestern 2-1 to reach the Division II state semifinals for the first time since 2000.

"We could have lost to Springfield Northwestern – they didn't care if they scored," Smallwood recalled. "Heather Rains scored a spectacular goal. We usually subbed right after a goal, and that gave me a chance to say something to the team. I said, 'That's the Player of the Year, right there!'"

Now, the Rams were set to face Bexley in the state semifinals at Kettering Fairmont High. Bexley is a fashionable Columbus suburb, the home of Capital University and the site of a great book by former Chicago Tribune columnist Bob Greene entitled, "Be True to Your School", about growing up there in 1964. Four decades later, no one realized that this 2005 meeting between two regional girls soccer powers represented the first of three straight years the schools would go toe-to-toe with soccer highs and lows riding on the outcome.

On this particular night, getting to the game was Badin's biggest problem, a rush hour traffic jam in Hamilton making the Rams terribly late. (Hamilton is a city of 60,000 people ... except at rush hour, when it seems like it must be a city of 600,000 if you're trying to get in or out of town from the east side.)

"The bus driver was pulling in and out of alleys in Hamilton to try to get around a traffic jam on High Street – I think the girls must have thought they were on an amusement park thrill ride," Keith Harring said. "We got there about 15 minutes before game time. The officials added 10 minutes to the clock."

Lindsey Smith, who would go on to play soccer at the University of Findlay, remembered it as well.

"We pulled up to the field late, and we see that Bexley is already there in an extravagant charter bus, warming up on the field," she said. "It didn't quite intimidate the team, but we were all kind of taken aback.

"We had to rush to get ready, and as we are sitting in the lockerroom, waiting for Coach Harring's pump-up speech, I looked up to see that the quote we had put on the back of our warmup shirts was right there on the wall:

"Coming together is a beginning, staying together is progress, and working together is success." – Henry Ford

"We all instantly became excited and knew that we were going to win after God sent us that sign!" Smith said. "We all couldn't believe it. We had shirts made at the beginning of the season, and the saying just happened to be in that room. It was just so cool to see that in a random lockerroom right before your team is getting ready to play in the state semifinals!"

Badin was late to the field – running right through the Bexley players as they were warming up – but early to the goal. The wind was raging that night, and it was an ill wind for Bexley. The Rams scored a soft goal early, quickly tacked on another tally, and dominated en route to a 5-1 victory. It was a more competitive contest than the 2000 thrashing of Springfield Greenon, but for Badin, both outcomes led to the same result ... an opportunity to play for the Division II state championship at Columbus Crew Stadium.

"I don't think there is one word to describe my experiences playing for Badin," Kristina Anderson said. "It was wonderful, exciting, challenging, emotional and most importantly, fun. It was a group of girls who loved soccer and loved each other. We supported one another, on and off the field.

"Just like the community of Badin, the soccer team was a family and we stuck together and we played our hearts out," she added. "We wanted to make each other proud."

That the Rams stuck together would become very clear the morning of the state title game. Doylestown Chippewa was the opponent, and while Badin was ranked No. 1 in the state, Chippewa wanted to say something about that. The Lady Chipps were undefeated at 21-0-1, and had been to the state semifinals in 2004.

"The elevator incident ... how can you ever forget the elevator incident," Harring laughed in thinking back on it. "After that, the team was loose and relaxed."

That morning, Emily Flum suggested that the entire team should get on the hotel elevator, "because I thought it would be fun," she said. So, 25 girls got on the elevator ... which proceeded, of course, to get stuck.

"The weight capacity was 2,500 pounds," Heather Rains said. "So that means we all had to weigh 100 pounds or less, which is definitely not the case."

For 20 minutes, the girls sang the fight song and other popular tunes until the local fire department was able to free them. Then, they posed for pictures on the fire truck and with their rescuers. It was not your typical pregame preparation, but it certainly made for one helluva story.

"We went from being regretful and scared to relieved and excited," Rains said.

Doylestown Chippewa certainly did not help itself in the run up to the game that day. Coach Ruth Coney, the Ohio D-II Coach of the Year, noticed that the color of Badin's jerseys and shorts did not match – the Rams were in green jerseys and white shorts -- and insisted to the officials that Badin needed to go into the lockerroom and change.

But Badin assistant Brian Smallwood knew the rule ... the jerseys and socks have to match, but the shorts do not. There would be no changing.

Keith Harring, in the meantime, had seen a Chippewa player on crutches, obviously sidelined by injury. He had his own injury, senior co-captain Kellie Beadle, out with illness. He proposed a ceremonial ball drop to open the game to get both players on the field for just a moment before play started.

The officials thought that was a nice idea ... but the Lady Chipps would have to go along with it. Coney refused. Harring pleaded with the Chippewa coach. She wouldn't have it. Some Badin fans had apparently written on the Chippewa bus, and she was irritated.

"She said, 'I'm not going to give you an unfair advantage' (with the ball drop)," Smallwood recalled. "I said 'You just did!' (by her refusal)."

Of course, psychological advantages ultimately have little to do with the physical point of the game – putting the ball in the back of the net. Neither team was doing that. While Badin was controlling the encounter, out-shooting Chippewa 9-1 in the first half, it was a scoreless deadlock at the break.

It got worse for the Rams. Early in the second half, Chippewa's Chrissy Summers intercepted a throw-in by Badin sophomore Megan Reimer. She rushed up the left sideline and found an open Natalie Villers, who chipped one over the head of Badin goalie Jenny Rosen. Chippewa was up 1-0 off the miscue with 33:29 left in the game.

"We knew that wasn't it," Chippewa's Coney told the JN afterwards. "We knew it would take at least two goals. A soccer game is never over at 1-0. Never."

"I remember when they scored on us, (defender) Ashley Roberto pounded her fist into the ground," Smallwood said. "We used that energy."

"How do you win state?" Keith Harring mused. "You've got to believe. You've got to have the right attitude. You've got to play together on the field and win as a team."

Badin knew that it had to counter quickly to reverse the momentum … and did. Just six minutes later, Kristina Anderson was awarded a free kick. She drilled it into the box, where it bounced off Chippewa keeper Samantha Hoffman in traffic. Megan Reimer cleaned it up, and with a bit more than 27 minutes showing, it was 1-all.

"I was there on the backside" for the rebound, Reimer said. "I felt like the goal they scored was my fault, so that felt really good."

Badin continued to dominate, but the scoreboard continued to say 1-1. For the game, Badin out-shot the Lady Chipps 16-4, and had 10 corner kicks to none for Chippewa. In the end, they would play overtime.

"I will never forget the feelings of walking into the stadium, leading the team in warm-ups, lacing up my cleats, putting on my uniform, performing the coin toss and kicking off," Heather Rains said. "Before I knew it, the game went into overtime. The nerves were unbearable. I never wanted anything more in my life up until that point and was willing to do whatever it took to accomplish it."

"I can still remember to this day being so exhausted in the state finals and then looking over and seeing Kelsey Fontaine cheering her heart out – that gave me motivation to keep going," Anderson said. "I am actually smiling and almost tearing up while I think about this, the memories and the moments with that team are so special. They cannot be described in words. They make my heart swell with joy and pride."

At the start of the overtime, Harring made a tactical switch that was the difference maker. Abby Milillo approached him and asked to play up front. He made the move.

"I had been playing midfield the whole game, so I asked him to put me up front," Milillo said. "I knew if he put me up there, I could get something started, and I did."

"Intestinal fortitude," said Steve Milillo about what made his daughter an excellent player. "God blessed her with ability. She had skills, but rarely was she the best player out there. Mentally, she was a strong person. A goal setter.

"When she got to be 12 or 13 years old, the greatest and worst thing of her life happened – she swallowed the soccer pill," he laughed. "She wanted to play. That was her dream. Before she came to Badin, she was invited to play in Europe through the Olympic Development Program. That was special."

Emily Flum was another difference maker. Her minutes had been cut earlier in the season when she was switched from defense to midfield because of a change in the defensive rotation. On this day, though, Smallwood sent her into a midfield spot in the second half, and her energy and stamina kept her on the field for the rest of the afternoon.

Flum, in a letter to the 2013 team (it's reprinted in the Addendum), explained exactly what happened a little more than four minutes into the overtime period.

"Abby Milillo get the ball in the center of the field, and if you know anything about Abby, you better watch out! I see her making her way up centerfield towards the goal, I'm on the right side of the field making my way to the goal with her.

"She spots me on the outside closing in on the goal. She crosses the ball right in front of the goalie towards me. It was slow motion for me running towards the ball and realizing the goalie is closing in on the ball as well.

"So I lit some fire under my rear and ran as fast as I could. I beat the goalie to the ball and tapped it into the back of the net. Before I realized I had scored the winning goal of the 2005 state game, I was on the bottom of a dog pile."

Asked about the play that day, Flum said, "I didn't really know what happened until (Heather Rains) jumped on me. Then I just started crying."

The Rams, 18-3-2, were the Division II state champions. They had been to the mountain five times ... and now they were finally standing on top.

"Watching Emily Flum score that goal was the best feeling a senior captain could ever feel," Rains said. "Winning state was a wonderful accomplishment – one that I will never forget. I will love that 2005 team forever and have a special place in my heart for Badin soccer. It gives me chills reliving it."

"Winning state was the best feeling the world," Anderson said. "It was like everything froze. Every fitness test, every long practice, every drill. It all paid off. All of our hard work won us that game.

"Were we the best team?" she wondered. "Maybe not, but we were a group that loved soccer and had a passion for the game. We loved each other and had a desire to win. To us it didn't matter how we won or who scored – because we won. It was never an individual effort."

"Badin soccer was by far my favorite part of high school," said Flum, who would go on to play in two more state championship games as a member of the Class of 2008. "It is something I miss often. The thing that sticks out are the people who went through the experience with me. It is something that we will always share.

"We, the 2005 state championship team, had a special connection," she added. "We all worked well together."

"I saw these girls go wire-to-wire," Harring said, calling it a "tremendous" feeling. "They started the year ranked No. 1 in the state, and not too many teams who do that go on to win it all.

"They wanted to come here and establish their legacy, for Badin High School and for themselves," he added. "And that's what they did."

"As a parent, from an athletic standpoint, there was no prouder moment," Steve Milillo said of the title. "Especially in soccer, so many of these girls had played together from the time they were 5 or 6 years old. We knew all of the other parents – so to see those girls win it all, to experience that, how proud for all of us."

Heather Rains is from a talented athletic family. Both of her parents played for Badin, and both of her sisters – one older, one younger -- were standout softball players for the Rams who also earned college athletic scholarships. Heather ended her career by helping lead an Akron squad to its first-ever Mid-American Conference divisional title.

Badin girls soccer still runs in her blood. When reminded of the story from Strongsville, of grabbing the ball out of the net, of making her point at the very start of a season that would end in state championship gold medals for Rains and all of her Badin teammates, she smiled and said simply, genuinely, from the heart, "I love Badin soccer."

2006

Senior Kristina Anderson placed the ball down as the Badin faithful looked on in loud anticipation. Badin's version of "Supergirl" had a free kick from 28 yards out, and that was right in her wheelhouse. There were no guarantees – at 5-foot-6, she may have not have had much of a view of the goal over the wall of Bexley players arrayed 10 yards in front of her. But if she made it, the Badin girls soccer program would be on its way to Columbus Crew Stadium to defend its 2005 Division II state championship.

No pressure.

After the game, Anderson would probably be a walking bag of ice. She had bruises on top of bruises, including a problematic muscle issue in her back that would fully heal only when she stopped playing soccer ... permanently. That thought was nowhere on her radar screen ... soon, she would sign to play Division I college soccer at Ball State University and subsequently be selected to the Mid-American Conference all-freshman team.

On a Rams roster stocked with skill – senior defender Ashley Roberto, in fact, would be named the D-II Player of the Year in the state – Anderson was the face of the program. Off the field, she was quiet and friendly, with a megawatt smile. On the field, she was high energy personified, with an intense "no quit/never lose" attitude that was contagious.

"She was so natural, just flowing, so graceful," head coach Keith Harring said of Anderson. "You could play her anywhere on the field. She had a beautiful foot. She could put the ball just exactly where you wanted it."

When Anderson raised her hand briefly to let the teams and officials know she was ready to attempt the kick, everybody affiliated with the Badin contingent – teammates, coaches, parents, fans – had the same thought: She's going to make it.

"What a special player," BHS assistant Brian Smallwood said of Anderson. "To me, she is the most talented player who went through the school in the four years I coached at Badin."

Badin was on another tournament roll, and why not? Ranked No. 1, they were playing with experience, skill and confidence in the wake of last year's state title, racking up a 9-2-4 regular season record and allowing just two goals in the post-season to date.

"That was just a year of tremendous talent," said parent Steve Milillo. "That was the year everybody had been pointing toward. The senior class was loaded. There was so much leadership on that team, they almost got in each other's way. It was tremendous team."

The veteran seniors in the starting lineup included Anderson, Sammi Burton, Janie Jeffcoat, Ashley Roberto, Lindsey Smith and goaltender Jenny Rosen, who fashioned 13 shutouts on the year. Juniors Emily Flum, Erin Golden, Courtney Gray, Jessica Hammond, Emily Leisge, Tori Mathews, Abby Milillo and Megan Reimer all contributed to what, in retrospect, represents basically a Who's Who in Badin girls soccer annals.

Anderson would play college soccer at Ball State, Roberto at UNC/ Charlotte, Smith at Findlay, Rosen at Xavier, Milillo at Ball State and Reimer at Gardner-Webb as Ram talent spread far and wide. Others certainly could have played college soccer had they chosen to.

The Rams had run up against the Alter jinx once again this year, and knocked it on its ear – a 2-0 win during the regular season, and then a verdict in a penalty kick shootout to capture a second straight district championship.

The Badin girls soccer program had endured a lot of high profile heartache. After last year's 2-1 overtime state title victory over previously unbeaten Doylestown Chippewa, they were hoping that was behind them.

"It just clicked and everything came so naturally," Lindsey Smith said of the team. "If I was playing inside mid(fielder), I wouldn't even have to look up to know that Kristina Anderson was on the outside flank making an unstoppable run to help start an attack. We all just read each other so well."

"I attribute a large part of our success to our mental game," Abby Milillo said. "We had a solid performance routine before every single game, including positive self-talk and imagery.

"Also, we had a collective focus cue for every game, which we would all write onto our arms. For example, we would write '110%'

or 'control the controllables' or 'let the game come to you' on our arms," she added.

Sammi Burton, friendly and self-effacing, couldn't help but look back and smile.

"I was a total tomboy, video-game loving, secret fantastical fiction writer and total dork!" she said. "I joined forces with the gorgeous Janie Jeffcoat, the hilarious Abby Milillo and the popular Jenny Rosen. I could outrun half the football team, Janie could defend any all-state striker, and Abby could fancily tip-toe and tap her way around the biggest defenders.

"Badin's soccer team brought together the talents of amazing women, from completely different walks of life," Burton added. "We played because we were talented, and we won because we became sisters."

Jeffcoat had recovered from a serious knee injury to join Roberto as a shutdown defender. Her mother, Kathy, was a popular English teacher at Badin and her older sister, Megan, had been a soccer player as well and the valedictorian of the Class of 2005.

"Persistent, competitive, hard-working," Janie told the JournalNews when asked her best attributes as an athlete, admitting that her game-day breakfast consisted of "a Pop Tart and that's it. But I have to have a strawberry Pop Tart with no icing. Why? I don't know."

Badin girls soccer at Hamilton Soccer Stadium, on Fair Avenue across from Garfield Junior High, was the place to be.

"It was incredible to see the support from all of the people in the Badin community," Anderson recalled. "I remember one game, it must have been a night game because we were playing under the lights, I looked over and people were tailgating! Imagine that ... people were actually tailgating for a girls soccer game!

"I just remember being on the field and being so happy and proud to be playing for Badin," she said. "No other school had a fan following like we did. It made playing that much more fun!"

"The fans and their support – unforgettable," Courtney Gray said. "From the beginning to the end, we always had an incredible fan section. Whether they realized it or not, as a player looking up into the stands, it is truly motivating to see so many people there supporting you and your team. Parents, siblings, teachers, classmates – they helped us get to the end. We couldn't have done it without them."

The Rams were 7-1-3 when Kettering Alter came calling for an unusual Saturday mid-day game at the Hamilton field. It was that day that Kristina Anderson certainly put herself into the collective memories of BHS soccer fans.

She took herself out of the game and off the field midway through the first half. What no one knew at the time is that she was back in the lockerroom, throwing up. What they remember is her coming back onto the field for the second half, after her mysterious disappearance, and scoring both of Badin's goals in the 2-0 victory. "Want to" is what Anderson possessed, according to an item in a subsequent Badin alumni newsletter. A whole lot of "want to."

Nor did people realize, according to Brian Smallwood, that Anderson had been up late the previous night ... laying on the grass at midfield of the stadium, looking up into the stars, visualizing the game.

"Yes, that's a true story," Anderson said. "I was so excited to play Alter on our home field. We always had such a great crowd.

"It was really peaceful being out there at night. I laid right at centerfield and just imagined the game the next day, imagined the passes I would make, the tackles, the shots, everything! One thing that really helped me as a player was visualizing myself and my team being successful.

"I didn't imagine not feeling well in the game, but things happen!" she laughed. "That game is a special memory for me."

Anderson had told the JournalNews that her favorite television show was "Smallville", because Superman was her favorite superhero. So she became Badin's Supergirl.

"I'm a hard-worker," she said modestly of her own skill. "If I do something wrong, I'm not going to give up. (Opponents) are going to be busy."

And she called the best part of Badin girls soccer "the closeness of the girls on the team. Like every team, we have our disagreements, but we respect each other. We always have each other's back."

Smallwood recalled another experience with Anderson that ultimately left a permanent positive impression.

Anderson's corner kicks were typically flawless, with plenty of scorers in the box to try to finish them off. But Badin also ran a tap-in play, where Anderson would simply tap the ball into a teammate and the Rams would try to get a 2-on-1 advantage on the way to the goal.

One night, Badin called the tap-in play from the bench three consecutive times ... but each time, Anderson ignored the instruction and booted the ball into the box. Aggravated, Smallwood asked

Harring if he could pull Anderson off the field. Harring agreed.

"She came off the end of the bench and ended up behind me," Smallwood said. "We gave the players the freedom to countermand us, but this was too much. I told Kristina that one kick was one thing, but doing it three times was too many. She went down the bench and dumped the cooler and cups all over the field."

The Badin coaching brass let the incident go that night, but Smallwood planned to address it with Anderson the next day at practice.

"I got there early, because I was going to talk to her," Smallwood recalled. "She was already there, running sprints up and down the field, drenched in sweat. She came over to me and asked for a ball. I told her she could take the whole bag, so she did.

"She was practicing corners and running suicides," he continued. "She came up to me and said, 'It will never happen again.' Her parents had handled it at home. ... Like I said, she was a special player."

While Badin had plenty of marquee talent on the field, the contributions of goaltender Jenny Rosen were substantial. Tall, talented, and reliable in the net, she turned in 22 shutouts over two seasons and handled her stressful task in rock-solid fashion; well enough that she went on to play D-I college soccer.

When the Rams faced off against Kettering Alter in the district finals, that was Rosen's night. She picked the right time to shine.

"It was exciting, pretty much what I live for," Rosen told the media afterwards. "I like to have all the pressure on me."

Badin had been rolling in the tournament, beating Eaton 4-0 in the opener when the Eagles failed to get off a single shot on goal; and then turning back a previously unbeaten Monroe squad 4-1 in the sectional final.

"We're getting everybody's best game, and we have to deal with that," said Sammi Burton, who had three goals in the two games, as did Tori Mathews. "Now that we're in the tournament, the pressure is just amplified."

It brought the defending champs face-to-face with No. 2 seed Kettering Alter, 13-4-1, in a wet, muddy showdown at Kettering Fairmont High. In the aftermath, Keith Harring called it "a war," adding, "Jenny (Rosen) was unbelievable."

Both teams had scored in the first half, Milillo knotting things at 1-all off of an Anderson corner kick for the Rams before the defenses took over. No one scored in 40 minutes of second half play or 30 minutes of overtime.

There weren't many goals in the shootout, either.

It was 2-1 on penalty kicks – Anderson and Janie Jeffcoat having connected on PKs for the Rams – when Rosen stepped out of the goal to take what was Badin's fifth and final penalty try. If she made it, the game was over. If not, Alter had a fifth kick.

Rosen was wide … but she didn't let that faze her. She turned right around and faced off against Alter's Courtney Chihil. If Chihil scored, the match would go to sudden death PKs.

She didn't. Rosen deflected the kick … and Badin, winning by an unusually slim 2-1 margin on penalties, would play on.

"I didn't hear it hit the post," Rosen said, after diving to get a hand on the attempt. "I just looked up and saw my team coming at me."

Rosen and the Badin defense kept up their stellar play, shutting out Cincinnati Hills Christian Academy and Seven Hills in the regionals 5-0 and 3-0, respectively, to set the stage for a second straight showdown with Bexley in the state semifinals.

Bexley, 19-1-2, had been to the state Final Four seven times in the previous eight years under head coach Scott Dempsey, but had yet to win the title.

The Lions were very good -- and played possum with the Rams.

"Badin is fast and physical, and I think we've got the world's smallest high school varsity team," Dempsey said. "I don't know that our speed necessarily stacks up with Badin, but how many teams do stack up with Badin? Not very many."

"Last year, we just ran right around them," Harring said, referring to the 5-1 triumph en route to the state finals. "I think we can really go after them."

In fact, the Lions played Badin nearly stride for stride. Their speed was good and their skill was solid. There was no running around them. When Anderson raised her hand for the free kick with 12:09 showing in overtime at Clayton Northmont, neither team had scored.

"I wasn't the least bit nervous," Anderson told the JournalNews. "I like having the game on my shoulders."

Bang! Back of the net. Ballgame! Anderson had delivered an emphatic "yes!" to all of the Badin expectations. Bexley had no chance to make a play on the ball.

"I was thinking, 'This is for my team, this is for my school, this is for the Crew,'" Anderson said. "Now we can think about winning another state championship. We just want to bring it home."

Badin, 15-2-4, was headed back to Columbus Crew Stadium to defend its Division II state championship.

"The journey to the state tournament was unforgettable," Courtney Gray said. "We took it one game at a time, but we always had the state championship in the back of our heads. As a team, we truly focused on the task at hand, whether it was at the regional or district level. We kept a level-headed mindset, and I do believe that helped us get to the end – exactly where we wanted to be."

Parma Heights Holy Name, 17-3-2, would be the Rams' opponent, making its first-ever trip to the finals.

"I'm not nervous," Keith Harring said in the run-up to the game. "I'm very proud of this team. They've had a huge load to carry this year, but they've stepped up to the challenge. They will not back down.

"All we want to do is play our best game," he added. "But no matter what happens, these girls are all winners for the rest of their lives. They're wonderful young ladies. In my eyes, in God's eyes, they'll all be champions."

Janie Jeffcoat, one of eight seniors on the team, was somewhat wistful on the eve of the game. "All the seniors play only one sport, so this is our last game as a Badin Ram," she said. "I think we're all pretty sad about that. It will be very difficult for me to walk away. I've been on varsity for four years, and now it'll just end. I'll probably cry. I might cry even if we win."

Emily Flum, back to her accustomed spot on defense as a junior, had scored only one goal a year ago … but it had been the game-winner in the title tilt.

"I don't really like to take credit for it," she told the JournalNews. "I know it's weird to say that, but I like to say the team made it happen for me. It was a team effort."

"Badin girls soccer – it's always about the team, never about the individual," Steve Milillo said. "The girls really propelled each other. They were always very happy for each other."

"The feeling (after the game-winner) is so hard to explain," Flum added in the JN interview. "It's like a rush. You're in shock for a little bit, then you're ecstatic and everybody's hugging you. There's this joy and excitement. It's everything combined."

Flum said it would be fine if someone else scored the game-winner this season. "Let somebody else experience it," she smiled. "I'll still be there to celebrate."

For Badin, though, there would be no celebration.

It was déjà vu all over again from 10 years ago. In 1996, the Rams had lost to a Chagrin Falls team they felt they would have beaten on any other day. In 2006, the Rams lost to a Parma Heights Holy Name team they felt they would have beaten on any other day.

On penalty kicks.

"Holy Name ... they were bullies. We knew that all along," Keith Harring said looking back on the game. "Their player threw Ashley Roberto down, and there was no call. That was uncalled for. I said something to the female referee and she said, yeah, maybe she missed that one.

"A few minutes later, Kristina Anderson was thrown down in the box. Again, no call," Harring said. "I think we got a yellow card on that, we were so angry. We dominated the game and couldn't put the ball in the net."

"We knew they would instigate a pause because they did not have a deep bench, and they did," Brian Smallwood recalled. "Their coach was on the field coaching his team, but the referees wouldn't do anything about it. We had to get our fans to quiet down."

Badin controlled the game, but the scoreboard read zeroes. The Rams hit the post twice, and had other opportunities go awry during the course of the afternoon. Neither team scored ... not in 80 minutes of regulation, not in 30 minutes of sudden death overtime.

Just as the Rams' first trip to the state finals in 1995 had been a scoreless tie that had come down to penalty kicks, this 2006 championship match would as well.

"We don't yell at our players at halftime," Smallwood said. "That's my only regret in four years at Badin. We should have yelled at them that day, and we didn't. We all know that now."

Should have yelled, in other words, to put some fire and urgency into the Rams.

"We were playing well and there were no changes needed," he said, indicating why there was no halftime yelling. "We beat them (Holy Name) at Strongsville in 2007," during the annual pre-season set of scrimmages the following season – but by then it was too late.

Too late to salvage the penalty kick shootout that went Holy Name's way in the most heart-wrenching of fashions.

"That's one of the downsides to soccer," Steve Milillo said. "Penalty kicks. But how do you finish the game?"

Badin, shooting second, matched Holy Name kick-for-kick in a 3-3 deadlock, seniors Kristina Anderson, Sammi Burton and Janie Jeffcoat scoring for the Rams in what was the final time they would swing their foot in earnest for BHS.

When Emily Balodis scored for Holy Name, it was 4-3, and Badin sophomore Lindsey Donges headed to the penalty kick line for the Rams.

Donges, a midfielder, had earned ever-increasing playing time throughout the season. On this day, Harring had given her the task of marking Holy Name's all-state senior, Lynnea Pappas, and Donges had held her to one shot on goal. She had played a big game.

"As a sophomore, I was excited to play with the older girls," Donges said in looking back. "I had to play 110 percent harder than the year before. My game got a lot better. I looked up to all of them. It was nice to play with them."

In practice, Donges was also one of the Rams' most reliable PK shooters.

"When it comes down to penalty kicks, who do you put out there?" Smallwood said, responding to the second-guessers who wondered about sending a sophomore to the line on such a veteran team. "You're darned if you do and you're darned if you don't. Lindsey was the best penalty kick shooter on the team."

"It was nerve-wracking for sure," said Donges when asked about it these many years later. "I remember it like it was yesterday. It hit the inside corner of the right post, rolled down the goal line, and barely missed the left post ..."

Barely missed the left post, no good. When Jessica Bound stepped up and scored for Holy Name, the Green Wave had won the championship, 5-3 on penalty kicks.

"I hate PKs," Harring said afterwards. "It's not fair to Lindsey Donges. It's not fair to Jenny Rosen. It's not fair to anybody."

"(Coach Harring) said my task was to guard the No. 1 player on the other team. I had a job to do, and that went well," Donges said. "I think we out-played them 100 percent. ... You just think that maybe there was something we could have done during the game that would have changed the outcome."

"Big deal – off the post. Big deal," Harring said that day. Today, he points out that high school goal posts are typically rounded, so Donges' kick may very well have bounced into the goal at a high school field. But with the flat posts at Crew Stadium, it bounced out.

"Lindsey played an awesome game that day," Harring said in retrospect. "She had stepped up all year, and she really shut the Holy Name girl down. But what does she think about? Hitting the post. That's not the game."

In a post-game column that hit all the right notes, JournalNews sports writer Jay Morrison quoted the late Steve Cummins, the cerebral and outstanding boys soccer coach in the Lakota district who had died much too young at the age of 50 in 2003: "Soccer is a cruel, cruel game," Cummins would say. "It'll break your heart every time."

The Badin girls soccer family, as it would do, enveloped an understandably heartbroken Donges that day.

"I just held her for a few seconds before saying anything," Ashley Roberto told Morrison. "Then I just told her it wasn't her fault, which it wasn't. We never should have gone to PKs in the first place."

Wrote Morrison:

Hopefully in a few days – or maybe weeks – Lindsey Donges will be able to look back on Saturday's experience and hear more than just a ball hitting a post. Hopefully the sounds that resonate will be those words of support and encouragement she received from her teammates.

"I'd turn the world over to those girls," Harring said. "They are class, and they are going to be successful in whatever they do. They will come back from this game. Because that's what it is, it's just a game."

It's a game all right, a game that will break your heart.

Fortunately, it's played by people who know how to mend it.

Eight seniors put their Badin girls soccer uniform on for a final time that Saturday afternoon: Kristina Anderson, Sammi Burton, Amanda Hessling, Janie Jeffcoat, Emily Lawall, Ashley Roberto, Jenny Rosen and Lindsey Smith. Collectively, Morrison pointed out, they had gone 17-3 in the postseason for the Rams.

A repeat state championship, though, was just not in the cards.

Kristina Anderson said she learned "many things" at Badin, but that one item she still kept close was a Kairos senior retreat note from "the one and only Mr. P.," Brian Pendergest, now the principal at BHS.

"He wrote, 'Stay true to yourself and never forget where you came from,'" she recalled. "I still have it in my desk drawer. I take it out whenever I need a reminder that the place I came from taught me to have confidence, to value myself and to never stop fighting for what I believe in and for what I deserve.

"It taught me to take pride in myself and the things that I do. The place I came from is one of incredible strength and support. The place I came from is Badin. And there aren't enough words in the world to explain how special of a place that is."

2007

"I believe in us!"

Badin senior Courtney Gray was emphatic in her declaration after the Rams reached the Division II state finals for the third consecutive year with a 2-1 triumph over Madeira High in the semifinals at Mason.

As hard as it is to get to the state finals even one time, this was the second time that Badin had made three straight trips to the championship game. The Rams did it a decade apart, going in 1995-96-97 and now 2005-06-07.

"Unforgettable – that's the word that sums it up," Gray said. "I take great pride and feel very fortunate to have been a part of that three-year run," she said. "The journey, the competition, the fans, the tradition, the team. It's something I will always cherish in my heart. It was all simply unforgettable."

There were 12 seniors who didn't know how to do anything else but win, racking up a 10-5-1 regular season mark that included victories over Fenwick, Madeira, Mariemont, McNicholas, Mother of Mercy and Ross, always tough opponents.

"That was so unexpected – that was a fun team," Keith Harring said. "They had an attitude, and they played together. They just played really well. That's one of the teams I'm really proud of. They weren't supposed to be there at all."

That was a case, said assistant coach Brian Smallwood, where the whole was better than the sum of its parts. "That was a team that accomplished more as a unit," he nodded. "It was a very classy team."

"That team had a lot of role players from the previous year," said Steve Milillo, "and they just jelled together so well. They didn't have all that tremendous talent, but they had great desire. They were fun to watch.

"That team over-achieved," he added. "You couldn't say the previous two teams over-achieved, but that team did. They believed, and they rose to the top."

Two early injuries had an impact, but the Rams had the confidence to recover.

The soccer gods were not at all kind to junior Lindsey Donges, who was no doubt hoping to put that penalty kick pain of 2006 behind her as quickly as possible. Instead, she blew out her knee in the first game of the season and missed the whole year.

Donges, though, held her head high. She came back to co-captain a team that missed making a fourth straight trip to the Final Four by a single game as a senior, was an officer in Badin's National Honor Society, then graduated magna cum laude from nursing school at the University of Cincinnati. Today, she is a nurse at Mercy Hospital/ Fairfield, one of the top hospitals in Greater Cincinnati. And, ironically, she works on the same floor as fellow nurse Emily Flum, who scored the game-winner in the 2005 title tilt.

Donges had to bear an unfair burden from that 2006 final, but she has gotten well beyond it. She may remember the penalty kick "like it was yesterday," but she is quick to add, "I would go back again, I would. I would go back to freshman year and do it all over again right now. Playing soccer was probably the best part of high school for me, honestly. I miss it."

Told the working title of this book was, "The Family", Donges said, "That's a perfect title. Those girls are still some of my closest friends. We always talk and catch up. They are definitely a part of my family."

Senior Abby Milillo could not play at all, either.

She injured her knee the day after the 2006 championship game and it simply got worse.

"We had decided that she would take a couple of weeks off from soccer after the championship game," her father, Steve, recalled. "So we're driving home from the game and she got a call from her club coach. He said the club team was playing tomorrow at Princeton High, and could she play? She said 'OK.'

"I said, 'Wait a minute … what did we just talk about?' She said, 'It's only one game.' Well, she made a slide tackle in that game and I notice she's gimping around a little bit. She played the entire club season on a bad knee. She'd torn the meniscus on that tackle. We didn't know that at the time. She finally had surgery and even though she stayed off of it for six weeks, she just couldn't come back for her senior year."

Being sidelined was not easy on Abby Milillo.

"She really struggled with not being able to play," her father said. "Psychologically, it was very difficult for her."

While Milillo and Donges watched the season from the bench, others were there to step up ... including freshmen Allie Crossley and Abby Stapf, standouts on four consecutive district championship teams.

"I always talk about roles, and the kids knew their roles," Harring said. "We had a lot of injuries that year, so we were constantly changing the lineup. That team found a way."

The Rams were coasting along at a pedestrian 5-5-1, having just lost to St. Ursula and Kettering Alter, when Harring made a move that turned the season around. He revamped his defensive alignment, switching from a "flatback four" backfield to a diamond defense, which still had four in the back but challenged the opponents' attack more quickly as well as giving the defenders a chance to be part of the offense.

Senior Courtney Gray was the stopper up top, with junior Christina Walsh at sweeper in the back. Seniors Emily Flum and Emily Andes guarded the flanks.

"Courtney Gray was terrific that year," Harring said. "Emily Andes had a great year as well," and was certainly a player who stepped up for the Rams. Andes had been rostered for both previous championship games, but hadn't gotten on the field either year.

Junior Megan Woodrey had succeeded Jenny Rosen in goal, and she was a revelation as Badin didn't miss a beat in the nets.

"Woodrey really carried us a lot that year," Harring nodded. "She was really good off of her feet."

The Rams suddenly found their mojo, and were unstoppable. They rattled off 12 consecutive wins on their way to the finals, served up nine shutouts, and allowed only four total goals in the other three games. It was a remarkable run, unmatched by any previous finalist. The 1997 Rams had won 11 in a row before facing Columbus DeSales in the championship, but the 2007 squad went them one game better. Not that it was easy. In soccer, it never is.

In the sectional finals, Badin faced off against rival Middletown Fenwick in a constant rain at West Carrollton. Each team had a lead in regulation ... Fenwick snapped Badin's string of six straight shutouts with a 1-0 advantage before the Rams' Tori Mathews knotted it in the final minute of the first half; and Badin led 2-1 on a Megan

Reimer goal before Fenwick tied it at 2 midway through the second half.

And then the teams just kept playing. Through regulation, through the first sudden death period as well as the second. And the rain kept coming.

Finally, it was time for penalty kicks. And not just penalty kicks, but sudden death penalty kicks.

Badin, shooting second, trailed 4-3 in the regular PK rotation when it got to its final kick. It was up to Emily Andes to force sudden death, or the Rams' season would be over. She was up to the task, and now whoever scored without the other team matching would win, or, on this particular soggy night, survive.

Fenwick blinked first, the Falcons putting their opening sudden death PK over the top of the goal. Now Badin sophomore Michelle Seither was up. It was, she conceded, "nerve-wracking, definitely." But she was just the latest to put her name into Badin's circle of clutch players, pounding it home. The Rams had advanced.

"When I shot it, it wasn't what I thought it would be," Seither told the JN that night. "At first, honest to God, I was in shock. But then I heard everybody screaming, and that's when it started to set in."

Survive and advance – in the tournament, that's what it's all about.

That's exactly what Badin did in the district finals, a 1-0 tally over Cincinnati Hills Christian Academy.

"When I was coaching the Zigs," said Brian Smallwood, referring to the Kolping club team that had included Badin's Erin Golden, Courtney Gray and Tori Mathews, among others, "if we scored first, the game was over. That's the way we always felt at Badin, too. If we ever scored the first goal, we never lost."

It set up the third straight tournament showdown with Bexley in the regional semifinals. The previous two games had been in the state semifinals, but with five D-II district champions in Southwest Ohio, Badin had drawn into a tournament bracket that would send it out of town into the Southeast regional.

Bexley was unbeaten at 19-0-1, ranked No. 1 in the state, and had allowed only two goals all season.

Make it three, after Badin's Erin Golden knocked home a rebound with 21 minutes remaining for what was the only goal of the game.

"That was a total team effort," Keith Harring said that night. "We made a lot of (lineup) changes, and everybody did what we needed them to do. I'm so proud of these kids. They have so much character and play so hard together."

A year ago, Bexley head coach Scott Dempsey had said, "It was an appropriate game for the state semifinals. Badin's a tremendous team. They've got team speed and tremendous technical ability, and they play with a style and physicality that's second to none. I hope they take care of business Saturday at Crew Stadium."

This time around, he was not so sanguine about Badin's physicality.

Asked by JN sports writer Rick Cassano if he expected Badin's physical performance, Dempsey said, "Of course. Everybody in the state knows they play on the edge."

On the edge, wondered Cassano. On the edge of what?, he asked. "Just on the edge," Dempsey responded.

Smallwood read that comment with a knowing smile.

"We actually had something that we called 'edge training' during two days in the preseason," he said. "It was training on your tactical and physical edge. With our ability, if someone isn't falling, you're not going hard enough."

It was Badin's Golden, though, who had taken at least one hard edge of the action, when she collided with Bexley goalie Katie Sarvas going for a ball early in the second half. Sarvas made the play, and Golden was banged up, hurting one side of her rib cage in the collision, and the other side when she hit the ground.

"I just needed to get my breath and get right back in there," Golden said. "It was exciting, overwhelming," she added of the win. "It's great to know that you can accomplish something as a team that you've worked so hard for all season long."

It could almost be considered the second straight year that Golden, a little 5-foot-2 red-headed spitfire, had beaten Bexley.

In 2006, it was Golden with a sensational heads-up reaction midway through the second half to maintain a scoreless tie in the state semifinal. With Jenny Rosen out of the net on a scramble play, Golden had instinctively raced over to cover the line, and while still on the run, knocked a Bexley shot clear that was no more than a blink away from crossing into the goal. In a game that went overtime, that play likely kept Badin from absorbing a 1-0 setback in regulation.

Now she had scored to eliminate No. 1 Bexley in the 2007 regionals, and the Rams played on.

"When I picture Erin on the field, I see her backside sprinting after a ball with her messy bun ponytail flopping in the air," said lifelong friend and teammate Courtney Gray. "Relentless would be a good word to describe her as a soccer player. I don't think I've ever seen someone more determined and focused than her. She gave her all every single game, every single practice."

When Erin's family and the Badin soccer community thinks about Erin Golden, they have to smile broadly at the memories. Sadly, tragically, that's what they are – memories. Golden was diagnosed with a rare brain cancer in January of 2012, and passed away in March of 2013 at the age of 22.

Badin hosted the funeral in Mulcahey Gym, and "the family" was out in force. Golden was, in her own word, "fearless" in the face of death. Badin faced it with love and affection for her. That didn't make it any less heartbreaking.

"Effort was a big part of her game," said Smallwood, who coached Golden for the Zigs as well as BHS. "She was a take-charge player. There wasn't a shot she didn't think she could make. She played with spit and vinegar."

Smallwood recalled one practice where the Rams were running sprints; Golden, obviously not feeling well, was crying. He felt like she should take a break.

"I said, 'Get those tears out of my grid!' And she just looked at me and said, 'Blow the whistle!' (for the next sprint). She had a toughness about her. That was it. She just said, 'I'm fine!' That was Erin. That wrapped her up in a bow."

"Erin never seemed to get tired, and if she did, it didn't show," Gray said. "She hated subbing out of the game. I always thought that was funny – you could tell when a sub yelled her name, she just wanted to roll her eyes and tell the coach that she didn't need a sub. On the sidelines, Erin would stand by the coaches so in case they needed to make a quick substitution, she would be the first player they saw.

"She loved the game, she loved winning," Gray added. "Some of my fondest memories with her on the field come from celebratory hugs after a scored goal. Most players will give high fives, but Erin always seemed to come up with a big smile and an accompanying hug. And her hugs were the best."

Bexley High can be forgiven if the name "Badin" seems like a four-letter word to them. The Badin girls basketball team knocked Bexley out of the regional finals in 2004, and now the Rams had bounced Bexley out of the girls soccer tournament in 2005, 2006 and 2007. Each game was different ... each team was different. And Badin just kept winning.

"The competition we encountered was unforgettable," Gray said. "We put our blood, sweat and tears into each and every game. Some games required more than others, but that made it fun."

Badin traveled north to Dublin Scioto – scene of two previous state championship failures in 1996 and '97 – for a regional final battle with Coshocton. The stress level was high, because Badin was trying to reach the Final Four for a third straight year. The competition, surprisingly enough for that stage of the tournament, was not. Badin thrashed Coshocton 5-0 in a game that could have been much worse had Harring not had his squad pull in their horns in the second half.

Mission accomplished – the Final Four, again, and the foe would be a familiar one … Madeira, coming out of the Southwest region that Badin had vacated this year, a very strong program winning its first regional title.

Both teams were on a roll – Badin coming in at 16-5-1 off 11 straight wins, and Madeira at 18-2-2, having won 13 in a row and giving up only one goal in the process.

The Amazons' last loss? A 3-2 home setback to Badin in mid-September.

That earlier game underscored the old adage, "Never give up on the ball …" Late in what was shaping up as a 2-2 tie, Badin had booted a long ball that senior Megan Reimer went sprinting after.

It was beyond her reach, and the Madeira goalie was set to gather it in. But with Reimer bearing down on her, the goalie muffed the ball … which popped directly to Reimer, with no one between her and the net 15 yards away. She finished off what was her third goal of the afternoon, and Badin snuck out with a victory.

"I'm almost glad we lost to Badin the first time," Madeira coach Dan Brady said. "I think it's going to be hard to beat us twice."

And in fact, it *was* hard to beat Madeira twice. But Badin did it, perhaps its big game experience telling the tale after nearly 55 minutes of scoreless soccer on a cold night at Mason. Megan Reimer scored twice, and the Rams prevailed, 2-1.

It meant that for the season, the scoring tally had been Reimer 5, Madeira 3 … and, most importantly, Badin 2 wins, 0 losses.

"I wish I knew what it was," the low-key Reimer said of her magic against Madeira. "I just finished my opportunities."

Badin had made the key tactical move in the second half, moving Reimer up to striker and pulling Tori Mathews back to center-mid

... allowing Reimer to attack, and Mathews to use her skills to help control the middle.

Mathews, nicknamed "The Tiki Monster", was a second-team all-state selection. Small, strong and quiet, she was an outstanding athlete who was also a starting guard on Badin girls basketball teams that reached the D-III regionals in 2007 and 2008.

Smallwood remembered Megan Reimer as an 8-year-old, and was proud of how far she'd come as a soccer player. "When she was 8-years-old, she was scared to go onto the field. She would hold onto the goalpost.

"She had single-handedly beaten Madeira during the regular season, so she was heavily marked in the tournament game," he said. "At halftime we knew we had to do something to make it harder for Madeira to mark her. She had been crying, hiding her face in her shirt. ... We put her in at striker. At that point, she wasn't coming off the field."

With 26 minutes left in the game, Reimer drilled a left-footed shot from 27 yards out into the upper corner. At the 13 minute mark, she found herself one-on-one with the goalie off a breakaway, and finished.

Madeira's Brady had not meant to challenge the Rams with his "hard to beat us twice" comment, but that's the way the girls took it. With the score 2-0 in the final 10 minutes, one normally mild-mannered Badin grandfather made the point quite loudly during a stoppage in play: "We ARE going to beat you twice! We ARE going to beat you twice!"

"I thought we dominated the game," Harring said after Badin's 12th straight win had earned the Rams a third straight trip to the D-II state finals. "(Madeira) played their hearts out, but we were winning the ball."

It got a little hectic at the end, when the Amazons scored on a penalty kick with 4:04 showing, but Badin's defense – the group that had keyed the 12-game run, led by Andes, Flum, Gray, Walsh and with Woodrey in the goal – continued to stand tall.

"By the end of our journey, we faced the toughest competition of all," Gray said. "I will never forget having to tell myself, 'Don't let this be the last run you ever make' ... 'Don't let this be the last defender you ever face' ... 'Don't let this be the last shot you ever take' ... 'Don't let this ...'"

When the Rams stepped onto the field at Columbus Crew Stadium for their third consecutive D-II state title game, eight of the girls in the starting lineup were seniors – Emily Andes, Emily Flum, Erin Golden, Courtney Gray, Jessica Hammond, Emily Leisge, Tori Mathews and Megan Reimer. Veteran seniors Ashley Crossley, Kaitlyn Spradling and Asheton Whitaker were there as well, with Abby Milillo on the injured list.

Milillo battled her way through numerous injuries during a college soccer career at Ball State University, but persevered. Before what turned out to be the final contest of her career, a Mid-American Conference tournament game at Western Michigan, Milillo was asked to do the pre-game lockerroom talk.

She said to her teammates, "Close your eyes and think about the most fun you've had playing soccer." She'd made a collage of all her years playing for Badin, which she shared with her fellow Cardinals. "This is why I play today. I had forgotten what it was like to have fun and play soccer."

Badin would face Shaker Heights Hathaway Brown in the 2007 D-II state title tilt. Hathaway Brown, a private girls school from the east side of Cleveland, had only fielded a team for eight seasons, but in those eight years had put together a strong program – winning the 2004 D-II state crown along the way.

"Our mind-set is we have to win," Badin's Flum said. "We can't lose. We aren't going to lose. That's basically it. We're going in with a positive attitude and coming out with a win."

"These kids ... believe in themselves," Harring said. "It's not a swagger. It's confidence."

"The team – *the* team. We believed we were THE team," Gray said. "The team that deserved the state championship. The team that could defeat any competition. We came and we conquered. And what an awesome feeling that was.

"I believed in us from the very beginning," she added. "I knew our strength, I knew our depth, I knew our hearts and I knew our bond. I believed that we would be the state champions."

They were not.

Five minutes into the game, Hathaway Brown nearly scored. It was at that point that Badin followers looked around at each other and said, "Uh-oh." It was clear that Hathaway Brown was bigger, faster and stronger than the Rams. It was clear that the Blazers were better than the Rams. It was clear that this was going to be a long day for BHS.

Merrill Bachouros tallied 20 minutes into the game for HB, and Lani Smith scored with 11:35 showing in the game, and that was the final – 2-0, Hathaway Brown, which finished 20-3-1 for the year.

"The hardest part," Erin Golden said afterwards, "is coming so far only to lose."

"Hathaway Brown – they were a great team," Steve Milillo said. "I would have put them up against anybody in the state in either division."

In fact, Badin played about as well as it could play in losing the final. The Blazers kept BHS from doing much at the offensive end, and kept the Rams busy at the defensive end. There could be no second-guessing about this setback. No shame at all in losing.

"They were a fast team, and they were moving," Harring said afterwards. "It was like that first shot as a boxer. It kind of startled us. Then we didn't get our game going, and I think it was caused by them. … We were just on our heels."

A year earlier, Badin – much to the subsequent regret of the girls – had been a bit ungracious in defeat following the penalty kick setback to Parma Heights Holy Name. Many of the Rams walked away from the post-game medal ceremony and took their medals off -- just as Badin had done following the 2004 district final loss to Kettering Alter.

This, however, had been after a second place finish in the entire state, which is still a tremendously successful season. That did not go over well with the Ohio High School Athletic Association, with Parma Heights Holy Name, nor with the Badin administration.

"That wasn't right," Keith Harring remarked. "The girls put their medals down, and they should not have done that. But they were just so frustrated."

The appropriate apologies were made, and Badin girls soccer moved on.

Now fast forward a year, to the 2007 finals, and Hathaway Brown were not such gracious winners.

With Badin trailing 2-0 and the clock winding down, there was a collision on a slide tackle in front of the Blazers bench. The HB player got up and stepped over, rather than around, her Badin counterpart.

Courtney Gray, on top of the play as well, raised her arms in a "What the heck is going on?" expression to the officials.

Behind her, a Hathaway Brown assistant coach lingered close to the sideline.

"I've never felt so disrespected by a grown adult in my life as I was by that coach," recalled Gray, noting that the coach was calling, "Scoreboard, number 12! Scoreboard!" into her ear. "I can remember exactly how he was standing when he muttered those words. Left arm folded over his chest with his right arm upward over his mouth. His right index finger rested on his nose and there was just a little space for me to see his mouth, with a devilish grin.

"Don't ask me why I remember those details, I just do," Gray shrugged. "It was very uncalled for, especially coming from a coach. If it were another player (trash talking), I'd have understood."

Harring had plenty of respect for his 12 seniors. "I'm going to miss these ladies," he said. "They'll have a special place in my heart for a long time."

JournalNews sports writer Jay Morrison paid particular notice to the fact that the Rams composed themselves well when asked to huddle up and smile for a picture with the state runner-up trophy.

"As ridiculous as the request was," he wrote, "the Rams complied. And not just with the kind of eye-rolling, sideways smirk that teenage girls are famous for. These were bright, beaming loud and proud smiles."

"They should be proud," Harring said. "They played their hearts out, and they deserve to be proud. … They had an incredible season. Twenty years from now when they come back together, they can never lose that. It will be more meaningful in the future. It really will be."

"Hathaway Brown was full of talented players," Gray said in looking back on the game. "We simply got outplayed, but we gave it our all.

"I believed we would win the state championship game all three years that we were there. Even though it was only one year that we won the title, I wouldn't change it for the world," Gray added. "I look forward to the day when I can reminisce about my Badin soccer experience with my children. Today, I beam with pride and excitement any time the subject comes up with friends or teammates."

Hathaway Brown won another D-II state championship in 2009 with a 2-1 victory, but shortly thereafter was forced to forfeit the title for using an ineligible player.

Some people around the Badin soccer camp might call that "karma."

There was a bit of chutzpah involved by the Blazers, who felt the ineligible player – apparently one of the better players on the team, though never publicly identified -- should still be eligible even though she had reportedly spent the spring semester at a soccer academy in

Florida. She was a Hathaway Brown student, they argued, who just happened to be going to school in Florida.

Ineligible, said the Ohio High School Athletic Association.

The recipient of the 1-0 state championship win by forfeit? Bexley, making its 8th appearance in the Final Four, and its second in the title game following a runner-up finish in 1999. The Lions had to figure they'd suffered enough soccer heartache over the years. They'd have rather won the title on the field, but their program was certainly worthy.

And while Badin did not return to the state championship game for six years, it's not as if the girls soccer team vanished from the headlines.

In 2008, the Rams started out 1-3-2 before righting the ship and battling their way to the regional finals, the Elite Eight. Captains Lindsey Donges, Christina Walsh and Megan Woodrey pulled the team together, and young veterans like Allie Crossley, Michelle Seither and Abby Stapf were joined by new names, like Sydnee Fields, Sammy Koerner ("the Koerminator") and Caitlin Shafor, along with a trio of talented freshmen, Kim Golden, Ashley Mahoney and Lauren Mathews.

"Success breeds success," Athletic Director Sally Kocher said in looking back. "You have girls playing for good club teams, and they want to continue playing for a good high school team. In many cases, that was Badin girls soccer. If you're good at soccer, you get to play at a smaller school like Badin."

Sydnee Fields represented that reality. She had transferred to Badin late in the summer before her junior year after being cut from the soccer program at Ursuline Academy – apparently because she was too small! File that under, "it's not the size of the girl in the fight, it's the size of the fight in the girl." (And as Ursuline Academy expressed some ongoing dismay over the fact that Fields was starring for Badin, well, they had cut her, so there wasn't much they could say about it.)

Fields, a girl with personality who took to Badin like she'd been there her whole life, was a two-time first team all-league selection for Badin, inducted into Badin's National Honor Society (lest someone think she was only about soccer), and went on to play four years of Division I soccer at Xavier University, where she captained the team as a senior. In this case, Ursuline's loss was clearly Badin's gain.

Unbeaten Madeira finally got the better of the Rams in the regional finals, getting a goal just 3:24 into the game and making it stand up for a 1-0 victory, denying BHS its fourth consecutive trip to the Final Four. Instead, it was the Amazons' second straight appearance in the D-II Final Four – where they were knocked out by Middletown Fenwick, which was on its way to the 2008 state championship.

In Southwest Ohio, it was just as Kocher put it – success breeds success, as the same schools kept showing up in the tournament year-in and year-out to knock each other out. Madeira would get a state championship of its own in 2010 (defeating, by the way, Shaker Heights Hathaway Brown!).

That 1-0 setback for Badin was the first of four consecutive years the Rams would end their season with a 1-0 tournament defeat … Madeira in the regional finals in 2008, Wyoming in the regional semifinals in 2009, Indian Hill in the regional semifinals in 2010, and Summit Country Day in the district finals in 2011. That latter loss represented Badin's first trip to the Division III tournament after enough high schools were playing girls soccer that the OHSAA could add a third division to the post-season, and the Rams found themselves in the smallest school bracket.

In 2009, it was Madeira once again that provided the Rams a boost – though it was totally unexpected. On the road to face the Amazons in the regular season, Badin goaltender Katie Maus broke her hand in warmups. With freshman backup keeper Morgan Walker not quite ready for the varsity wars, Keith Harring pulled talented senior athlete Caitlin Shafor off the field and stuck her in the goal for the second half.

Shafor was, in a word, terrific.

Badin still had an excellent team, and Shafor was the glue behind a strong defense. The Rams were 11-4-4 when they faced unbeaten Wyoming in the regional semifinals at Centerville.

No one knew it at the time, but it would be the final game for head coach Keith Harring – and it would be decided by a crazy play that had Badin fans shaking their heads as if to say, "Well, that's soccer …"

Badin was controlling the game but could not score on Wyoming's excellent goaltender, Alexa Levick, who was en route to Vanderbilt University.

With just more than four minutes remaining, Shafor came off her mark to keep Wyoming sophomore Michelle Jolson from getting an easy breakaway attempt. Shafor made the play as the two players collided, sending the ball bounding back towards midfield.

Shafor was playing on a bad leg, and she was down after the

collision.

The ball was 35 yards away from the goal … but Badin couldn't cover the line as the Cowboys' Hailee Schlager sent the ball back towards, and into, the net for the game-winner.

"It was just a fluky play," Harring said at the time. "I told our girls they have to be proud of what they've done. How many teams can say they made (the Sweet 16) five years in a row?

"Sometimes you have to learn from losses in life," he added. "It's tough for the kids to understand that right now, but every one of them I put out there gave everything they had and I couldn't be more proud of them."

Five years later, Harring has not changed his view of that game. "That was an incredible game," he said. "The girls just played so well that night. It was a fluky goal, but I was so proud of our effort."

He's similarly proud of his days as the Badin High girls soccer coach.

"It was a treat, a pleasure, it really was," Harring said. "God blessed me. He gave me the opportunity to coach some great girls. They weren't just athletes, they were ladies. It was a privilege.

"The next thing I'm looking forward to is seeing what kind of people they become," he added. "I'm sure I will be proud of looking at them as they grow up over the years. They really were great girls."

The 2005 state champions knocked off Doylestown Chippewa, 2-1, in overtime. Co-captains Kellie Beadle, Kelsey Fontaine and Heather Rains pose with the trophy in front. The winning goal was scored by Emily Flum, second from right in the top row.

With head coach Keith Harring, seniors on the 2006 state runner-up Rams included, front row from left, Kristina Anderson, Ashley Roberto, Janie Jeffcoat and Mandy Hessling. At rear are Harring, Jenny Rosen, Lindsey Smith, Emily Lawall and Sammi Burton. Photo by the author.

Courtney Gray (left) and Erin Golden, members of Badin's Class of 2008, played in three straight state championship games for the Rams. Photo courtesy of Courtney Gray.

Three Badin seniors were all smiles on Signing Day in the spring of 2012 – from left, Ashley Mahoney (Kent State), Kim Golden (Morehead State) and Lauren Mathews (Miami University). Photo by the author.

2010

Ashley Mahoney crow-hopped once and ran out toward her teammates in the Badin lineup. Though she was only a junior, she had been the last player introduced on this particular Monday night in late September 2010. Mahoney had verbally committed over the weekend to play women's college soccer at Kent State University, and that news over the p.a. had earned her a warm reception from the crowd at Virgil Schwarm Stadium.

"I just love to play," Mahoney had said with her typical modesty when asked to describe what made her such an excellent player. She was the first of what might be termed Badin's "Big Three" in the Class of 2012 to commit to play D-I college soccer, joined soon after by Lauren Mathews (Miami University) and Kim Golden (Morehead State).

"I'm just determined to make the most of myself out there and keep trying all the time," added the fleet-footed Mahoney, whose distinctive running style made her easy to spot on the field – though generally you knew where to look because she was the one making the strong defensive play in Badin's end of the field.

A four-year starter on defense, Mahoney had Badin fans used to thinking "Never fear, Ashley is here" as she turned away yet another opposing threat in the BHS zone.

On this night, Mahoney and her mates were turning away Wyoming, 2-0, in a dominant performance that perhaps gave some small measure of revenge for the last game of the 2009 campaign, a 1-0 setback to Wyoming in the regional semifinals.

That loss had been Keith Harring's final game after a spectacularly successful eight-season run as head coach of the Rams. They'd won five straight district championships, been to three state finals, and captured the Division II state crown in 2005.

Though his departure may have come as a surprise to some in the Badin girls soccer community, he had been thinking about it for awhile.

"That was really difficult," Harring said of making the decision. He'd originally planned to coach Badin for five years, and stayed on for eight, compiling a stellar record of 101-43-23, putting the BHS girls back in every soccer conversation in the process. "I know the first time I was driving to Badin to give them the news that I was stepping down, I chickened out. I just couldn't do it. I turned around and drove back home to talk to my wife, Pam, about it some more."

Harring, age 64 in March of 2010 when he stepped away, conceded that age was a factor.

"You need so much energy to be a head coach, and I just don't have that energy at this point," he said at the time. Looking back, he added, "They needed someone else to get some kids into the program. I really think some people were looking at me, saying, 'Who's this old guy?'

"But it was an experience that I will cherish for the rest of my life," Harring said of his eight seasons at the helm.

Steve Tabar, 26, was the next man up, with a solid playing and coaching background. He was a standout goalie at Colerain High School and then Cincinnati State and Northern Kentucky University during his playing days, and had subsequently coached in the Olympic Development Program through the University of Notre Dame, directed club soccer teams, been an assistant at Mason High, the largest high school in the state of Ohio, and the goalie coach for the women's program at Miami University.

"We're going to play an exciting brand of soccer," said Tabar, a Hamilton resident who had been drawn to the opportunity by the ongoing success of the Badin program. "You play hard from the first whistle to the last. You leave everything out on the field. Let's go score some goals and win some games.

"Soccer is not a very entertaining game," he added, "but let's try to make it entertaining."

It had not been a straight line from Harring to Tabar, though, because finding a new head coach in a high-profile program like Badin girls soccer was never an easy task. High expectations collided with a modest (at best) salary schedule, and that was problematic.

Badin had an outstanding athletic tradition. Longtime head football coach Terry Malone, for instance, had been the winningest coach in the history of the Ohio prep ranks when he retired following the 2003 season, with 360 victories and the 1990 Division III state crown on his resume. The school had dubbed itself "The Home of Champions" after winning six team state titles and four more individual titles since its opening in the fall of 1966.

But the Rams were also fortunate in many cases to get dedicated, successful coaches who were willing to take on the expectations for not a lot of money. Maybe they were Badin grads who wanted to add to the tradition. Maybe they liked the opportunity to coach well-disciplined athletes who were willing to work hard to win. Maybe they were relatively new to coaching and Badin gave them a chance.

But they had to appreciate the psychic benefits that came with coaching in Ramland, because the dollars were not really there. Indeed, an estimate by a committee doing strategic planning work for the school in 2012 said that Badin would have to spend $100,000 a year across the board just to get its coaching salary schedule up to the scale the Greater Catholic League recommended … and even that fell well short of its public school counterparts.

In other words, coaches were not lined up out the door to apply for the girls soccer gig – even at a school that had been to the state championship game seven times in the previous 15 years. Craig Manahan guided the Badin girls soccer program to its first three state finals in the mid-1990s in his first three years as head coach, so obviously he knew what he was doing. But he was also just five years out of Northwest High School when he took over the program, so he was quite a find.

In this case, though, the Badin brass felt comfortable that they had two candidates who could step up to fill the girls soccer void -- former assistant coach Brian Smallwood, or 1996 BHS grad Stacey Kuhl Rhodis.

Smallwood had been a valuable assistant for Harring during those four seasons from 2004 through 2007. While Harring took care of the Big Picture and was a supportive influence for the girls, Smallwood was a strong tactical presence who was also a corrective force on the sidelines and in practice. It wasn't quite a Nice Coach/Tough Coach dynamic, but Smallwood had played a crucial role in the Rams' success and would have been a relatively seamless transition from Harring.

Kuhl Rhodis was another positive force who had been the captain of the first Badin team to reach state in 1995, had played for Xavier University in the NCAA tournament, and was a well-respected club soccer coach who was well-versed on the Badin girls soccer roster.

Feelers were put out to both coaches … and both, much to Badin's surprise, politely declined.

Smallwood had the simultaneous opportunity to take over the program at Hamilton High School, and he felt like he just had to do it. He'd been co-head coach for a club team that had future Hamilton girls in the pipeline, helping them go from last in the seventh division of a 70-team, seven-division league, to first in the first division of that league. He couldn't walk away from those girls.

"I couldn't have been more honored that Brian (Badin principal Brian Pendergest) called me," Smallwood said. "But I just really felt for that Hamilton High program. There was so much work to be done. I told the (HHS) girls, 'This is not your fault.' The program was in disarray.

"Now we have meaningful halftimes," he added of the situation after four years at the Big Blue helm. "No one listens to you when you're behind 3-0."

Kuhl Rhodis, meanwhile, was pregnant … and the timing simply wasn't good. Would she have liked to talk about the job? Absolutely, she told Badin athletic director Sally Kocher. But under the circumstances, it just wasn't going to work.

Now, Badin girls soccer was in the hands of Steve Tabar.

"Badin girls soccer had been successful for a long time," Tabar said, "but when I got there, things were in a little different mode. The numbers were down. We only had five freshmen come out that first year, and one of them, Crystal Rains, we had to recruit to get her out on the field."

Harring had seen that situation arising.

"They had those three excellent players," he said, referring to Golden, Mahoney and Mathews, "but maybe they didn't have enough players to support those three. I thought somebody else could come in and bring some additional players into the equation.

"I think another thing that happened, when we had those good teams," Harring added, "was that some girls looked at it and saw maybe they wouldn't play right away and decided to go someplace else. I know we had at least one girl we thought was coming, but she ended up going to Ursuline Academy because of our (talent) situation. And I don't think she ever played at all at Ursuline."

Still, Badin was too used to winning to simply flame out. The players' own personal expectations were too high to throw in the towel. Each of Tabar's three seasons on the sidelines ended in tournament disappointment, though for most schools, three trips to the district finals and one to the regionals would be cause for a parade. At each juncture, though, the Badin players were not ready to be done. They may not quite have been state championship caliber teams, but most athletes know when they have gotten to "the end." For Badin, three years running, the girls didn't feel like they had reached the end.

"Expectations were high," nodded Tabar. "Again, you go back to the numbers situation. We were playing 8 v. 8 or 9 v. 9 at the junior varsity level, then dressing up a number of those girls to play varsity the same night. That's a huge challenge."

Indeed, one night in 2011 at Wyoming High is one that Ram squad will never forget. Badin AD Kocher had called to remind the Wyoming staff that Badin would be playing 9 on 9 in the reserve game. But when the Rams showed up, Wyoming – like Badin a strong program annually -- refused to play short-handed in the reserve contest. So the JV game was played at 9 on 11 ... yet even down two field players, the determined Badin squad managed a tie.

Kocher, a mild-mannered veteran AD who was slow to boil, was boiling over at this insult. She called the Wyoming athletic director the next day and cancelled the series.

"One thing about high school soccer is you have a lot of players who are at different levels," Tabar said. "Some are playing a high level of club soccer, and others aren't even looking at a ball once the season was over. I tried to change it up so that the girls played not only during the season, but in the offseason as well.

"Badin is a very good name on the soccer field," he added. "I felt like we were able to get more of the girls playing club soccer, and then by the third year our total numbers were up. That certainly helped."

Three weeks after Ashley Mahoney committed to play at Kent State, Lauren Mathews indicated that she would be headed to Miami University, just about 25 minutes north of Badin in Oxford.

"Everything was a 'yes'," Mathews said of her college search checklist coming up 'Miami.' "I couldn't find a 'no.' It just clicked. Miami was where I wanted and needed to be."

"Dedication," she added of what helped propel her into the top levels of soccer. "Making the right moves that you have to make on your own to get better. Pushing yourself to your highest potential and not stopping there."

And Mathews called her favorite thing about soccer "the intensity. It's that one place in life where nothing else matters except being part of the team. ... It's your family outside of your family."

Mathews was the first girl Miami had recruited off the Badin campus to play soccer, and that eased some ongoing BHS angst toward veteran Miami women's soccer coach Bobby Kramig. (Former Badin goaltender Caitlin Wolf had transferred to Miami from the University of Dayton, but Mathews was the first Ram inked by Miami right out of high school.) The Rams had some outstanding D-I caliber girls soccer players in the past two decades, but Miami – right up the road -- had not even attempted to recruit any of them. That had Badin soccer followers gnashing their teeth over the years.

Perhaps the personal connection that Tabar enjoyed with Miami had made an impact. Mathews certainly made one in Oxford … by the end of her freshman season there in the fall of 2012, she was starting and playing nearly the entire game for a Redhawk squad that advanced to the second round of the NCAA tournament.

"Badin soccer was a unique experience that taught me so much in what was actually a very quick four years," Mathews said in looking back. "When I thought about getting to high school, that's what it was all about – playing soccer for Badin," she added, noting that she had grown up watching her cousin, the very talented Tori Mathews, play for the Rams.

"I wanted to be a part of that tight family chemistry of the team and enjoy those special traditions that had been carried on for years," Mathews said. "Though all the games were special, tournament time is when you could feel the true magic among the team and the community. Each game day I got to look forward to seeing the newest inspirational quote taped to my locker, I could feed off the energy of the crowd of Rams that came out to support the team, and I got to be a piece of a unified goal."

The 2010 Rams, after a modest 6-7-3 regular season, captured the program's sixth consecutive district championship, with crucial back-to-back 1-0 tournament wins, over Kettering Alter in the sectional finals, and Jamestown Greeneview in the district finals.

That win over Alter meant that since absorbing a penalty kick setback to the Knights in 2004 – the last time Badin had failed to win a district crown to that point – the Rams had knocked Alter out of the tournament the next four times they had met, in 2005, 2006, 2009 and 2010. Badin didn't beat league foe Alter very often in the regular season, but when it came to tournament play, Badin had Alter's number.

"We had an amazing bond that was like a family," Mahoney said of the BHS program "We could go to each other when we had problems with anything and it was like a support system. Before every game we would all be in a room and talk about what we wanted to do for the game and how we could succeed in that. This really helped us get our minds right for the game and make sure we were pushing ourselves.

"We may have had some differences with one another off the field, but that didn't affect our play on the field," she added. "We put aside anything that was wrong with our lives and played our hardest every game.

"Soccer meant a lot to all of us," Mahoney said. "There were some struggles we had to battle through, but we also had our victories … like the games we won, but also pushing through any problems and not letting our team fold and give up. I was glad to be a part of it."

Badin got knocked out by a vaunted Indian Hill squad in its regional Sweet 16 game in 2010 – Indian Hill was en route to the state Final Four, and had beaten Badin 2-0 during the regular season – but with a bang, not a whimper. The 1-0 setback wasn't over until the final seconds, when Braves senior goalkeeper Katie Markesbery made a superb deflection of an Allie Crossley shot ripped right on top of her that had "OT" written all over it.

The following year, though, it was a listless 2-0 regular season loss on a Saturday afternoon at Indian Hill that brought some festering Badin girls soccer woes to the surface. There had been some pushback between Tabar and the team, the team and Tabar, even among the team itself. Some parents were grumbling. The Badin girls soccer family was slightly fractured.

"Any coaching gig is tough," Tabar said. "There's never an issue that doesn't pop up here and there. High school soccer is a little more difficult because of the different levels of play. There's always some humps in the road."

And yet, two nights later, the Rams circled the wagons and played what was arguably their finest game in Tabar's three-year tenure – because that's what Badin soccer girls do. They play soccer. In this case, a dramatic 0-0 tie at archrival Middletown Fenwick.

Tabar set the tone with a savvy tactical move. With starting goalkeeper Morgan Walker sidelined by injury, the Rams had to go with untested sophomore Michelle Hessling in the varsity nets. So, like the French at Verdun in World War I, Tabar basically said, "They shall not pass!"

He put his two Division I stalwarts, Ashley Mahoney and Kim Golden, in the middle of the defensive wall to protect Hessling and simply dared Fenwick to score. He wasn't too concerned about Badin being able to score – in a game where scoring was already at a premium, the Rams under Tabar had a particularly hard time putting the ball in the net, which was one of the team's underlying problems – but set up his team to keep Fenwick off the board.

Lauren Mathews was not playing. She had blown out her knee in club soccer in the spring of 2011, and was sidelined for the season. She was able to come back in the middle of the girls basketball season, and book-ended her Badin athletic career by starting at guard for back-to-back Ram basketball teams that made the Division III regionals.

But, in another move that put Miami University in a good light, women's soccer coach Bobby Kramig had immediately told Mathews not to worry, that the soccer scholarship she had verbally accepted in October 2010 was secure. Not every school would do that. In fact, many schools would not. Mathews has done well at Miami.

In March of 2011, Kim Golden had committed to play college soccer at Morehead State. It meant that three Badin girls soccer players in the Class of 2012 were already ticketed for D-I college play while still juniors in high school, quite a coup for the small Catholic high school. That the three were also inducted into the National Honor Society as juniors, not an easy task at Badin, tells you a lot about that trio as well.

Golden was a tall athletic blonde, typically at least a head taller than most people she would play against – which, she laughed, meant that she got called for a lot of fouls. She had followed her older sister, Erin, to Badin from St. John the Baptist on Dry Ridge Road in Colerain Township, and both left a great legacy at BHS.

Kim ultimately went off to Morehead State to study math education. On some days she said she wanted to be a college math professor, on others, that she wanted to come back to teach math at Badin – which would certainly be great for Badin. On the night she graduated in 2012, she was awarded the Stephen T. Badin medal as the most outstanding member of the class "by every measure." It was well-earned on her part.

"At St. John's, Badin really wasn't that well heard of, but Erin had played with a lot of girls on her club team that were going to Badin. That's how we heard of the school," Golden recalled. "Erin and my parents fell in love with Badin. And I couldn't wait to come to Badin games!

"From the outset of Erin being at Badin, I could tell you the whole team in order on the numerical roster," she said. "I always wondered, 'Whose number do I want to have?' Ultimately there was no question that I would choose No. 1 (Erin's number).

"She was so feisty," Kim said of her late sister. "We'd joke that she was the littlest player on the field, but she didn't know that. I remember she saved the ball on the goal line (against Bexley in the 2006 state semifinals) and that saved the game. That summed her up. She was always making that extra effort."

Asked about her own skill – as a sophomore in college, she started on a Morehead State team that reached the NCAA tournament, after having won but two games the year before – Golden said, "I never remember soccer not being a part of my life. I had a very supportive family behind me. It makes it easy when you have all kinds of people rooting for you.

"Also, it's the love of the game, the passion for the game," she said. "I'm already halfway through my college career, and I wonder what I'm going to do when I don't have soccer as a part of my life. When I have a few weeks off from soccer, I don't know what to do with myself."

Golden's all-Ohio skills enabled Tabar to play her anywhere on the field … and she wasn't particular about where that was.

"I play wherever the coach wants me to play," she said. "When I'm *not* on the field, that's when I want to do everything I can to get *on* the field."

Golden was rarely off the field at Badin.

"I love the wow factor of playing up front, the security of helping on the back line, and the freedom of playing in the middle," she said. "Just don't put me in the goal. My hand-eye coordination is terrible!"

On that evening at Fenwick, Tabar moved Golden from the front to the back and it all clicked. The rookie Hessling played a spectacular game, with a number of athletic saves, and the Badin defenders – seniors Golden, Mahoney, Paige Bresnen and Theresa Salerno anchored the effort – kept the Fenwick chances to a minimum. The Rams were 1-5-1 going into the game, and Fenwick was en route to the state Final Four. They ended the night dead even.

"The girls played terrific that night," Tabar said. "It's a game I'll never forget. Just thinking about that game brings back some great memories.

"That night, you've got four or five impact players who are sitting there in warmups and rain boots. You look at your lineup and you've got to make some adjustments.

"And Michelle just played out of her skin," he added. "Out of her skin" – it's the same phrase Tabar used with the JournalNews for its article the next morning.

"We knew Fenwick had a good team and good players," Golden said. "Being next to Ashley (Mahoney), that was fine. I had played with her my whole life. We knew we could depend on each other.

"Michelle Hessling played really well that game," she added. "She had to be nervous – how could you not be? I told her you have to believe in yourself. At that point, we were her defense – so talk to us. Don't worry about the age difference, that she's a sophomore and we're seniors. Just be the command presence."

When Hessling put together a sensational senior year in goal for the Rams, everybody who was at the Fenwick game on this night pointed to it and nodded ... she had shown exactly what she could do.

"In that moment, I had to step up to the plate a little bit," Hessling recalled. "It helped with Kim and Ashley in front of me. They're not just talented players, but leaders on the field."

And Hessling couldn't help but enjoy the sub-head in the newspaper the next day, which read, "Sophomore goalkeeper for Rams steps up in first varsity start." It was certainly something for the scrapbook, and something to build on.

"I was super excited, but you always feel the nerves sinking in," Hessling told the JournalNews. "I did not want to let anyone down."

"Every girl that stepped on the field tonight played hard," Tabar said. Two girls who played hard for Badin actually got knocked out of the game ... junior Colleen Monaghan and sophomore Crystal Rains. "If you look at our record, you can tell that things haven't gone the way I or the girls wanted them to go. This was a step in the right direction. It's a sign that we're here to battle."

The Rams battled, but the season remained a struggle ... a 5-9-2 regular season that had the squad scrambling come tournament time.

"When I was a freshman, I would say, 'There's no way we're not going to win this game,'" Golden said, thinking back on the 2008 regional finalists. "After all, we were Badin girls soccer.

"As a senior, we had a losing record, and now I'm wondering if we're even going to get a home game (in the opening rounds of the tournament)," she said. "But we did, because we were Badin. I have to thank all of the girls who played before me for that. We had that legacy. Otherwise, with our record, we were just another team."

The Badin girls got to enjoy that final home game with a 5-0 tournament triumph over Xenia Christian, and now a date with a tough Jamestown Greeneview outfit loomed in the sectional finals. Greeneview had given Badin all it wanted the previous year before BHS prevailed 1-0 in the district final.

"Going to districts, as a Badin girls soccer player, it's expected," Golden said. "But some schools never get that far. From a distance, you respect that success.

"The love of the game, the support we got, that's one thing that always helped Badin get as far as it did," she added. "Playing for Badin was so much fun. I couldn't wait for the season to start. I was playing with all of my best friends.

"It's always so exciting," Golden continued. "It's such a family-oriented school. The lockers are decorated, people are rooting for you. Just listening to the National Anthem. There was nothing better. I still quietly say, 'And the home of the ... Rams!'"

During the Anthem, Badin had an ongoing tradition of lining up and kicking each other's heels, down the line, and then back up, as they stood single file, holding hands, facing the flag – sometimes having to hurry to get finished, depending on the speed of a particular singer. When the public address announcer wanted to play the Anthem before introducing the teams -- that always drew a frown from the Ram players.

Badin's 3-2 overtime triumph over Greeneview was not only a thrilling affair that put BHS into its eighth straight district championship game, but it also reminded BHS fans that while talented players graduate each year, others are there to step up and take their place. On this night, freshman Madi Kah was front and center.

Kah had put together a strong freshman year – she would commit to play Division I women's college soccer at Ohio University even before the start of her junior campaign – and was a girl Badin could count on at the scoring end of the field. She showed just exactly why under the lights at Monroe High.

After a scoreless first half, Greeneview had fashioned a 2-0 advantage with 28:23 remaining when Kah decided enough was enough. Barely 10 seconds later, she pounded one home from 25 yards out .... and then tied the game at the 22 minute mark after dribbling between several defenders in the box and knocking in the equalizer.

Just for good measure, Kah assisted on the game-winner less than two minutes into the extra session when she found senior Victoria

Heflin with a through-ball that Heflin converted from point-blank range.

"That's the way Badin girls play," Steve Tabar said. "They play with heart, they play hard."

"It was amazing," said Heflin, whose iced ankle was such that she was actually leaning on Kah for support during a post-game interview. "It came from my little freshie here, Madi. I knew it would. She had an amazing game. We all did."

The "little freshie" Kah was making a name for herself … and would go on to rack up more than 100 points on offense by the time her junior year was over.

"It helps that I play midfield," Kah said of her scoring prowess. "It helps when you have good teammates. It helps when people get you the ball where you want it."

"Madelyn was born to be a soccer player," Terry Kah said. "The first time she stepped on the field, she was naturally gifted. She had good balance and good vision and she decided that it was something she wanted to do, 365 days a year. She's been fortunate to have good people in her corner, too."

"It's fun," said Madi. "I wouldn't play if it wasn't fun. Coaches have really helped me. They've made me the player that I am. When you make a good play, when you win games, when you see all of your hard work pay off, that's fun."

Kah was enjoying the hard work at Badin.

"The traditions, the team bonding, all the stuff you do pre-game, all the people that come see you play," she pointed to. "You get really close with everyone. It's all really good."

Terry Kah was pleased that his daughter had decided to attend Badin.

"It's definitely a family atmosphere. You don't see that anywhere – but Madelyn saw it right from Day One," he said. "It was apparent that she was going to get some playing time as a freshman, but all the players embraced her. Every single player. That never happens.

"They had the winner's mentality (in Badin girls soccer)," he added. "They wanted to win, and in (freshmen) Madelyn and Morgan (Langhammer), they saw two girls who could help them win. That goes a long, long way toward success."

Now it was a matter of continuing that success in the district championship game against Summit Country Day … where a familiar coach, former BHS head man Keith Harring, loomed on the other sideline. Harring was an assistant to head coach Michael Fee at

Summit, but it was Harring who had Badin the girls' attention.

"That was the most difficult game I ever had to coach in my life," Harring said. "I wanted to talk to the Badin girls before the game, but they wouldn't look at me. They would just walk the other way, or put their head down as they went by. Even after the game, I wanted to talk to them. But I thought better of it. I knew that wasn't the time."

The reality is that Badin players were not happy to see Harring coaching an opponent. Although he'd indicated when he left that he would probably serve as an assistant elsewhere – he had done some work with Brian Smallwood at Hamilton as well – the girls were a little bitter about it. He had retired … but here he was on the other sideline. They wanted to prove that he was on the wrong sideline.

It didn't happen. Summit CD was on one of those magical runs that concluded with a D-III state championship victory two weeks later. On this night, they were one goal better than Badin, 1-0.

"We dominated the game," Tabar said, accurately. "It stings a little bit when you play better soccer and the end result doesn't come on your side."

Summit had scored in the final minute of the first half. Badin, obviously tiring as the clock ticked down, had subs at the line, but couldn't get them in. Summit freshman Emily Wiser managed to navigate the end line off a long ball and keep it inbounds, and then fired a perfect centering pass for sophomore Meredith Schertzinger, who knocked it home with 46 ticks showing.

Badin attacked hard in the second half, but ongoing scoring woes continued to torment the Rams. When a clean header off a corner kick failed with 30 seconds left, Badin's string of six straight district titles was at an end.

"We definitely had chances in a lot of games," Tabar said, "but unfortunately, soccer is one of those games where it's just hard to put the ball in the net."

It was the end of Badin's district title run, and it was the end of the run of three Division I seniors in the Class of 2012, Kim Golden, Ashley Mahoney and Lauren Mathews.

"We definitely missed having Lauren on the field in 2011 – she was such a good player," Tabar said.

"When you think of all three together as a group, their work rate and their effort was phenomenal," he said. "They were good – but it was their work rate that made them Division I college players. They had motors that wouldn't stop. Their competitiveness really made them excel."

Golden recalled that competitiveness with a laugh. The Rams were not going to practice one afternoon, they were just going to have a pleasant game of flag football instead.

"We couldn't even have fun – we were just so competitive!" she said. "We were still getting mad about it! That's not something to be that competitive over, but we were."

As a sophomore, Mahoney had indicated in an athletic leadership interview that her goal in life was to play women's professional soccer. It was not a ridiculous notion, based on her skills ... and the fact that she was willing to voice that aspiration in front of her peers said a lot for her desire.

Her shins, however, betrayed her. After a solid freshman year at Kent State, where she played nearly half of every game, she had to give in to her chronic lower leg injuries. They had plagued her in high school as well, and now her career was over.

"It's exciting to see Badin girls soccer continue to succeed," Mahoney said. "Badin definitely helped me get to play at Kent State. It was a great opportunity. On the field, every girl had each other's back. I wouldn't have changed anything. I'm proud to say I played soccer for Badin."

2013

It was early May 2013. The Badin High girls soccer program didn't have a head coach. But it did have Renee Balconi.

In a surprise move at the May organizational meeting, Steve Tabar announced that he was resigning after three seasons in charge. Tabar was a phys ed teacher in the Mason City School District, and his wife, Jennifer, was expecting their second child. The family was moving to not-so-nearby Lebanon, and the logistics of trying to coach Badin girls soccer in Hamilton just no longer worked.

"We were all freaking out when he resigned," Madi Kah said. "We had no idea who was going to take over. It was getting toward the pre-season, and we didn't have a coach!"

"When Coach Tabar left, it was a big mix of emotion," Amy Seither remarked. "I thought there was no way we'd get a decent coach in time. We'd be way behind."

"I walked into the meeting late," Rachel Riley said. "Michelle (Hessling) and Holly (Reed) were on the verge of tears. It was like, 'oh, no!' We thought we were going to have a bad season."

After two straight sub-.500 regular seasons, the Rams had put together a strong yet ultimately disappointing 2012. Badin roster numbers were up, the schedule was a bit lighter, and the Rams fashioned a solid 11-2-3 campaign. Sophomores Kah, Annika Pater and Kate Bach were playing well, and an infusion of freshman talent included Riley, Malia Berkely, Gabby Geigle, Shelby Lamping, Taylor Smith and more. The "young Turks" could play!

Badin had powered its way into a ninth straight district championship game, with unheralded Troy Christian on the other end.

Troy Christian begged to differ about the unheralded part. The Trojans scored off of a defensive error five minutes into the game ...

and almost before a text could go out announcing the score was Troy Christian 1, Badin 0, scored again on a through-ball to a sprinting forward Badin fans howled was five yards offside. The offside flag never came up.

That was enough. A frustrated Badin squad kept charging ahead, with little to show for it. The Rams finally narrowed the gap to 2-1 on an impressive Kah blast with scant minutes remaining, but could get no closer. Once again, the Rams felt that their season had ended prematurely … but believed the returning roster could be poised for a big run in 2013.

Except that now they needed a head coach.

"It was tough to walk away knowing there was a good team there," Tabar said. "The thing about teaching and coaching is that you spend all day with literally hundreds of kids, and then I'd get home and have maybe 15 minutes with my own kids. I always told the girls to make time for family. I had to make time for my own family.

"High school athletics is a pretty neat thing. One of the cool things is all the extra bonding that goes on," Tabar added. "I wouldn't change a thing about my experience at Badin. I'm happy for all of the success the girls had (in 2013). That's a heckuvan accomplishment. I'm proud for them and their families."

There was, obviously, a void to be filled. Yet behind the scenes, Terry Kah had quietly handled the preparation and fundraising for a conditioning program that would pay huge dividends for the Rams.

Kah had been talking to Steve Tabar in the offseason, suggesting that the Rams needed to be in better shape. Some friends of Kah's daughter had been telling her all winter about the Balconi training program. Tabar gave Terry Kah the go-ahead to see what he could arrange.

"Renee Balconi would train only four teams, and one of those was not coming back," Terry Kah said. "She would interview the coach and a parent. She had seven schools interested in her one open slot. She wanted to know about the makeup of our team. She ate up the work ethic and the family aspect of it."

"Terry Kah put together the Balconi training," Todd Berkely said. "That's something the girls desperately needed. They were out of gas against Troy Christian. It's no slouch of a cost – but Terry made it happen without cost to the girls."

Kah arranged for an overnight "lock-in" at an indoor amusement center, and Badin soccer girls brought friends with them from all over

Greater Cincinnati. The place was packed. The money was raised.

"Renee knows how to appeal to girls," Berkely said. "It makes you wonder why we didn't do it sooner. You've seen the training scenes in the Rocky movies? It's like that ... only faster!"

"Renee Balconi was even more remarkable than I expected," Kah said. "She is very tough. The players were like, 'If I can get through this, I can get through anything.' But she was tremendous. And she was a great bridge between coaches."

That was the key – while Badin was in search of a new girls soccer coach, the girls weren't sitting around waiting and wondering. They were training, and training hard for the dynamic young former University of Cincinnati women's soccer captain.

"Balconi training – it was awful, and it was wonderful," Seither said. "Renee was a big part of why we got as far as we did. She was everything to us. She got us in shape. It was lovely."

"Balconi training was definitely hard, but it was well worth it," Annika Pater said. "She pushed us every second, but not in a mean way. She was fun to be around. She was cool about everything. But she didn't let us slack off."

"I was terrified for Balconi training," Morgan Langhammer said. "I thought, oh, this is going to be bad. She is the most in-shape person you've ever seen. You look around at us, and we're not. ... But it was one of the key facts that led us to state."

"Balconi training helped us a lot," added Madi Kah. "It gets you in shape. It pushes you. It helps you with your footwork. She's very inspirational. She doesn't let you stop."

And in the meantime, the Badin administration was searching for a head coach. They checked the Badin rolodex, and just as they had in March of 2010 following the departure of veteran girls coach Keith Harring, put out feelers toward two people with solid Badin connections -- 1995 team captain and current club coach Stacey Kuhl Rhodis, and former BHS assistant Brian Smallwood.

Smallwood had just completed his third season as the head coach at Hamilton High, and he was prepared to stay on with the Big Blue. A strong group of club players he had been involved with was coming into the freshman class of 2017, and Smallwood was going to see it through. Kuhl Rhodis, meanwhile, had extensive family and work commitments that simply would not enable her to devote the time necessary to a program of Badin's caliber. She cared about the BHS program too much not to be able to give it the appropriate attention.

Who else was in the pipeline? Out of earshot, parents Terry Kah and Mike Langhammer were quietly lobbying for Todd Berkely to get the job. Berkely had coached the Fairfield High freshman girls for the past three seasons, but he had just stepped away from that post because he wanted more of an opportunity to be involved with his own three children.

Berkely recalled that throughout the May meeting at which Tabar had announced his resignation, he could feel Terry Kah's eyes boring a hole through him, as if to say, "You should be interested in this job!"

"I had gotten to the May meeting about an hour early with my wife (Sherrie) and (fellow parent) Pat Bach," Kah said. "Steve Tabar was there and he told us what he was going to tell the girls. We were like, 'Heck, now what are we going to do?' At the same time, when we left, we thought, 'Well, it's not the best thing, but maybe it creates an opportunity ...'"

Berkely was good friends with the Fischer family ... Kurt Fischer had been Malia's club coach for a number of years, and Heather had been the Fairfield High varsity girls coach who brought Berkely aboard to coach the freshmen in 2010.

"I reluctantly expressed an interest in the Badin job," Berkely said. "Heather said I'd be ideal for it. We went back and forth on the phone for two hours about it. She said Badin needed someone to step forward and give them hope."

But Badin was not quite ready to offer the job to the parent of a player, even a player as dynamic as Malia Berkely. Instead, an offer went out to a well-regarded young coach with a strong local soccer organization. He thought about it for a few days ... and turned the job down.

"I knew at some point that Badin's backs were against the wall in terms of hiring someone, that much I knew," Berkely said.

He had asked his family what they thought about the possibility of him becoming the Badin girls soccer coach.

"Malia said it would be good and bad – that I knew what I was doing, but then her dad would be the coach," he laughed.

"My dad asked me what I would think about him being the head coach because people were encouraging him to do it," Malia said. "I had played for my dad before and I loved it. I knew he was a good coach. You see how it turned out."

His wife, Nicole, told him not to worry – that if it came to pass, she would handle the family logistics at home.

"My first thought was, what is Malia going to think?" Nicole said. "He had coached her before, but now he was not only going to coach her, but her friends, and in high school, which is such an impressionable time.

"I knew he was good with kids. He can handle it -- camaraderie, communicate, connect," she added. "But would the players respect him, or would they just think he's there to look after his daughter? I had mixed feelings. It was a little scary. But it all worked out."

Terry Kah told Berkely that all he had to do was coach … Kah and others would mobilize all of the things that needed to happen for the program behind the scenes.

"It was tough for him to coach, because he was missing a lot of things with his two younger children," Kah said. "But we knew he'd be a very good coach."

"Everything happens for a reason," said new Badin Athletic Director Geoff Melzer, on the job for barely a month but already tasked with filling one of the school's more prominent coaching positions. "We offered the job to a young coach who turned it down.

"You don't necessarily want to hire the dad of a player," he added. "But Todd Berkely had interviewed very well. He answered all the questions well. There's definitely a plan – we just don't always know what it is."

In this case, it came back to the fact that sometimes the best things to happen are things that don't happen. A coach had turned down the job, and now Todd Berkely was in the catbird's seat, or the hot seat, depending upon your point of view.

Berkely's phone rang at home. It was Morgan Langhammer. "I heard a rumor …" she said. Berkely shook his head. "I had known Morgan for years – she never calls me!"

Madi Kah had heard the same rumor, though in this case the rumor turned out to be true. Todd Berkely was the new head coach of the girls soccer Rams. Kah went upstairs, put on her running shoes, and went out the front door. She knew she had better get ready to run.

2013

When Todd Berkely took over the Badin High girls soccer program in the summer of 2013, he hit the ground running – literally.

"I said that Badin will be the most fit team on the field – and we will play as a team," Berkely said of his overview of the Rams.

Berkely had not been waiting and wondering just in case he got the job. He had been thinking and planning. He had some thoughts from the previous season, when he had just been in the stands as a parent, watching his daughter, Malia, play for the Rams. He had some ideas he had put into effect with the Fairfield High freshman girls soccer team that he had coached the past three years. And he had the perspective of someone who'd been around soccer all of his life, growing up as the son of Croatian parents who loved "the beautiful game."

"As soon as I got the job, I said, oh, God, I've got to get to work – we were a month behind," he said. "I knew that we were going to have a good team and be able to play. ... But talent is never enough. The focus has to be – let's get better."

Terry Kah mobilized parents to handle all of the behind-the-scenes activities, people like Tim Hessling, Etta Reed, Jennifer Scowden and others. Fairfield High girls coach Patrick O'Leary sent Berkely the Indians' old practice schedule, so that Berkely could wrap his mind around what needed to be done, when.

"So many people stepped up," Berkely nodded. "I was worried about the logistics, but I have so many people to thank. My strength is working with kids, my strength is coaching, my strength is getting the kids to believe."

"You know he knows what he's doing – just look at his daughter," Madi Kah said of Berkely being named head coach. "He had so much experience that I knew he was going to be a good coach."

"The first pep talk from Coach Berkely – it gave me chills, it was awesome!" Amy Seither said. "I liked what I was hearing. I had a good feeling about it."

"We had our first meeting in the Little Theatre, and I didn't know what to expect," Annika Pater said. "Everything he said – I was so pumped up, and I looked around the theater and I could tell that the whole team was pumped up. I knew from that moment on that everything was going to be fine."

Berkely's attitude was to work hard and focus on the positive.

"I had some negative experiences in sports growing up, so that pushed me towards the positive side," said Berkely, who had played tennis at Moeller High School and is a graduate of the University of Cincinnati. "Negativity breeds negativity, and it's tough to recover from that. Even with a negative, you have to look for a positive to come out of that."

While Malia Berkely had been growing up, obviously showing some soccer skill, her father looked very carefully for the right club team to put her on. He settled on a squad coached by Kurt Fischer, whose wife Heather was the Fairfield High girls head coach who subsequently brought Berkely on to her staff.

"I saw enough of the wrong type of thing and the wrong type of coaching," Berkely said. "Kurt Fischer did things the right way. And Heather Fischer is one of the most underappreciated coaches I have ever met. Her attitude for the freshman team that I coached was develop, develop, develop, not just win, win, win."

Berkely appreciated his three years of being on the soccer staff at FHS, first with Heather Fischer and then Patrick O'Leary.

"Working with Fairfield High was absolutely outstanding," Berkely said. "It helped me round out my coaching philosophy. I watched it all and soaked it all in. Heather had the 'one voice' coaching philosophy. You reinforce what the coach is saying – you don't have five different coaches saying five different things. And Patrick always encouraged his assistant coaches to be involved, to make suggestions. It was a very good working environment."

Following on the heels of Balconi training was what Todd Berkely affectionately, almost jokingly, refers to as "Berkely Camp." From a conditioning standpoint, it was no joke.

"There's one word for it – hell," said sophomore Rachel Riley, smiling amid her recollection of the anguish. "It was hell. But he knew how to make it interesting so that we weren't crying all the time."

"You've got to build the individual," Berkely said. "Then, you've got to build the team and connect everything together. You have to continually improve as a team, because playing as individuals doesn't work in the state tournament."

Berkely looked back on the 2-1 loss to Troy Christian in the 2012 district championship, and saw opportunity. "You could see a team there ... they just hadn't quite grown to fruition yet," he said.

Even in the loss, he saw a positive ... the fact that Kate Bach had played sweeper/keeper the last eight minutes of the game as Badin sought to score the tying goal. "That she was willing to do that ... that's a team commitment right there," Berkely said. "That's a team dynamic. Out of a negative, something positive."

Berkely's first commitment, though, was to get the team in shape.

"That was an intense summer," senior Maggie Adams said. "Sometimes we'd go through training, then we'd go to practice. It was a lot different than what we were used to."

"He really pushed us, that's how he motivated us," junior Kate Bach said. "He'd tell us how hard something would be, and then maybe it wouldn't turn out to be quite so hard as we expected it to be. So that was good. In bits and pieces we were coming together to be one."

"I was excited about Coach Berkely coming in, because I knew he tried to make players better," sophomore Shelby Lamping said. "He's stern, but we needed that a lot. He created some heavy competition in practice."

"Practice was definitely different," junior Brianna Scowden said. "We did a lot more conditioning and a lot more technical stuff. I knew Coach Berkely and I liked him. But I was also kind of scared of him. He's definitely intense."

"Even though it was hard, Coach Berkely made it fun," sophomore Taylor Smith said. "It was physically and mentally exhausting, but he was always smiling. He won't talk down to you. He constantly boosts you up and pushes you to be better."

"The biggest drawback of Todd being the head coach," said his wife, Nicole, "was no overnight guests. No one would come spend the night with Malia, because they were all worried that Todd was going to put them through a workout!"

Berkely's signature drill was what came to be known as "Ram Runs", which he had brought with him from Fairfield. At Fairfield, whose teams are nicknamed the Indians, they were known as "Indian Runs" – and generically, that is how they are referenced, as Indian

Runs. But Berkely was not going to have Badin run a drill named for a rival school, so he revised the name.

The soccer Rams would line up, single file, and run around the practice field at Queen of Peace School in Millville. At all times, the girl at the back of the line would have to sprint to the front. Once she got to the front, it would be time for the next girl at the end to sprint forward. So, the line would always be running … and one girl would always be sprinting.

Berkely generally split the team into two groups, so the sprinter would only have to pass a dozen or so girls to get to the front of her line … but they'd typically run four laps around Queen of Peace, which made the total run about 1.5 miles.

"Soccer is not based on a sprint or a distance run – it's a combination of both," Berkely said. "The Ram Run for fitness closely resembled what I wanted to bring to Badin."

The girls had their own view of the Ram Runs.

"Oh, gosh, I hated the Ram Runs," smiled Pater. "We'd pray for no Ram Runs at a particular practice – I'd try to get a hint from Malia if we were going to have to do them. Usually we would. Your legs are so tired – but the truth is, that's the way the games are going to be. We always felt like we were the fittest team out there."

"They were awful, just awful," said Scowden. "Even our recovery runs were another two laps. But at the same time, they were helpful. We knew that."

"Sometimes it would only be three laps, and we'd get really excited," Kah said. "But we definitely had more energy than the other teams."

"They were a necessary evil," junior Morgan Langhammer said. "We would not have won the state championship had we not done them. Overtime was our time. That was lap five of the Ram Run. You're tired, but you have to keep going. You have to work for everyone else out there because they're working for you."

The Ram Runs were conditioning runs … and they were also bonding runs as the players supported each other on the way around.

"As much as we hated being told to get into two lines, we knew they would help us overall," Malia Berkely said. "Whenever someone would sprint to the front, we would cheer them on. Maybe someone wouldn't finish – we would go back and get them and run with them to the finish. It was a competition, and competition helped us."

"We would get after each other," nodded Gabby Geigle, "but if someone wanted to drop out, we'd say, 'just one more! … just one more!' We helped each other get through it."

"Watching all the practice drills, I didn't learn anything new that I hadn't seen in 25 years," said assistant coach Jeff Pohlman. "But I learned a lot about the value of running. Todd ran the girls a lot, he ran them hard, and he conditioned them well. When we got into some of those overtime games in the tournament, our girls were still playing and the other girls were exhausted. That was very impressive."

Pohlman was one of those "desperation leads to inspiration" hires for the Rams. Berkely was scrambling to pull a coaching staff together, and would-be reserve coach Allie Crossley had to step aside because of scheduling conflicts. Parents Pat Bach and Shawn Pater suggested Berkely contact Pohlman, who had been coaching their daughters in club ball for years and whose daughter, Katie, was a sophomore member of the soccer team.

"My wife told me I'd better do it," said Pohlman, a 1977 Badin High grad who is a successful area businessman. His wife, Ellen, is also a Badin grad, and Katie is the fifth Pohlman child to come through BHS. "She reminded me that I'd been wanting to coach high school girls soccer for a while.

"I'd always enjoyed watching the Badin girls play soccer," he added. "It's like all of the other sports at Badin – the kids are dedicated. Every time we play, other teams know, no matter what division they're in, they're in for a fight."

Pohlman's arrival was much appreciated by Todd Berkely. "I was exceptionally glad to have an experienced coach, especially someone with Jeff's background, come onto the staff," he said. "He knows the players, he knows what he's doing. You need someone with a steady hand. He made it a ton easier. He's the foundation for you to be able to build your house."

While the delay in finding a reserve coach added to the scramble mode that Berkely found himself in, it also enabled him to get a closer look at the junior varsity squad that he might not have gotten to see otherwise.

"I think it's another example of what a good job Todd Berkely did pulling everything together," Athletic Director Geoff Melzer said. "You start late, your junior varsity coach can't continue, so now it's a fire drill to find a JV coach. Jeff Pohlman comes on, and now he's a great addition to the staff."

Berkely also brought Ken Murrell back aboard as an assistant. Murrell had been a "super scout" for head coach Keith Harring and the state teams of the mid-2000s, and was well familiar with Badin girls soccer. He had a folksy way about him that the players embraced.

"I got an e-mail from Todd Berkely that said simply, 'Help, Ken, help!'" Murrell laughed. "I had sent Sally Kocher an e-mail letting her know that I was interested in coming back in some capacity, not realizing that she was retiring. I had a lot of good memories from Badin girls soccer. I wanted to get back in it."

"Ken was a big help – another mature voice. The players liked him," Berkely said. "We all had a common goal. I'd love to say that it all (the staffing) fell together easily, but that wasn't the case. But while it didn't come together easily, when it came together it was a good fit."

Pohlman liked the course Berkely had set.

"He was very positive – there was definitely a change in attitude," Pohlman said. "There was no negativity at all. Everything out of his mouth was positive. He made the girls believe in themselves."

Pohlman and his wife had already scheduled a Rhine River cruise for early in the season, so he had to miss some games. But that was a minor glitch in the big picture.

"One of my goals was to actually do some things with the reserve team," Pohlman said. "Too often I've heard JV players say, 'We didn't do anything' … they'd just practice with the varsity and play their games. I wanted to do some instruction with them.

"It was a very enjoyable year," he added. "I felt like I could take some of the burden off Todd, talk to the girls on the sidelines during the varsity games, suggest some things. It worked out well."

While Berkely was taking a careful look at his roster in preparation for the season, he made a shrewd move early that defused potential drama and proved that he was not just a "my way or the highway" coach. It was a major boon to the team.

He had said that Badin would play with three captains … and he was trying to decide whether he would have three seniors, two seniors and an underclassman, just how it would work he was uncertain. But the Rams had four seniors, and all brought certain skills to the table. Who would be left out of the captaincy?

Maggie Adams was perhaps the most popular girl on the team, not quite the den mother but a girl the players weren't afraid to talk to, a girl who made up for her lack of foot-speed by being technically sound in all areas and, incidentally, not afraid to knock an opponent onto her rear if being knocked onto her rear might be called for.

Michelle Hessling had worked hard as she waited for her hoped-for opportunity to play varsity goalie as a senior, and was turning heads with her obvious ability. She led by example on the field, and there was no doubt that her example was worth paying attention to.

Amy Seither had recovered from a freshman knee injury to log a lot of varsity minutes over the years, and she was also in the Top Five in her class. She would earn $1.5 million in college academic scholarship offers, and head to Butler University to major in pharmacy.

Holly Reed had started for three seasons … but now was in a position where she could not play at all, her career having been curtailed by one too many concussions. Her teammates understood that she was a very good player who couldn't play, through no real fault of her own, and they listened to what she had to say.

Berkely, in fact, had made the presence of Reed on the team a priority as he went through the coaching interview process. He didn't think she should suffer for being an energetic player – he figured that her not being able to play was punishment enough. He had her on the roster in every single game the Rams played.

In the end, Berkely made a decision that resonated well with the Rams. He made all four of his seniors co-captains. They all had skills, they all had constituencies, they all cared deeply for the Badin girls soccer program. It was a significant step toward success.

"Collectively, they balanced the team," Berkely said. "Which of them do you not select? They all took being a captain seriously, and made a difference throughout the season."

He frequently used Seither as a go-between to deliver messages to the squad.

"Coach Berkely put a lot of trust in me," she nodded. "Lots of practices, I would stay after at the field and talk to him about everything. He treated me as a captain right from the beginning, and I was grateful for that. A lot of times he treated me as more of a coach than a captain. I always had an insight to what he was thinking. … Being a co-captain was fun."

"Respect – she was just looking for some respect," Berkely said of the fact that overall, Seither didn't feel like she was having such a great experience at Badin. "She earned it. She deserved it. She did a good job as captain. They all did."

"Being a captain was nice, but it could also be a pain," Adams said. "All of these girls are my friends – so you don't want to have to yell at them. You don't want people mad at you. But sometimes you have to. It was an honor being the captain of this team."

"Being a goalkeeper, you're not only playing the position, you're playing a leadership role," said Hessling, who was still sharing goalkeeping duties on the JV as a junior. "I had to show that this was my team, my position, my role. I knew if I was going to succeed, I had to be better than I was. With that came a lot of responsibility, a lot of pressure. I think I had something to prove."

"I think they did pay attention to me," Reed said. "I did all of the conditioning, all of the non-contact work. They never once said, 'well, you can't play.' They never once treated me like I was different."

"I think the captains did a really good job," she added. "They didn't start any drama. The captains understood that this was bigger than our senior year."

"I'll miss the seniors," Morgan Langhammer said. "They were the best seniors we could have had … the best leaders we could have had. They kept us together. After all, we're high school girls."

Talented defenders in 2013 who helped keep the ball out of Badin's net were, from left, juniors Brianna Scowden and Kate Bach and sophomores Shelby Lamping, Taylor Smith and Gabby Geigle. Photo by the author.

Leading Badin's 2013 offensive attack included, top to bottom on the left, juniors Morgan Langhammer, Madi Kah and Annika Pater. Top to bottom at right are sophomores Malia Berkely and Rachel Riley. Photo by the author.

Above, members of the Badin High 2013 state champions were honored by Hamilton City Council and given a sign for the school. Below, the girls show off their new state championship rings. Don't mind the outfits … it's Mismatch Day during Spirit Week in early 2014! Contributed photos.

2013

Badin High girls soccer coach Todd Berkely knew that he would have a solid team in 2013 – the Rams had gone 13-3-3 the previous season, and most of the key players were back – but it was not a ready-made team.

Who would be in goal was one critical question that had to be answered, and Berkely was preparing to introduce a new system of play, which would require a lot of practice for the team to get comfortable with. The Rams definitely had their work cut out for them in the pre-season.

"I never worried about the season – that part was so far into the future," Berkely said. "I had to focus on the training. If we had the right training attitude and mentality, then we had a chance to improve. Keep the visor low, that way you can't see the horizon."

Senior Michelle Hessling would have the first shot to earn the starting nod between the pipes. Badin had played a pair of sophomores in goal in 2012, and both had played pretty well. But Mackenzie Eagan had transferred out to a home school situation, and Mandy Lucking had been involved in an August car accident that left her with a severe concussion that basically sidelined her for the year.

Hessling had spent the entire spring and summer working on her game – and working on her game very effectively.

"Not playing (varsity) as a junior was really hard on me," she said. "I pushed myself in the spring to get quicker, faster, stronger. I always expected myself to be this good, but I had to work hard to make myself this good. I might have even surprised myself a little bit."

"Michelle had just never been given the opportunity back there," Berkely said. "She had the hands, the smarts, the footwork. She had great hand-eye coordination. When it's clutch time, you want Michelle Hessling in the goal. You could count on her to make plays."

Hessling was familiar with Berkely, and was initially skeptical when he landed the job as head coach. She quickly came around.

"Being 100 percent honest, I thought hiring a parent was going to be a bad idea," she nodded. "Having a parent as head coach, I was afraid there was going to be a lot of drama. But he handled it very well. The first few practices I complained, but I owe him a lot."

Berkely was a goaltender himself, and he well understood the pressure and the rigors of the position.

"Coach Berkely said we had some homework, to set personal goals and team goals," Hessling recalled. "My personal goal was that I wanted to be better than I had ever been. He said, 'Don't worry … you'll get there.' He trusted me. He put a little faith in me."

Hessling was concerned that the fact she was only 5-foot-4 would be a problem.

"I said that one of my weaknesses was that I was short, but Coach Berkely told me that it wasn't a weakness, that I had the ability to get to high balls," she said. "I think I can see the field better than a lot of people, and I'm good with my hands. … I had to get comfortable with this position, with this group of girls."

And Hessling looked back at that 2-1 loss to Troy Christian in the 2012 tournament as one of the toughest of her career. Senior goalkeeper Morgan Walker was a good friend of hers, and other than playing well on Senior Night in a rainy 1-0 shutout victory over Landmark Christian, Walker had mostly been relegated to the role of spectator that season.

"I remember all of our tournament losses vividly," Hessling said. "I talked to the girls and said I never want to get to that loss part. When you're an underclassman, the season's over and you start a new season. When you're a senior, your career is over and you're done with those girls. It'll never be the same group again.

"I had to sit next to Morgan and watch the last game of her career, of her senior year, knowing that there was nothing she could do about it. That was hard," she said. "At least this year, my senior year, I knew that I would have the opportunity to do something and fail rather than not have the opportunity at all."

With Hessling appearing to be solid in goal, the Rams also had what looked to be a potent scoring punch at the other end of the field. But Berkely was going to reconfigure the attack as well.

In 2012, his daughter Malia had been the tip end of the scoring spear for the Rams, notching 17 goals. But Todd Berkely felt that putting Malia up top made her easier to defend. He wanted to pull her back, and match her up more with running mate Madi Kah. Junior Annika Pater would make a strong striker in the new setup.

"Madi and Malia offensively – there's no better combination of players," Todd Berkely said. "They're like two gunslingers out there. They're 'Thunder and Lightning'. They know each other's moves, what to look for, where to go. And then you add Anni to the mix, and she's the wild card. Very tough to stop."

"This year we looked past everything and focused on what was important for the team," Malia said. "There was no real drama, no real issues. That was huge. Drama affected our field play last year. This year we pushed all that aside."

"The pre-season really got us ready," Kah said. "After the first couple of games, we realized how good we were. We played really well together. That was our best thing. We knew how we all played and we played well – and we had the drive to keep on winning."

"I was a little nervous at first because we had a new coach and I felt like I had to prove myself all over again, and that was a little intimidating," said Pater, also a starting guard for the BHS girls basketball quintet. "Some of the practices we looked good, and that was a positive."

Pater's older sister, Morgan, had been a fleet outside defender for the girls soccer Rams, and had set the girls basketball record for career three-pointers when she graduated in 2011. The Mathews girls were her cousins, "and I felt like I had to live up to all of them. I loved going to all of their games. It was fun. I've enjoyed every moment of Badin girls soccer."

Pater is named for golfing Hall of Famer Annika Sorenstam – it's amazing how many apparent non-golf fans there are butchering her first name over public address systems all over Southwest Ohio – and her dad, Shawn, had been pointing to her as a future standout athlete for the Rams since grade school. He was right.

"Growing up, I don't remember a time where I wasn't playing soccer," Annika said. "It's all I wanted to do. My dad has been such an influence. I get a little annoyed with him sometimes, but I wouldn't be where I am without my dad pushing me.

"My older sister had a big impact, whether she knew it or not," Pater added. "I love competition. I don't like to lose. When you win, it just makes you want to keep going and win some more."

"She's a tireless warrior," Berkely said of Pater. "She's one of the most gifted natural athletes I have known. I am convinced that if you taught Anni a new sport that she had never seen before, she would be able to play that sport at a very high level faster than any other person you could find."

As he looked around the Queen of Peace practice field, Berkely felt like he had 13 battle-tested players he could send into the fray night-in and night-out – Hessling in goal and 12 field players to rotate around the 10 starting positions. Co-captain Holly Reed would also be a staple of the varsity roster, though she could not play. And he had a number of other solid players who could swing between reserve and varsity and be ready for some key minutes as necessary.

"I think the difference between 2012 and 2013 was a little more maturity," said Joe Geigle, whose daughter Gabby was a fixture in the starting lineup. "That was a great team (in 2012), but the next year there was a more mature attitude; the kids had more of a belief in themselves. And Coach Berkely knew what buttons to push, and when."

Berkely would "jigsaw puzzle" the rest of the starting lineup between seniors Maggie Adams and Amy Seither, juniors Kate Bach, Morgan Langhammer and Brianna Scowden; and sophomores Geigle, Shelby Lamping, Rachel Riley and Taylor Smith.

Others he expected to see regular varsity minutes included junior Emily Henson, sophomores Lydia Braun and Ali Kalberer, and freshmen Sabrina Bernardo and Samantha Lehker. As time went on, sophomore Katie Pohlman and freshman Lindsey Brinck played their way into the mix as well. Sophomore Anna Glen and freshman Nicole Visse would backstop the reserve team and be available for the varsity as needed.

Geigle had started on defense as a freshman, and would do so again.

"Soccer is fun. I like playing outside … the feel of the ball at my feet is a great feeling," she said. "I like being on a team, playing with people you like. As a kid, I just kind of fell in love with it."

Geigle was one of the fastest players on the team, and certainly utilized her speed along the back line.

"There's a lot of pressure when you play defense, but you know that," she said. "You have to keep the ball out of the net and help the keeper. You're the last one there – it's your responsibility. But at the same time, you know they have to go through the whole team to get to you. You can't be too discouraged when the other team scores. When you make a big play on defense, that's all the better."

Kate Bach was another returning starter; an excellent athlete whose dad, Pat, had been Badin's starting quarterback for two seasons in the mid-1980s and was the president of the athletic booster club. She was a free spirit with talent and a sunny disposition.

"Badin soccer feels like my second family," she said. "I can be who I want to be around my teammates because they act just as crazy as I am. As a team, all the girls connected. We agreed on the things that mattered. I never dreaded going to practice because I enjoyed seeing my teammates."

"She has a fantastic attitude," Todd Berkely said. "She approaches the game with an engine that never quits. We got her settled down on the field and that was a key to her success."

"Coach Berkely definitely made me a lot better player over the year," Bach nodded. "I was a more controlled player, more calm on the field. He taught me to use my speed as a weapon during the game.

"And he's the most positive man you'll ever meet," she added. "He'll never put you down. He never meant to be rude. He's the best coach I've ever had … the best coach I've ever had!"

Shelby Lamping was a high-octane player who was often compared by Badin soccer observers to 2007 graduate Kristina Anderson for her tough, no-quarter style of play. There was no higher compliment.

"I'm intense – I push myself," said Lamping. "When I see someone who's fast, I want to be faster. … Playing for Badin, there's a lot of bonding; you're always together with everybody. But it's a very competitive environment; you've got to work hard."

Lamping had come to Badin from Fairfield Middle School after Madi Kah preceded her by a year. Some of her club teammates like Malia Berkely, Gabby Geigle and Lydia Braun were coming as well … "so I knew it must be a good place," she said.

While Lamping was impressed with how friendly everyone was as she had considered Badin, she nearly left after freshman year.

"The classes were harder, and I wasn't ready for it," she conceded. "My grades weren't that good. The (seven-point) grading scale was frustrating. I realized I had to work a lot harder. I did that, and was able to raise my (grade point average) from a 2.9 to a 3.4. I'm glad I stayed."

"She has no 'off' switch," Berkely said of Lamping. "There is no work rate superior to hers on the field. She will literally run herself until she is at the point of collapse. Finding a spot where she didn't kill herself was a challenge.

"When college coaches come to see us play, she is a player who is on their list every time," he added. "I just have to smile to myself when they ask about her. She is like a burst pipe … you can't stop it, you can't even slow it down. You just have to shut it off at the source – usually by taking the halftime break."

Taylor Smith – whose parents still refer to her as "Boo", a club soccer nickname she was hoping to outrun at Badin -- was another hard worker who played her way into being an impact player for the Rams.

"She's got that hard-nosed tenacity," Berkely said. "She's very coachable with a solid work ethic. I love her approach to the game. She made us better on defense with her great raw instincts."

As an 8th grader at Colerain Middle School, Smith was well aware of Erin and Kim Golden and Ashley Mahoney, whose parents were family friends and who had made such a soccer impact at Badin. She took a look around and, much to her parents' delight, said that she would wear Badin green.

But, just as quickly as she had made that decision, Smith suffered a bout of cold feet in the spring and determined she would stay at Colerain. Then, in May of 2012, Smith came down to the breakfast table one morning, looked at her mother and said, "I think I'll go to Badin after all."

Barbara Smith, a McAuley High grad who wanted Taylor in Catholic education, said that was a great day at the breakfast table.

"High school soccer is a family thing – they know you better than anyone else," Taylor Smith said. "You see your teammates more than you see your family. You can rant about what's going on in your life. It's a very helpful environment."

Smith was another one who had to be convinced that the father of a current player would make a good head coach for the Rams.

"I didn't like him at first – I like him now," she said of Todd Berkely. "He showed that he cares a lot about you. He cared about where we'd go and what we'd do. He never brought us down, ever.

"He's focused on education," she added. "He made it clear that grades came first over soccer. We learned to manage what little time we had and help each other out."

Like Smith, Rachel Riley is from northwest Hamilton County, a St. John Dry Ridge student whose family ran in similar club soccer circles. Riley's older sister, Kelsey, had transferred to Badin from Ursuline Academy as a junior over the summer of 2011, and Kelsey made such a positive impact in just two years at BHS that she earned the Archbishop Leibold graduation medal for "outstanding service to the school and community."

"I was thinking about going to Badin even before Kelsey transferred in," said Rachel, though the fact that Kelsey had such a good experience certainly didn't hurt. "Erin Golden used to babysit me. I talked to the Mahoneys. Everyone was so positive about Badin."

Tall and fast, Riley possesses such speed that her soccer teammates suggest she should be a sprinter on the track team in the spring.

"She has a heart of gold and is a great teammate," Todd Berkely said. "She's a special kid. I pick on her in practice, but she can take it. She has a physically dominating look on the field of play, but she's a big teddy bear. You'd run into her, and she'd apologize."

"We're all very close," Riley said. "It's a very family-like atmosphere. We push each other to do well. You learn to like people that you generally wouldn't spend much time with. ... We felt like this was going to be our season. We had talked about it all freshman year."

Berkely saw a huge upside in the talented Riley.

"I spent the majority of the season working on her technique," he said. "I put her on the spot in practice whenever I had the chance as far as demonstrating technique. She always took it as a challenge with a smile even when she knew she was going to mess it up."

"I'm fast, I'm athletic," she nodded. "I'm not such a technical player – I'm more of a runner that you can play the ball into. I was scoring a lot early in the season and that taught me that I had the ability to be out there and score.

"And then I stopped scoring and that kind of got to me a little bit," Riley said. "But I make outside runs so you really get the ball to your feet maybe one out of every 10 balls. I understand that."

Brianna Scowden had been under-utilized as a sophomore defender; quiet and skilled, she was always in the right spot and opponents rarely ran past her. Her bright white hair band and lime green soccer shoes made her easy to find on the field; Berkely was familiar with Scowden from club soccer and felt she would earn plenty of playing time.

"Bri is all about angles and positioning," he said. "She knows where the ball is going to be three passes before it gets there. ... She may not be the fastest and she may not be the strongest, but she is definitely the smartest, and in soccer that counts. She's a gamer."

"Playing for Badin is pretty cool – it's definitely a big family," said Scowden, who often answers to the nickname 'Breezy'. "I thought we were definitely well-prepared for the season considering the short amount of time we had to get ready.

"Coach Berkely put me at center-mid to start," she noted. "I didn't know if I'd like that, but it turned out OK. He was trying to find out what worked best for the team. He did a lot of that (shuffling players around)."

Scowden would be inducted into the National Honor Society just a few days after the season ended, one of four Badin girls soccer upperclassmen in the school's NHS chapter -- seniors Holly Reed and Amy Seither and fellow junior Morgan Langhammer.

Langhammer was like a "bonus player" for the Rams ... the star who comes off the disabled list and gives the team a massive jolt of talent.

Starting at sweeper for Badin during her freshman year, Langhammer had torn the ACL in her right knee in the fourth game of the 2011 season. Then, trying to come back for her sophomore year, she'd torn it again during club play in June of 2012. That latter mishap had come, ironically enough, during a scrimmage against a boys' team.

"Especially after the second injury, I wondered if I would play again," Langhammer conceded. "I wasn't sure if I wanted to risk it. ... But after all the trials and tribulations, after all the pain and frustration, it is soooo worth it. ... My right knee may never be the same. I've come to terms with that. But I don't think twice when I go into a slide tackle."

Todd Berkely insisted repeatedly that before her injuries, Morgan Langhammer would have been the best player on the team – quite a statement considering the talent on the BHS roster. Even with the injuries, he still thought she was very nearly the best.

"She is one of the most talented and focused kids I have ever known," Berkely said. "She could have said enough is enough ... but instead she has come back from the abyss not once but twice – not only to play, but to lead. She's Badin's own version of the Terminator. You simply can't stop her."

"It was nerve-wracking not having a coach in May, but in hindsight, I was super-OK with it because we got Coach Berkely," said Langhammer, well familiar with Berkely through all of her club days with Malia. "Especially since this was going to be the first time I was getting a full year of high school soccer in. That was stressful.

"Coach Berkely commands respect," she added. "He's very knowledgeable about the game. He honestly wants what's best for the team. He didn't come for any other reason. He sacrificed a lot for us."

"Morgan is one of the best players, one of the best leaders on the team," Berkely said. "What she went through with those knee rehabs was unbelievable. I had her play outside mid to get fit, to get healthy, to get back her love of soccer. She would ask me sometimes if she could go back and play defense. I would just have to look at her and say, 'Morgan – no!'"

Senior co-captain Amy Seither was a key leader on the team – she appreciated it, and took it seriously.

"Soccer is one of the main reasons I came to Badin," she said. "I loved Badin soccer. It was a bumpy road, sometimes it was miserable. But we made it work."

"Amy is one of the most mature players I have ever met," Berkely said. "I put the burden of leadership on her shoulders even when I knew the weight would be difficult to bear, and she handled it. Her maturity and no-nonsense approach to things is something the team needed."

"We had a talented group, and we worked well together," Seither said. "We all had our roles, and we knew our place on the team. Renee Balconi talked about heart, talent and family. She said we had the talent, we were a family, and it all came down to heart. We wanted to make the season last as long as it could."

Senior co-captain Maggie Adams was the popular big sister, the "go-to" person for her teammates with her wide smile and sparkling eyes. She wasn't afraid to play the big sister role of enforcer either, if necessary, to look after the interests of her "sisters" on the field.

"Playing soccer has been one of my favorite parts of high school," said Adams, whose mother, Sharon, is a Pate – one of the largest extended families in the history of Badin High. Maggie's cousin, Courtney Gray, had played a leading role in all three state tournament runs in '05, '06 and '07, and Maggie had long dreamed of being a part of the BHS girls soccer family and wearing Courtney's number, 12.

"I loved every one of my teammates," she said. "It was awesome to play with Malia – she might be famous some day! She was an amazing player to watch and be on the field with. ... I enjoyed playing with everyone. We worked so well as a team."

"The girls looked up to Maggie in many ways," Berkely said. "She was the single most improved player on the team. We could not have won without Maggie on the field."

"I always tried to give it my all," Adams said. "My toughness definitely helps me ... though it can hurt me, too," she chuckled, as she was constantly getting called for fouls simply because she was often the bigger of the two girls involved in a play.

Senior co-captain Holly Reed was one-half of the answer to a trivia question involving the Badin girls soccer program: Who were the only two students at Badin who had district championship medals in girls soccer?

The last time Badin had won a district title was 2010, so they had to be seniors who had played varsity as freshmen. The answer – Holly Reed and Crystal Rains, which made it even more unusual since neither were playing any longer. Rains – the younger sister of 2005 headliner Heather -- had stepped away from soccer following her sophomore year to concentrate on softball, and would earn a softball scholarship to the University of Indianapolis. Reed, so mature she could have passed for a senior as an 8th grader, was sidelined by concussions.

Berkely insisted, though, that Reed be a part of the program every day.

"Holly is one of those kids who you instantly root for as a coach or a parent," he said. "She needed to be a part of the dynamic, a part of the Badin soccer family win or lose."

"It was hard not playing senior year, I'm not going to sugarcoat it," said Reed, who'd suffered four concussions by the end of her junior season. "It was hard to be on the sidelines and not play. But the girls never made me feel like a burden; they treated me well. I was lucky.

"My best friends are all on the soccer team," she added. "We're not just teammates, we're like a family. We can be dysfunctional sometimes, get mad and competitive with each other. But at the end of the day, we've got each other's backs and love each other."

That family bond had been strengthened by a new coach, forged by tough training and preparation, and now the road test loomed in the regular season. The Rams felt like they were ready.

2013

Todd Berkely had given the Badin girls soccer team "homework" heading into the regular season – personal goals, and team goals.

The team goal, as the Rams prepared to open on the road against Edgewood High, was pretty much unanimous. Win the Division III state tournament. Of course, that was the goal nearly every year – but this year, the girls felt like they truly had a fighting chance of making it happen.

"Every Badin girls soccer team, at the beginning of the season, goes into it thinking they'd like to win the state championship," Michelle Hessling nodded. "If you don't set your goals high, you're never going to get there."

On the sleeve of their practice shirts, Berkely had put the logo 7/8 … meaning that the Rams had been to the state finals 7 times previously, and the goal this year was to make trip number 8.

"I think we all came in thinking we had a shot at state this year," Malia Berkely said. "We couldn't let that go to our heads – but we were excited to give it our all. We felt that vibe throughout the whole season."

"Last year we joked around that we were going to state, and then we got knocked out in the district tournament, and it was very disappointing," Shelby Lamping said. "This year we said it, and we really meant it!"

"I'm thinking we're going to state," Annika Pater agreed. "That's what we said. That was in our head. Whether it was a joke or not, honestly, I didn't see that far ahead."

The Edgewood game was the first time the so-called "Magnificent M's" – Madi Kah, Malia Berkely and Morgan Langhammer – had been on the field together for the Badin girls soccer program. Berkely was still in the 8th grade for the 2011 season, and Langhammer had been injured and out the entire 2012 campaign.

The veteran Kah opened the year with her usual solid outing, a goal and an assist, and the Rams used a tally in the final 10 minutes to get clear, 3-1. Badin was excited to win its opener for its new head coach – but perhaps a little less than exhilarated about struggling to beat the Cougars. That view should have fully vanished by the time Edgewood turned in a strong 13-2-1 regular season.

Kah had committed to play for Ohio University over the summer, but Todd Berkely still felt like she was "the single most underrated player in Southwest Ohio, maybe the entire state."

"She's a dynamic 'wow!' kind of a player," Berkely said. "She has a gift for deception with the ball. No one makes more defenders look bad than Madi Kah – she constantly makes people miss. She's the girl nobody wants to play against."

Kah wanted to study meteorology in college, and that soccer/ weather combination was just the ticket for OU.

"The recruitment process was stressful," said Kah. "Some people like the spotlight on them and coaches trying to get you to come to their school. I did not like that at all. I was glad to get it over with. It was a big weight off my shoulders."

Before the start of the 2014 season, the other two "Ms" would also make their college commitments – Malia Berkely to Florida State, and Morgan Langhammer to the University of Evansville – as Division I colleges continued to call on the Rams.

Todd Berkely – "keeping the visor low" – had quietly divided the 16-game season into four-game quadrants in his own mind. He wanted to see ongoing improvement at each quarter pole of the year.

"My thought process isn't to go undefeated," he said. "It's just to keep working together, to keep getting better as a team. You're trying to find the right fit and the right formation. I could just send them out there as individuals and let them go beat somebody, because they had the skills to do that. But that doesn't work come tournament time."

And he was in the process of changing the Badin game plan to a different style of play, to build the attack from the back of the field. It got more players into the offensive zone, and kept the ball away from the other team in the process.

"It's a possession game," nodded Berkely. "You keep the ball away from the other team, and by the end of the game they wished they had picked another sport to play. It's the equivalent of running a cross country race by the time they're finished chasing you around the field."

"Todd Berkely's team does not play high school soccer, and it frustrates the hell out of other high school coaches," Terry Kah said. "He got Badin to play a pretty possession game instead of just kicking the ball and going to get it."

Even then, Berkely's first formation failed to work. Building from the back, he went with four defenders, five midfielders and a striker (4-5-1) – but the midfielders were lost in translation. So he switched it up to a slightly more traditional plan with four defenders, two midfielders, three forwards and a striker (4-2-3-1), which the players found easier to execute.

The two outside defenders were thrown into the offense, along with one of the midfielders. The other midfielder would be a "holding" mid, assisting on defense with the two center backs. That put seven girls into the attacking plan, a lot of numbers to try to defend against.

"I knew we wanted to be offensive-minded, because I'm an offensive-minded coach," Berkely said. "Let your cheetahs run, don't let 'em get trapped in a cage!"

"My first formation was an abject failure," he noted, "because all it did was confuse the heck out of the players. We did some trial and error the first few games. Then you try something else – that's how failure can lead to success."

"It probably took 'em 25 percent of the season to get comfortable with the formation," assistant coach Jeff Pohlman said. "Once you figure it out, all of the sudden you've got seven players in the attack and all kinds of weapons. It took the girls awhile to get used to it, but once they did, it was very effective."

When the Rams lost to a strong McNicholas contingent on the road in Game Three, 2-0 in an outcome that wasn't really that close, there was no attacking, just a "Not Ready for Prime Time" wake-up call.

"That was awful," Rachel Riley said. "It was like, OK, we've got to step it up. It created some tension within ourselves. It was like, 'You guys aren't as great as you think you are.'"

Berkely, however, would not let the girls get down on themselves.

"Confidence is the No. 1 enemy of girls," he said, underlining his relentlessly positive mantra. He'd use his lengthy postgame talks in the middle of the field to accentuate the positive, but also to get the players to think about what else they could have done, and could have done better.

"I would talk to the other parents and ask them how everything was going," said Nicole Berkely, who was both the parent of a player and the wife of the head coach. "I didn't want them to feel awkward talking to the coach's wife. Sometimes I would say, 'So, what's with this 20-minute postgame talk?'"

"Coach Berkely was definitely different than any coach I had ever had," Amy Seither said. "He certainly liked to talk a lot. People started timing his post-game talks. He took on more of a role of teacher than coach.

"When the season started, some of us were afraid to say it – state," she said. "We just kind of knew – we were going to state. It felt right."

"The goal was to win the state championship," Jeff Pohlman said. "The girls really bought into it. They gave it their all."

Forget state – the Rams were just trying to win a game in Game Four, trailing rival Hamilton High 1-0 at halftime, having been shut out for three consecutive halves. BHS fans were a bit miffed, too, since even though it was Badin's "home game" at Hamilton's Virgil Schwarm Stadium, Big Blue fans were sitting on the home side.

The reality was that former BHS assistant Brian Smallwood had done a nice job turning Hamilton High into a formidable competitor that would no doubt only get tougher. Badin's 3-1 win the previous year had been a close encounter as well.

Junior Brianna Scowden was back from a quad injury for the Rams, and she made her presence felt. After Madi Kah scored early in the second half to knot the score, Badin finally won it late on a perfect ball from Scowden to Malia Berkely off of a free kick.

Hamilton defenders were caught off guard on the play, since Scowden could conceivably have tried to pound the free kick into the net. Instead, she chipped it short to Berkely in the middle of the defensive zone, and Berkely quickly did the rest.

"The Hamilton game really stands out from the regular season," Kate Bach said. "It's kind of a big deal to step up and win against them. They wanted the field to be theirs – but it was ours, too."

Bach was a talented player who was at home with her teammates.

"I love to play soccer," she said. "It's a stress reliever – everything else in my life is completely gone. I like the friends and family atmosphere. It's good to be part of something. You push yourself to get better. It's something to strive for."

Malia Berkely had stepped up in a clutch spot for Badin with her game-winning goal – but one of the key realities for the Rams in 2013 is that it did not have to be 'all Berkely, all the time.' Badin had plenty of offensive firepower to go with her.

In 2012, Berkely had gotten off of a red-eye from California and hustled to the district final game against Troy Christian. She was exhausted, but her teammates perhaps expected too much from her in that outing. Now, Berkely could be Berkely – but other players had the confidence that they could be factors as well. Nobody was standing around watching, waiting. It made her that much more of a factor.

"A lot of practice with 1 v 1's and with penalty kicks against keepers," said Malia when asked about her goal-scoring ability. "You have to be dynamic with the ball and try to find different ways to put it in the net. You have to be cool, calm and collected and not just hit it as hard as you can. It's about placement and getting the ball past the keeper.

"Though sometimes," she added with a laugh, "I do take my anger out on the ball."

Badin didn't have any trouble putting the ball in the net during a 10-0 pounding of Northwest in Game Six, but Todd Berkely wasn't the least bit happy about it.

"That was a tough game to coach," he said. "Our girls were cocky, arrogant, playing in an almost disrespectful way. When you lose, lose with class. But you'd better win with class, too. The Northwest center back played with more heart and gusto than anybody on our team that night.

"When we beat Chaminade-Julienne 3-1 in the next game, that had everything to do with the conversation after the Northwest game," he said. "Play team soccer. That's what we're all about."

The Rams definitely tried hard to play team soccer off the field each season. They had plenty of pre-game rituals that had been passed down over the years and were a key part of the soccer family dynamic.

This year, Terry Kah had arranged for a local restaurant, Texas Roadhouse, to be a team sponsor. You could almost see the restaurant from the Hamilton High stadium. The Rams had all of their pre-game meals there before home games, and it was the same meal each time – grilled chicken, baked potato, salad and vegetables. Renee Balconi had stressed proper nutrition, and this was a part of it.

Of course, the girls loved rolls … and Texas Roadhouse rolls are particularly good. They were not part of the meal … but the girls always got them surreptitiously from the Texas Roadhouse representatives, Katie and Shane. The only time they missed out on the rolls? The afternoon head coach Todd Berkely unexpectedly showed up for the meal.

Cheese was another no-no … a restriction the girls generally followed. But junior Annika Pater was addicted to cheese … so one afternoon for the 4 o'clock meal, she could stand it no longer, and simply brought her own.

What the girls referred to as a "dance party" would precede the meal in the upper parking lot at Badin. Same three songs every time. Then the girls would pile in the same cars, leave the lot in the same car order, and head to the Roadhouse.

Once at the stadium, by halftime of the reserve game, the varsity would get together for what was referred to as a "séance" – a pre-game event that had been a ritual for years. No spirits were being conjured, but the girls would go around the circle and talk about what was on their mind, then enumerate their individual goals for that night's game.

"They could go long, though on the road we generally had to shorten them up," said senior co-captain Maggie Adams. "They were nice, especially if someone had a bad day, they could vent to the team. It definitely brought us closer."

Naturally, for the séance, the girls would sit in the exact same order every game … co-captains Adams and Amy Seither would start the session; co-captains Michelle Hessling and Holly Reed would end it, and then Reed would read some soccer quotes that were also part of the legacy.

Kate Bach recalled the night freshman Sam Lehker was pulled up to varsity. Lehker was small but skilled and had made a good impression with her constant effort. "We were in the circle and she didn't really know what to say," Bach said. "So she just said, 'Well, I guess I'm on varsity now …' We just laughed because we already knew that."

"We had a billion-and-one superstitions," Seither said. "We had our lucky rolls. We would do everything in the same order. Pre-game things went like clockwork. We all trusted each other so much. We had a bond that we'd never had before."

Once the pre-game introductions and National Anthem were over, the girls would huddle up to the side of the bench and say a "Hail Mary" prayer, then Madi Kah would shout the ongoing line of enthusiasm, "Let's play with some emotion!" and all voices would be raised in a cry of unity.

When the huddle broke, the girls had so many special handshakes on their way to the field that the officials and opposing team might be left waiting for a few moments. The Badin girls figured they had 80 minutes of soccer to play ... so that if it took them 10 seconds or 30 seconds to get to the line, there were still 80 minutes of soccer to be played.

Todd Berkely had added another wrinkle to help bring the team together ... what was referred to as the "Trust Circle" under the large trees next to the Queen of Peace practice field. Those were opportunities for girls to get things off their chest with their teammates, rather than let them fester. But the girls had to be prepared – if they were going to call somebody out, they needed to know that they might get called out themselves. It wasn't a one-way street.

"The honesty sessions were a humbling thing," Seither said. "We'd get things off our chest and feel closer. It wasn't like the season was a smooth sailing ride. We had problems like every family has. We'd get past them like families do."

"We all got along for the most part – we fought like sisters and we'd love each other like sisters," Annika Pater said. "Sometimes the Trust Circle would take up the entire practice. We'd talk about what we did wrong during games, what we needed to do to get better. We learned to trust each other and pump each other up."

"Calling people out if necessary – it worked," Kate Bach said. "We'd never fight, or if we did, we would confront it and get through it. Coach Berkely was very flexible about that. We needed to prove that Badin really was a family. We bonded a lot."

Assistant coach Ken Murrell recalled a practice session when the Rams were taking a water break.

"Some of the girls were fussing at each other about this and that," he said. "I just told them they needed to work to keep getting better, each practice, each game. They looked up and sort of acknowledged that. I never heard another squabble from then on. They just kept getting better."

Todd Berkely had had a trust session of his own, a mid-year "heart-to-heart" meeting with senior co-captain Maggie Adams.

"At first, I was terrified of Coach Berkely," Adams said. "But at mid-season, we had a talk, and I started to like him. He cared about us so much. That really stood out. He told me he believed in us and as captains we needed to get the team to believe, too."

"Good things come from strange situations," Berkely said. "Maggie was mad. She didn't think she was as good as the other girls.

I didn't feel that way at all. I told her, 'Go assert yourself and do what you do. Go lead and be a force in the game.'

"When Maggie became a leader on the field, we became a team," he added. "'Great leaders are humble but filled with infectious passion.' That's Maggie Adams. She's a great leader."

Todd Berkely and Terry Kah had put their heads together and come up with another nice pre-game routine, inviting former Badin standouts back to act as honorary captains and be introduced to the crowd. The eye-opening resumes of former players like Ashley Roberto, a high school soccer All-American, and Tori Mathews, who played on three straight state finalists, certainly got the current players' attention.

"You want to bring out the pride and tradition of the program," Berkely said. "Have the players come back and be recognized. This is a soccer program that is steeped in tradition and history, at a school that's steeped in tradition and history. Bring that back. You don't see that at other schools. Everywhere else it's all about now, now, now."

When the Rams thumped Roger Bacon 6-0 at home in mid-September, they were 6-2-0 at the midpoint of the season, having lost road games at McNicholas and Kettering Alter. Just as Berkely had hoped, they continued to show improved play.

"Turning a high school team into a possession mentality team is a daunting task," he said. "You're only playing together for about three months. I thought I could piece things together. We were going to keep the ball. It took a lot of sessions to explain just how we were going to do that."

"Todd Berkely did a great job," Athletic Director Geoff Melzer said. "It helps when you have talented girls in the program, but he got those talented girls to buy into his plan. The girls were willing to work hard. They worked hard, and overall they played very well."

In Game Nine, at home against Mother of Mercy, a capable Division I school, all the prep work came together in a "eureka!" moment with an impressive 3-1 victory. "After the Mercy game, we were on Cloud Nine," Rachel Riley nodded. "That was a really good win."

It was a really good win because it came against a good team, and in the ball-control manner that Berkely had been preaching. And it had been capped by one of the most remarkable goals of the season, when Malia Berkely amazingly went coast-to-coast in unheard of fashion.

With a 2-0 lead at halftime, Todd Berkely had put his daughter back on defense. It was an understandable move, since Berkely was still piecing his rotation together and certainly Malia could help keep things under control at the defensive end.

What happened next had to be seen to be believed.

Malia went airborne just inside the 18-yard-line to knock Mercy's attempted chip pass down to her feet. Then she started dribbling the other way, expecting to find a teammate to drop the ball off to at any moment. There were plenty of teammates available … but the more Berkely dribbled, the more open she became. No Mercy player challenged her. So she just kept going.

And going. She dribbled the length of the field, through the entire Mercy squad, unimpeded. Finally, at the other 18, the Bobcat sweeper stepped up. But Berkely just juked her with a back-tap of the ball, easily maintained possession, and was 1-on-1 with the Mercy keeper.

It was no contest. The crowd, a low roar building ever louder as Berkely continued dribbling, exploded. Berkely, shaking her head in amazement and disbelief, told her teammates that night, "Nobody ever cut me off!"

"That's probably my most favorite play that I've ever been involved in," she said looking back on it. "As soon as I got the ball, I just looked ahead. Nobody was coming at me. It happened so fast. It took me a minute to realize I'd just scored. That was a great moment. I loved that feeling."

It was a three-goal hat-trick for Berkely, and a signature win for the Rams.

"That was the best goal she's had in high school," said Todd Berkely. "But that was a good team win, too. We were playing our possession game, and Mercy didn't have a clue how to defend it or attack it. And beating Mercy, a good Division I school, did wonders for our confidence."

Badin, now 7-2-0, would need that confidence as it entered the meat-grinder portion of the schedule. In fact, the Rams would win just one more game the rest of the way. But they would play hard and well, get their rotation in order, and have plenty of reason to feel good about the post-season opportunities as Division III tournament time approached.

"Our philosophy was that the season would prepare us for state," Malia Berkely said. "We might have lost some games, but we were getting ready. Practices prepared us for the games, and the games prepared us for the state tournament."

"I knew we had a tough schedule, but that was OK," Kate Bach said. "The losses on our schedule were not shocking. I would prefer to have a tougher schedule. You become better by playing the best."

After 1-all deadlocks with Dayton Carroll and Madeira, the now 7-2-2 Rams hosted always tough St. Ursula Academy – the Bulldogs were headed for the Division I regional finals – and came out on the wrong side of a 5-1 final.

"The St. Ursula game, even though we lost, it helped us," Annika Pater said.

Todd Berkely felt the same way.

"This year, we prepared for the St. Ursula game like it mattered," he said. "A year ago, the girls went down there and lost, 6-0, and it wasn't that close. They knew they were going to lose even before they got there.

"We didn't approach it that way this year," he added. "You knew they looked at us like the lightweight on their schedule. It had all the ingredients for an upset."

The Rams trailed 2-0 when Morgan Langhammer scored the first goal of her high school career, and understandably shed tears of joy over putting one in the nets after all the injury trauma. St. Ursula battened down the hatches, and handled BHS from there.

"We were down 5-1, but we were still playing some of our best soccer," Berkely said. "We played so hard we were out of gas."

In fact, starting with the Mother of Mercy game, the Rams were in the midst of playing six games in 10 days. The St. Ursula game was the first of three games in four days. It was a tough stretch. And looming two days later was a road test at defending state champion and arch-rival Middletown Fenwick.

"Badin and Fenwick are two of the best programs in Southwest Ohio – this is always some great soccer," Berkely said. "It's like the Red Sox and Yankees. This is the one game everyone wants to see."

"We bring out the best in each other," agreed Fenwick coach Tom McEwan. "It doesn't matter if one team is up and the other team is down, they are going to rise to the occasion for this match."

On this night, like a lot of other nights, each team's best played to a draw, 1-1. In fact, it was the fifth consecutive year that Badin and Fenwick had played to a tie in the regular season, two proud programs battling for local bragging rights. Not since Oct. 8, 2008, had there been a winner in the game – 1-0 Fenwick en route to the 2008 Division II state championship. Neither team had scored more than one goal in any of the most recent games, either.

Badin's Gabby Geigle was still feeling down about the 2012

encounter, when she had been whistled for a foul in the box in the final minute of a Saturday afternoon game. Fenwick converted the penalty kick, and slipped out of Virgil Schwarm Stadium with a 1-all tie.

"It was a foul," said her father, Joe, about the call that had Badin fans up in arms at the time. "I know people were saying that the official was too far away from the play, but you can't trip somebody from behind in the box and not draw a whistle. That's a foul."

"But the thing I remember is how supportive her teammates were of Gabby after that game," Geigle added. "Nobody was pointing fingers or laying blame. She was a freshman, and they were all so supportive of her. It's neat the way they do that."

On this night, Fenwick drew early blood and led 1-0 at the half. Badin, summoning all of its resources, would not go quietly into the early October night.

With less than 15 minutes remaining, Rachel Riley, racing up the left side, gathered a long ball from Malia Berkely and attacked. She took a left-footed shot from a ridiculous angle some 15 yards out. From a distance, it appeared to settle on top of the net. And then, all the Badin players started running to congratulate her. Somehow, she had stuffed the ball into the upper near corner. It was a terrific goal ... and a 1-all deadlock.

"That was obviously one of my best games of the season," Riley said. "Malia played me a really good ball. I tried to beat the defense and played it with my left foot. I hit it perfectly. It was a good feeling."

"Rachel Riley made a great play for us," Todd Berkely said. "She is so fast. A very special kid."

Riley had to concede that the head coach had made a good point with her game.

"I'm right-footed, and I play right outside mid(fielder) for my club team. But Coach Berkely pointed out that I score most of my goals with my left foot."

Riley is a good player who just kept getting better through sound coaching.

"If Coach Berkely saw potential, he would just keep drilling and drilling and drilling a player to make her better," Amy Seither said. "He was harsh on us sometimes, but he drew out our potential. He was very down to earth with us."

Riley would have started for most teams on Badin's schedule, but she was primarily an "injury replacement" in the Rams' starting lineup. It meant she started a number of games because Badin, like all teams, had its share of bumps, bruises and illness. But when the team got healthy for the tournament, it also meant Riley would be coming off the bench.

"You always want to have a starting spot," she said. "I worked hard, started a lot of games, and thought I was improving. It was a little frustrating to go to the bench, but you get over it. You add up all of the minutes I played and I played as many as most of the others.

"Coach Berkely was very reassuring," she added. "He didn't say you weren't starting because you weren't good enough."

In fact, Riley was like having a strong sixth man in basketball. She would come off the bench with instant speed and energy. In that sense, she could hardly have been more valuable.

"The Fenwick game was huge for us," Malia Berkely said. "We overcame some obstacles that night – we tied them, and we did it without Madi (Kah, who was out sick). That really helped us" from a confidence perspective.

The very next night, the gauntlet continued for the Rams, who had to go on the road and play their third game in four days, facing Cincinnati Country Day, one of the top-ranked Division III teams in the state.

"I couldn't feel my legs that night," Annika Pater said. "We were all so tired."

Badin scored in the first 15 minutes of the game, but then exhaustion replaced adrenaline. CCD was a good team ... playing on a grass field that added to the Rams' leg weariness ... and had enough to squeeze out a 2-1 win over the now 7-4-3 Rams.

"We were on empty," against CCD, nodded Todd Berkely. "That game had nothing to do with soccer. We had played so hard against St. Ursula and Fenwick. We didn't have much left that night."

"That loss got to us – it was kind of an eye-opener," Rachel Riley said, as Kah was still sick and Malia Berkely was nicked up that night. "It was a blessing in disguise. It reminded us that we needed to play through things."

Unbelievably, the campaign was drawing to a close. Blink and it's time for the tournament – a 16-game regular season schedule behind the girls in less than two months.

Badin honored its four seniors on Senior Night, and the fans were in full throat when co-captain Holly Reed was sent out for several corner kicks. She notched two assists during the 5-0 triumph over Purcell Marian, and all involved were thrilled about it.

"I was definitely happy to get out on the field," said Reed, though her parents were cringing in the stands – particularly when Reed found herself a field player for a couple of minutes at one stretch when the ball stayed in play. She made sure to steer clear of contact … but playing Reed was yet another way that Todd Berkely, who'd also sent her in for corners against Mother of Mercy, showed his players that they meant something to him as people and not just athletes.

"The girls never worked harder to get Holly into the stat book," Berkely said. "Her career had been taken from her by an unfortunate injury, and she had earned the right to be a part of the Badin soccer family, win or lose. I have never been more proud of a group of girls to work so hard for a teammate."

Rachel Riley put it very simply: "Holly didn't get to play, so we were playing for Holly."

Badin closed the campaign with an 8-4-4 record after playing what amounted to a "country club tie" in the finale with a talented Mariemont squad, 2-2. The game had been postponed by lightning earlier in the year, and – with the tournament right around the corner -- both teams played their junior varsity in the second half to avoid any 11th hour injuries.

"Going into the tournament we weren't a great team, an undefeated team," Michelle Hessling said. "We have a tough schedule in general. You know you have some games where you play well and lose and other games where you don't play all that well and you win. That's just the way soccer works.

"Coach Murrell told us that in the tournament, everybody gets a little bit of luck," she added. "What team will get it at the right time?"

2013

When the Badin High School girls soccer team climbed off the bus at Mariemont High School, they knew it would be cold. What they did not expect on this late October evening was a field that was snow-covered and iced-over as they prepared to play Madeira in the Division III district finals.

What no one realized at the time is that Mother Nature was giving them a sneak preview of what would be the worst winter in anyone's memory.

"You show up at the stadium and you can't even see the field!" Rachel Riley said. "Our warmup was basically trying to break up the ice and snow."

The Rams had powered their way through their opening two tournament games, blitzing Yellow Springs and Xenia Christian, 10-0 and 7-1, respectively, to advance.

"I was a little naïve going into the tournament," head coach Todd Berkely said. "In the Greater Miami Conference (Division I teams, the large-school division in Ohio), the tournament opener is always a tough game. It's a wildcard -- you never know what's going to happen. So even though a team has a weak record, that doesn't mean anything to me.

"I basically went in treating that first game like it was a regional final," he added. "The team treated it the same way. They didn't take anything for granted. We did everything we needed to do. The girls showed a mental toughness."

Xenia Christian had already won two tournament games when they showed up for the sectional finals. The Ambassadors took the game to Badin for the first 15 minutes ... then surrendered an "own goal" ... and collapsed.

"Xenia Christian was a highly touted team," Berkely said. "I told the girls we were going to have a fight on our hands, and we did. Xenia Christian dominated the first 15 minutes, they really forced it down our throat. But we adjusted, and they did not.

"We withstood 15 minutes of non-stop pressure, and once they put it in their own goal, that was the beginning of the end," he said. "Then we just wore 'em down in the second half."

Junior Annika Pater had shown up big in the first two games. She scored seven goals and added two assists in those outings, including five goals against Xenia Christian. That explosion earned her Player of the Week honors by the National Soccer Coaches Association of America/TopDrawerSoccer.com. (And showed, too, that even though it might be his first year on the Badin sideline, Todd Berkely had a few soccer connections to get that kind of a national award for one of his players.)

Pater – who would commit to play Division I college soccer at Eastern Kentucky University late in the summer of 2014 – was a friendly, good-natured girl well known for always playing with a smile on her face.

Sometimes, Pater would be raising her arms to the heavens, because she couldn't believe what she had just done ... but she did it with a smile. Other times, she would be smiling at an official ... in disbelief about a call that either was or was not made. But again, she was smiling. She lived with optimism, and not much got her down.

"Those first two tournament games, Annika was absolutely unstoppable," Berkely said. "The girls just fed her the ball and she made something happen. She was just head-and-shoulders above everybody else."

"I'm not all that technical, but I try to be in the right spot," Pater said of her scoring ability. "You've got to be in the right place. You've got to know where to go.

"A lot of my goals come off crosses or deflections. You're not going to dribble through five players and score. It's a lot easier, in my opinion, if you're in the right place. You need to anticipate where you need to be. And you need to take shots when you're open. A lot of players don't know when it's the right time," Pater said.

"Annika was almost our secret weapon," Michelle Hessling said. "We had a lot of versatile girls who could step up and put the ball in the goal. That's a real asset. It takes away the opportunity for the other team to man-mark your players."

And now Badin found itself in yet another tough elimination game against Madeira High, whose girls soccer program had put plenty of hardware in its own trophy case over the years. The Amazons had won a state championship in 2010, and had knocked Badin out of the post-season the last time they met in tournament play, in the 2008 regional finals. That loss kept Badin from making a fourth straight trip to the Final Four.

The two schools typically played a regular season game that was a good gauge as to where they stood. This year's contest had been a 1-all deadlock in Game 11. Badin was making its 10th consecutive trip to the district finals, but the Rams had not won gold since 2010. Getting gold through Madeira would be no easy task.

"As I looked ahead, I knew there would be a lot of good teams to deal with in the district final, so we were getting ready," Todd Berkely said. "I felt like we had a chance to do something special, but we needed to get through this game."

"We were always so well prepared," Morgan Langhammer said. "I don't think Coach Berkely ever sleeps. I think he just stays up all night watching soccer video. I've known him for a while – he's intimidating. He knows what he's doing, of course, and we get along, but yes, he's intimidating."

Langhammer, in fact, was one of the girls who *would* go to the Berkely house during the course of the season. The families were friends. But she had more than just a social reason … she and Malia Berkely would go through workouts together as Langhammer got her game back into shape following her knee surgeries. (There would be no overnight, though!)

"That first Madeira game, we had played poorly," Todd Berkely said. "Madi Kah was sick, Malia got hurt on a slide tackle, and we were still trying to put together the right combination in the back. We just didn't play well that game."

When Berkely finally got Badin's back line in order, that was when the Rams were ready to rock – rock n' roll up front, rock-steady in the rear. And it was a simple concept, probably one that came to the head coach when he was watching those soccer videos in the middle of the night … "Fire and Ice."

"We used the regular season almost like the preseason to get the right fit in the back," Berkely said. "We were piecing it together and finally we just figured out that the 'Fire and Ice' approach would work (with Shelby Lamping and Brianna Scowden).

"Shelby is the Fire – you can't shut her down. She'll run herself into oblivion she's so aggressive. Sometimes the other kids will disappear off the map because she's doing all the work.

"So now you have to put someone who is complementary back there ... Brianna Scowden. She's the Ice -- cool, calm and collected. You can't ruffle her feathers with a shotgun. She perfectly complements Shelby. She has that calming effect, and she allows Shelby to concentrate on the most direct threat around her."

That decision effectively settled Badin's back line defense with Shelby Lamping and Brianna Scowden in the middle, Kate Bach and Gabby Geigle on the wings. Maggie Adams and Taylor Smith would be the center midfielders in front of them, with Malia Berkely, Madi Kah, Morgan Langhammer and Annika Pater on the attack. For all intents and purposes, then, senior co-captain Amy Seither and sophomore Rachel Riley were like having two starters come off the bench, with other solid players stepping up as needed. It was a strong roster.

"Our defenders were a really good group," Michelle Hessling said. "Shelby and Gabby had the hardest transition. Shelby was used to playing up front and being a distributor, and Gabby wanted to play in the middle. In the grand scheme of things, though, it worked out to our benefit.

"We had a lot of fun, and got along really well," she added. "They were a phenomenal group, and worked very well together. Shelby likes to step up and dive and get dirty. Bri drops in behind, very composed, and is always very smart about it."

Lamping had played center-midfielder much of the season, and had gotten comfortable there.

"I was really nervous, having just switched positions," she conceded as the tournament started. "I always felt that I had to prove my spot. After the (regular season) games, we'd have meetings to talk about what we did well and what we needed to work on. Playing center-mid, I could go to either meeting – but Coach Berkely always sent me to the defensive meeting. When the tournament started, that made sense."

The girls bought into the adjustments. They were excellent soccer players in part because they were perfectionists ... they didn't like making mistakes, so they worked very hard not to. This just made them work even harder.

"I was so excited and relieved (to be posted as a central defender for the tournament)," said Scowden, who called her primary defensive skills "patience and composure."

"When he put Shelby back there, that surprised me," she added. "But it was a really good decision. Our communication was great. We just clicked really well together."

"I really liked the four of us back there," said Lamping, who showed up with a powerful presence every night. "We had speed on the outside and patience in the middle.

"Playing in the middle with Bri, we're like total opposites," she said. "I'm a screamer and she's quiet. We really bonded. She kept me relaxed. I wanted to protect Bri. We protected each other. No one pushed us around. We're like family."

"We had a really strong defensive unit," Bach said. "When Shelby Lamping came back there, she was the rock that we needed. Shelby was the aggressive one, always winning the ball. Bri was the calm one, keeping everything contained. Then Gabby and I could make our runs on the outside."

"On defense, all of us are really close, so that worked out well," Geigle said. "Coach Berkely said the four of us have to be the best friends ever, working together to keep the bowl defensive shape. Step as one, drop as one. We were a tight-knit group, knowing how each other played."

"The defense had to experiment a lot during the season," Malia Berkely said, her goal against Mother of Mercy out of a defensive position being one of the highlight goals of the campaign. "We didn't really get it all together until the state tournament, but it was better late than never. I love having Bri Scowden back there on defense. She's so calm. She's a great soccer player."

All of the defenders gave a nod to goaltender Michelle Hessling, who was quick to cover their occasional errors.

"Michelle would save us – she always backed us up," Lamping said.

"Michelle was a great leader in the back; she guided us the entire time," Bach said. "She was the eyes in the back of our head. She took advantage of her chance to play. She was amazing."

"Michelle wanted to prove herself, and she just killed it this year," Geigle said. "She knows how to keep the defense calm; she knows how to keep everyone's energy up. She knows the game. She's a great keeper."

Scowden echoed the word "great," adding simply, "I loved playing in front of her."

And now, it was Madeira High in the cold, snow and ice of the district championship showdown.

"We had tied them during the regular season, so we knew it was going to be a tough game," Madi Kah said. "And it was just so cold."

"That was awful and exciting at the same time," Scowden said. "We didn't expect the snow and ice. My feet were totally frozen."

Annika Pater remembered looking over at the Madeira players, and they were all wearing long sleeves and leggings to ward off the cold. Only a handful of Badin players were dressed for the weather. "We thought we'd be tougher than they were," she laughed.

It was a battle for survival, and Madeira was surviving at the break, leading 1-0. The Rams went to their bus – rather than the lockerroom – at halftime just to try to warm up.

"That game was a mixture of nerves and excitement," Malia Berkely said. "We let our nerves get to us too much. We had so much adrenaline that we used up a lot of our energy to start the game. We didn't click as a team until the second half. The cold was just another obstacle to get through."

It was clear early in the second half that Madeira was simply going to pack it in and try to win 1-0. They went into a defensive shell, and had very little offense in Badin's zone for the rest of the night. If the Amazons could keep Badin off the board for the final 40 minutes, they were going to the Sweet 16.

"We knew what Madeira was capable of," Hessling said. "We expected a fight, and that's exactly what we got.

"With about eight minutes to go, I looked at the clock and we were still trailing 1-0," she added. "I thought, 'This is going to be my last game with these girls.' That really hit me. I started to cry a little bit. I said, 'I'm not ready for this to end.'"

Badin was relentless in its offensive zone. The Rams were on the attack the entire second half, and Madeira just kept turning them away. With about six minutes left, the ball came to Pater in the box. She was, as usual, well-positioned.

"It was left-footed … I don't know how it went in," she said. "Someone said 'shoot it!' and I just put my foot out there. It wasn't the right form or anything. And then I was just being attacked by my teammates!"

"When Annika put the ball in to tie it, that was a perfect moment," Hessling said. "I thought, 'my prayers have been answered.'"

Madeira had put all of its energy into winning 1-0. When Pater scored to make it 1-1, all the momentum shifted into Badin's camp. The game was going to overtime, and in 2013, overtime was shaping up to be Badin time.

"Madeira had spent the lion's share of the game defensing our attack, and they were out of gas," Todd Berkely said.

"Going into overtime is one of the scariest things because it's golden goal," Malia Berkely said. "You've got to make every play count. You never know if this is the play that will win the game for you or lose the game for you."

All of Madeira's energy was sapped. It took Badin barely five minutes to push the winning goal across. And it was Berkely involved in the play that won the game. She put the ball into her longtime playing partner Madi Kah, and Kah delivered Badin's first district title since 2010.

"Malia played the ball perfectly to me," Kah said. "But right then I had a cramp in my leg, and I was afraid I was going to miss it! Fortunately, I didn't."

What transpired, instead, was a mob scene on the field.

"We were running back down the field at one point against Madeira and I looked at Kate Bach and said, 'Don't give up!'" Shelby Lamping recalled. "I was really hurting that night. I had been clipped on the hip. We just said we needed to do it for the seniors.

"During the game I said we needed to go forward, always forward," she added. "When we won it in overtime, I was so happy. I'd had my doubts. It was joy and relief when they saved us. You always thought that someone would save us."

"When I passed the ball to Madi, and she slotted it by the keeper, that was a pretty great moment," Berkely said. "It was a huge night. That win really boosted our self-esteem. It really sunk in that we were on our way to state."

"There were tears when we won that game," Pater said. "That was the hump that we needed to get over."

"That was a nice one to win," Kah said. "We had not won a district championship, so it was very exciting."

"You could see that the girls felt like it was a huge win," Todd Berkely said. "It was a tough win, but a great win. The one scary thing you worry about as a coach is a letdown."

The Rams were 11-4-4, and thrilled to earn the gold medals of a district championship winner. But they were not satisfied … they had to win three more games to reach the Division III state finals at Columbus Crew Stadium. They were just getting started.

"I remember talking to Holly Reed when we got to districts," Maggie Adams said. "We said we were either going to lose at districts, or win state. That was our feeling."

Badin players were carrying with them the hopes and

encouragement of their predecessors, Badin girls who knew what it was like to win a state title: members of the 2005 state champions.

Adams had talked to her cousin, Courtney Gray, a then-sophomore who had been on the field for both goals during the 2-1 overtime win over Doylestown Chippewa in the 2005 title game. They had arranged for Gray and some of her teammates to send letters to the 2013 Rams.

"What stood out to me was the letter from Emily Flum," Michelle Hessling said. "Her letter was longer than anyone else's. It took us step-by-step through the state championship game."

Flum had scored the championship goal by putting herself in a position to receive a pass from a hard-charging Abby Milillo, then knocking it home.

"She ran to the far post," Hessling said in recounting the letter, "and then before she knew what had happened, she was at the bottom of a dog pile. I thought that must be the greatest feeling in the world. But I thought I would never be in that position."

There was plenty of soccer to be played, and the Rams were in the right frame of mind to play it. Todd Berkely had set the tone at the start of the post-season when he explained to the team that from this point on, the bench would get a little shorter, playing time for some would get a little leaner.

"The whole team was on the same page," Maggie Adams said. "Girls were willing to give up playing time if that meant we would get to state."

Badin was in the Sweet 16. Their attitude, though, had "state" written all over it.

2013

Brianna Scowden headed for the corner. Badin and Middletown Fenwick were in the fourth minute of the second overtime period of the 2013 Division III state semifinals, and the talented junior defender was operating under a simple directive – win the game.

Fenwick was basically out on its feet. The score was deadlocked at 1, and Badin was getting all of the chances at this point. Scowden was setting up another corner kick, another chance for the Rams to advance to the state title game at Columbus Crew Stadium.

"I don't know how I became the chip-kick girl," said Scowden, who was handling a lot of the corners for BHS as the season went on. "I felt like I was never good at free kicks. I don't know how it happened. I don't know how I became that girl."

Head coach Todd Berkely knew *exactly* how it happened.

He had a drill where players would line up behind the goal and chip the ball over the goal to a teammate, who would head the ball into the net. One afternoon at practice, Scowden chipped one over the goal, perfectly, to a teammate, who headed it in.

Berkely stopped the ongoing line of players and sent Scowden back to chip another one. Once again, Scowden chipped the ball perfectly to a teammate ... as easily as if she had walked over and flipped it off of her forehead.

That is how she became the chip-kick girl.

"Bri just air-mailed it in perfectly, twice in a row," Todd Berkely said. "I had not seen anybody chip the ball better than her. That was definitely a weapon we could use."

Berkely had unveiled the chip kick against Hamilton High in the regular season, and Scowden, from the middle of the field, had put one right on the foot of Malia Berkely for what turned out to be the game-winner in Game 4.

"That's where all the free kicks started," Scowden nodded. "Coach Berkely liked my practice chips, so he told me to go kick one against Hamilton. Malia scored on that one."

Depending on the situation, Scowden or Berkely would head for the corner to kick start the Badin attack.

Tonight, it was the state semifinals, and Badin was still attacking. The Rams had battled their way through the regionals and reached the Final Four for the first time since 2007.

"That team had so much resiliency – they just had the ability to always figure out a way to move on," parent Joe Geigle said. "It was amazing. It was remarkable. You could see their confidence growing."

"I was on the edge of my seat during the tournament," said Nicole Berkely. "I couldn't breathe. I was almost in panic mode because of the expectations Todd set. Is he going to be able to pull this off? And if we lost, then what? I was worried about everything. I couldn't have been more proud of how it all unfolded."

It unfolded in the regional semifinals with an unexpected matchup against Cincinnati Country Day at Madeira High. (How's that for irony? Madeira loses in the district final, then is the host site for a regional game that includes the team it just lost to. That had to have the Amazon soccer community gnashing its teeth a bit.)

Cincinnati County Day was 18-1-0, ranked No. 7 in the state, had beaten Badin 2-1 during the regular season, and had just knocked off Troy Christian. Badin had expected – perhaps *wanted* – to play Troy Christian, the team that had ousted the Rams in the 2012 district finals.

"That would have been a blood bath because of last year's game," Rachel Riley said of facing Troy Christian. "So we're on the bus (going home after defeating Madeira) and somebody said, 'CCD beat Troy Christian …' Well, that was OK with all of us because we felt like we should have beaten them the first time we played them."

To every Badin player and coach, that was the view – the Rams should have beaten Cincinnati Country Day during the regular season, and would definitely take care of the Indians in the post-season.

"They were a tough opponent," Todd Berkely said. "But everybody knew we didn't have our legs under us that first game," when the Rams were playing for the fourth time in six days and the second time in 24 hours.

"We were exhausted that first game," Hessling said. "Our legs were tired; we were mentally exhausted, too. We had something to prove against CCD, and we proved ourselves again."

Malia Berkely scored in the third minute of the game, and the Rams were off to a dominating 3-1 triumph over Cincinnati Country Day.

"We said we were definitely going to beat CCD," Malia Berkely said. "We figured if we scored first, they'd get down on themselves. We thought we'd be pretty well set."

Morgan Langhammer tallied midway through the first half off of a corner kick from Scowden, and when Madi Kah scored less than two minutes into the second half, it was 3-0 Badin and all over but the celebrating.

"I just remember I couldn't feel my legs during the first game (with CCD)," Annika Pater remarked. "Compare that to the tournament game – you can see the difference. We won the game that really mattered."

"In that first game against Cincinnati Country Day, everything that could go wrong, did go wrong," assistant coach Jeff Pohlman said. "When we beat them, and beat them as handily as we did, that was it right there. At that point, we all thought we were on our way."

Cincinnati Country Day scored late on a high, looping shot from 30 yards out, one of those balls that is either going in or it isn't, and there's not much the defense can do about it in any case. Other than that, Badin's defense had a fairly routine night of it – routine enough that Bill Getz, Brianna Scowden's grandfather, was heard to remark at one point – half in exasperation, half in amusement -- "I wish she'd stop playing with her hair!"

"I know I play with it all the time," Scowden laughed. "It's just a nervous habit. ... I'm nervous all the time back there," a candid concession from a player who is lauded for her defensive composure. She plays on the back line with composure, but that doesn't make it any less stressful.

Badin was in the regional final for the first time in five years, against a new opponent – Lehman Catholic from Sidney, north of Dayton, the furthest reaches of the Archdiocese of Cincinnati. Lehman had eliminated state-ranked Summit Country Day in the Sweet 16, and Summit had been the only other team to have beaten CCD before Badin knocked them out of the tournament.

Lehman Catholic was undefeated at 17-0-1, had a senior-dominated roster, and was loaded for state. The Cavaliers presented a huge challenge for Badin.

"The tournament is a long ride – rough at times, easy at others,"

Amy Seither said. "We got down at times, but we always came back. None of us were willing to give up. In past years, when we got down, we got down on ourselves. That was not the case this year. We won it more mentally than physically."

"People think everything was hunky-dory with our team, but we had our issues," Hessling said. "We were always able to work through them. The 'truth circle' always had a positive impact. We always came out better as a team."

The Rams faced Lehman Catholic at Lebanon Junior High on what was Hessling's 18th birthday. She was worried. She didn't want that to be the last high school soccer game she ever played. She didn't want to remember her 18th birthday like that.

"I didn't know it, but the girls had gotten me a birthday cookie to share at our pre-game meal at Texas Roadhouse," Hessling said. "Well, I didn't want to focus on my 18th birthday until after the game. So they quietly ate it at another table, so that I wouldn't know about it."

Badin came out determined to make short work of Lehman. For the first 10 minutes of the game, the Rams turned Lehman's goal into a shooting gallery. They were attacking so hard it appeared they had double the number of players that Lehman could defend against.

Lehman was unfazed. After the onslaught, the game was still 0-0.

"They had asserted themselves over every team they played," Todd Berkely said. "I don't think they looked past us, but I think we absolutely shocked them. We stunned them with our quality of play.

"We were a possession team rather than a kick-and-run team," he added. "Lehman hadn't seen a team like us all year. They struggled chasing us all over the field. They were trying to figure out what we were doing. But we started to show some wear during that game."

Late in the first half, Badin finally put one home, Malia Berkely scoring off an assist from Annika Pater to take a 1-0 lead to the intermission.

But Badin's opportunities were so limited, the Rams got exactly zero shots on goal in the second half. It was all Lehman Catholic. It was clear that if Badin was going to advance in regulation, it was going to be by a 1-0 count.

"That was a scary game," Malia Berkely said.

"I don't like games like that," Madi Kah agreed. "You're ahead 1-0 and you're just trying to hang on."

Hessling admitted that she was "stressed out and feeling so much pressure."

She was also playing hurt, which the Badin soccer family had done a good job keeping under wraps. Hessling had rolled her right ankle during a Ram Run, so she was no longer practicing during the tournament. She was working out to stay in shape, but she was not working between the pipes.

"Our trainer, Travis Snyder, would always tape it up," she said. "He said we'll get through the playoffs and then we'll take a closer look at it. I don't think he thought we would be playing quite so long!"

Before the game, Todd Berkely had pulled Hessling aside and told her that she had to be ready to make a "turn-tip save." Midway through the second half, that's exactly what she did, a leaping punch save off of a shot by Lehman's Lauren Goettemoeller. She punched another ball out off the ensuing corner kick, and Badin kept the Cavaliers from getting another shot on goal for the rest of the game.

"That was my best save of the game," Hessling said of her quick reaction on Goettemoeller's shot. "I won't ever forget that Coach Berkely said that to me. Somehow he knew."

"She saved that ball from point-blank range. It was a laser, an absolute blast," Berkely said. "It was the save of the season.

"The coach in me says that we shouldn't have given the Lehman girl that much room for an open shot," he said. "The dad in me says I was glad it wasn't my daughter having to deal with a ball coming that hard. But the coach in me also said, 'Thank God we have Michelle Hessling in goal.'

"That save absolutely inspired the whole team," Berkely said. "After that shot, Lehman Catholic didn't have a chance."

"That was a hard game," Gabby Geigle said. "They had a lot of close calls. At one point, I thought they might get it tied up. But we decided, we're not stopping. We have to keep going."

"The gold trophy is the best birthday gift ever," Michelle Hessling said of the regional championship trophy.

Lehman Catholic was a stunned squad after the setback. Their first loss had been their last loss of the season, and instead it was Badin – now 13-4-4, unranked in the state – that was headed for the state semifinals against Middletown Fenwick.

"Bring everybody!" Todd Berkely told the media of Badin's impending matchup with the Falcons. "It's going to be good stuff. It always is. It summarizes what soccer is all about with the rivalry, the makeups of the teams and the overall soccer savvy. It is going to be a good one."

Fenwick, 11-5-5, was the defending D-III state champions, adding the 2012 crown to the D-II title the Falcons had captured in 2008.

Badin had not beaten Fenwick since the 2007 post-season, when Amy Seither's older sister, Michelle, had converted a sudden death penalty kick to advance the Rams.

Fenwick, in fact, had won the last "decided" outcome between the two teams, in the 2008 regular season. Since then, the regular season games in 2009, 2010, 2011, 2012 and now 2013 had all ended in ties.

"I remember Coach Berkely said in the paper to bring everybody," Hessling said. "Fenwick is a phenomenal, phenomenal team. They push us to a higher level of soccer. We're an evenly matched pair. We knew they were going to be good. To beat them would mean a lot.

"I had some serious nerves coming into the game," she added. "I had to get used to living up to the expectations I'd set as a sophomore," when Hessling, pressed into service at Fenwick in what was her first varsity start, had delivered a tremendous performance in a 0-0 deadlock.

When the Rams walked off the field at Lebanon after capturing the regional, they had no idea where they would play the state semifinal. There was talk that the game would be at Clayton Northmont, northwest of Dayton, but that seemed like a ridiculous waste of travel for two schools 15 miles apart and a good hour away from the potential site.

Bill Stewart, athletic director at Lebanon High with close ties to Butler County sports, graciously stepped in and said he would make Atrium Field at Lebanon Junior High available once more. That was a comfortable trip for both schools, and a nice site for the Final Four matchup.

"We felt a lot of pressure, but at the same time we all felt like we had something to prove," said Gabby Geigle. "We were ready. We told each other we weren't going to lose this time. We came out with a lot of energy, and we didn't drop off."

"We knew it was going to be a crazy game," Malia Berkely said. "It was so intense. We just came in, like, we have to beat them!"

"It was a good game for us," Rachel Riley said. "We knew they were good, and they knew we were good. We weren't sure how the game was going to go.

"Coach said you've made it this far, just play hard and leave it all out there," she added. "We've made it so far, he said, it would be silly to lose and have to start all over again next year. Don't let Fenwick stop us from reaching our goal."

A large crowd – including a big Badin student contingent – had shown up on a Tuesday night in early November to see it happen.

Badin fans always travel well for sports, and this evening was no exception. It was a great night for a well-played game.

"Pound-for-pound in the playoffs, Badin vs. Fenwick, that's the best soccer you're going to see in the area, right there," Todd Berkely said. "The level of play is so much higher. I didn't even need to give a pre-game speech. I just told the girls to go play our game."

The two schools went to the intermission in a scoreless tie. Badin was getting the better of the play, but Fenwick was running an offside trap on defense that constantly tripped up the Rams, frustrating them with the number of times the offside flag went up.

"We knew they were a great team and it would be a battle," Pater said. "I definitely felt some pressure myself. I'd had a wide open goal during the regular season and missed it."

"I was freaking out," Shelby Lamping admitted. "The nerves were going right through me."

In the first minute of the second half, Fenwick's Margot Harknett controlled a corner kick from teammate Taylor Engle, and hammered it into the net. Just as they had in the regular season game, the Falcons had seized a 1-0 advantage.

"Morgan Langhammer was so upset with herself," Hessling recalled. "On the film, it looks like I'm yelling at her, but I'm really telling her that it was OK, trying to get her head back up.

"But we're down 1-0 early in the second half, and I was a little worried, a little bit heartbroken," Hessling added. "But I thought, we've come back once in the tournament (against Madeira) and we can do it again."

Co-captain Holly Reed had heard the crowd roaring while she was taking a halftime bathroom break.

"I heard the cheering and I was hoping it was for us," she said. "I came out of the bathroom and a bunch of our players looked like they were about to cry. I said I didn't realize the game was over. I looked at that as my job – to make sure the team realized that the game wasn't over until the clock ran out."

"Holly Reed – she was always there to tell us we'd be fine," Lamping said. "She was really our support system. ... I knew somebody was going to come through and save us."

"The tournament was crazy," Reed said. "I'm usually a calm person, but the tournament – it was crazy!"

The clock was wasting away, and the Rams' chances for a trip to Crew Stadium were vanishing in a flurry of offside calls.

"It was a little disheartening to go down 1-0," Todd Berkely said.

"But it was not so unexpected. We had been playing from behind all year. Our mindset was constant. The girls just kept playing."

Finally, with barely six minutes remaining, Annika Pater dribbled to the end line, then flicked it back to Kate Bach. Bach angled it to Malia Berkely, wide open in the box. Would the offside flag come up?

"I thought I was offside," Berkely conceded. "I didn't see a Fenwick player back there, but I figured just in case, I'm going to slot it in there. I just sort of pushed it by the keeper. I didn't realize the goal counted until my teammates came running to hug me."

Rob Berry, the outstanding girls basketball coach at Carroll High School in Dayton, was the side judge on the play. A year earlier, he had been the center official during Badin's district championship loss to Troy Christian, and Badin fans had been in his ear all afternoon. Now, he had his hand out, palm down, to indicate "play on."

Asked about the play six weeks later during basketball season, Berry pointed out that Badin had been trapped by the Falcons all evening ... but that on this particular play, a Fenwick player had fallen down and couldn't get up in time to put Badin in an offside position. So play continued.

"We were playing well against Fenwick, but we hadn't been able to score yet," Todd Berkely said. "We hadn't taken advantage of our space. The play was designed to go that way, and the girls executed it perfectly.

"The whole game was the culmination of a lot of practice," he added, "just doing things that we'd worked on."

Now, Malia Berkely had sent the game into overtime, and just like the district finals against Madeira, all the momentum turned Badin's way. But Fenwick was not in the mood to call it quits just yet. The Falcons were the defending state champs. They were not quite ready to relinquish the crown.

Badin, though, had some extra resolve in its tank ... and some extra energy, from the tough Balconi training and the difficult Ram Runs.

"Our fitness was a huge key this season," Malia Berkely said. "A lot of teams die at the end of games. We had that extra effort to give at the end."

On this night, it showed. Fenwick wasn't giving up, but it wasn't getting anything going, either. The game might go to penalty kicks ... but only because Badin couldn't find a way to put one in the back of the net. The longer the game went, the more the Falcons were clearly exhausted. They were basically running in place.

"Our Ram Runs prepared us," Hessling said. "They were awful. They were so hard. We were dying. But when you look back on it, I'm so glad we did them. It's like Coach Berkely said, the 80 minutes of regulation were like our Ram Runs, and then the overtime was like a practice. Just keep your legs going."

Scowden had been taking the Badin corner kicks in the overtime ... and Todd Berkely had added a new wrinkle to her efforts. Instead of booting the ball into the box, at the start of the second overtime he told her to kick the ball to the far post. He thought Madi Kah would be there for the Rams.

Four minutes into the second overtime, Scowden trotted over to make what would be her second corner kick of the period.

"Brianna played a tremendous game that night," Berkely said. "She didn't hit her mark on that first kick, which was unusual for her. I told her to hit it to the far post, and that Madi would be there. She put the softest touch on the ball. She floated it right past the keeper."

Badin assistant coach Ken Murrell had suggested to Kah that, rather than stationing herself at the far post, she wait until Scowden kicked the ball, and then move into position for a header, making it tougher for Fenwick to mark her.

"I took the corner, and it was awesome," Scowden said.

She put it right on Kah's forehead.

"Bri has really good aim and is really good on set pieces," Kah said. "I don't remember it happening. I just remember getting tackled. I can't really describe it. I just know that it felt real good."

"I remember Madi's face," Scowden said after Kah's header had given Badin a 2-1 sudden death victory in the state semifinals. "We just looked at each other and started running at each other. And then I was getting squished at the bottom of the pile."

Kah was a low-key star in the Badin constellation; not flashy, no drama ... simply an excellent player. Kah had delivered Badin into the regionals with the overtime goal against Madeira, and now she had delivered Badin into the state championship game with another OT game-winner.

"Madi got up to the ball because she has tremendous hops," Todd Berkely said. "She knew it was going in the net when the ball was in the air."

"There was just joy, nothing but joy," Hessling said. "Madi was in the dog pile ... I grabbed her arms and pulled her out so that she wouldn't get hurt. I told her we needed her! She was crying. She said they were tears of joy."

"You can't tell me that people didn't say that was one of the best soccer games they'd ever seen," Todd Berkely said. "If you're on the other side of the field, you don't feel so good about the outcome. But you have to feel good about the performance. Under the lights, a huge crowd, it was fantastic."

"That was such a rivalry game, but one thing I really took away from that game is how respectful Fenwick was to us," Annika Pater said. "I'd have been so mad about losing, but they were really nice to us, texting our girls and congratulating us. Usually our rivals don't like us very much. That really showed me something."

Dozens of Badin students had leaped the fence and were in the middle of the post-game hubbub, which didn't go unnoticed by the celebrating BHS soccer girls.

There had been some angst back at school from fellow students over the course of the girls' high-profile campaign. In the meantime, the Badin football team had been putting together its best season in 15 years, reaching the Division V Elite Eight. The girls volleyball team had played its way into the Division III district finals for the first time since 2007. There was plenty of attention and success to go around, but there had been an undercurrent of discontent directed toward the girls soccer team.

"There was some negativity at school because people thought we were cocky," Pater said. "We weren't cocky – we were confident. There's a big difference."

"We were confident," Bach said. "If we don't think that we're going to win, why would we expect anyone else to?"

The girls had noticed the huge student turnout on this night … and would notice the state title turnout to come. It washed away many of the hard feelings that might have undermined a trip to the state championship game.

"When the student section rushed the field, I just loved it," Pater said. "I was hugging people that I'd never even talked to before. I really appreciated that."

"After the game, with everybody on the field, that was the coolest thing I'd ever experienced," Gabby Geigle said. "I was tired, I was cramping, but I didn't care. I just dove right in there."

Up in the press box, with dozens of people milling around the field and the Badin faithful showing little movement out of the stands, Lebanon athletic director Bill Stewart looked on. He understood. A former Fairfield High athletic director, he was well aware of the Badin athletic tradition. He had a state championship ring of his own, as an assistant football coach on the Fairfield High team that took the big school crown in 1986. As the head girls softball coach, he'd guided the Indians to the state semifinals in 1991. He well understood the excitement that high school athletic success creates. He let the lights burn.

"That overtime goal was huge," Todd Berkely said. "At that point, I wasn't even thinking about the state championship game. I was just thinking about what we'd accomplished in this game."

"It was just surreal," Hessling said. "Me, Holly (Reed) and Maggie (Adams) sat in the middle of the field, talking, taking it all in. It was everything we'd ever dreamed of.

"Thinking about state – it's always there," she said. "The fact that we did it, yes, it's kind of shocking. Never in a million years do you think those prayers are actually going to come true. Somehow, we managed to come from behind again. It doesn't hit you until later.

"I would have been happy to beat Fenwick on just a regular day," Hessling said. "This was the state semifinals!"

And now, the Rams were headed to the Division III state championship game at Columbus Crew Stadium.

The lights burned on.

2013

Michelle Hessling was sobbing. It was halftime of the Division III state championship game, and the Badin High goaltender had tucked herself inside an open locker at Columbus Crew Stadium. Gates Mills Hawken led 2-0 at the break, and Hessling was wrecked.

"It was the best day and the worst day of my life, all at once," Hessling said.

The sign in the Badin student section read, "Don't mess with the Hess …" but here at the intermission, 'the Hess' was a mess.

Hawken had scored on a penalty kick, then converted a Hessling miscue, and the Rams were reeling. But head coach Todd Berkely brought an air of adult calm into the sea of teen chaos all around him. He looked at Hessling hunkered down in the locker and said simply, "What's wrong?

"I believe in you, the girls believe in you, and we're going to win this," Berkely said.

The Rams had been planning all week to win the state title as they prepared to face Hawken in the championship on Friday, Nov. 8. They were exhausted and yet exhilarated following their 2-1 double OT triumph over Fenwick in the state semifinals Tuesday night.

Berkely knew the girls needed to get their legs back under them … but had to be mentally prepared as well.

"We were tired, we were exhausted, we'd just played a double-overtime game," Berkely said. "So on Wednesday we had a skull session. I just said, 'Let's talk soccer.' That's about the best we had after playing 99 minutes the night before.

"We were talking about the game and what it meant to us," he added. "Annika Pater said, 'Oh my God, I love these!' We just talked shop. The girls were relieved. They were on the road to recovery."

Former Badin head coach Keith Harring came over to address the girls that evening. He'd taken the Rams to three state championship games, winning in 2005, and he gave them a pep talk about what to anticipate.

"It was nice to hear Coach Harring talk to us about state," Rachel Riley said. "Obviously you want to win, but he said it was also about enjoying it. You have to enjoy it. You want to remember every detail. It was a big deal ... embrace it ... don't be on your phone all the time. He wanted us to win."

Harring was always well-versed with what the opponent was all about, too, so he'd been on the phone pulling together a scouting report on the Hawks for the Badin staff. Hawken brought a record of 16-1-5 into the game, and had been to the state semifinals in 2012.

"I appreciated that, but my coaching mindset is, I really don't worry that much about the other team," Berkely said. "I worry about us. There's no reason to concern our team with a highlight tape of the other team so that they say, 'Oh my gosh, look at them!' It's about our players, and following the game plan."

"When we went to Columbus, that's when it really opened my eyes," Terry Kah said about the internal support the girls soccer program received at Badin. "It was just the perfect storm of things coming together – (athletic director) Geoff Melzer, (principal) Brian Pendergest, all the work everybody did.

"All the phone calls that were made, all the preparations that were made, all of the things that were donated," Kah said. "That was the whole family dynamic at work."

Melzer was not only in his first year as athletic director ... but this was his very first sports season. It was trial by fire ... but a good problem to have.

"I had a couple of sleepless nights," he said. "I really needed to make sure everything was turned in that needed to be turned in. I didn't want to be the guy who screwed things up."

At 3 o'clock Thursday afternoon, the girls were sent off with a big celebration on the front porch of Badin High School. Their friends from Texas Roadhouse stopped by with food for all of the girls, including the forbidden -- but much loved -- rolls. The Badin soccer parents had arranged for a tour bus ... and not a school bus or car caravan ... to take the Rams in comfort the two hours to Columbus.

"The sendoff was amazing," Maggie Adams said. "All the support outside from the students, all the hallway decorations. Going on the bus was a real cool team experience."

Along for the trip were four girls that Berkely had brought up from the reserve team to assist during the tournament – sophomores Morgan Deitschel, Gaby Ems and Jessica Stein, and freshman Maddie Smith. They had practiced with the varsity throughout the post-season, helped as ball girls at the tournament games, and were part of the state traveling party.

They couldn't be part of the 22-player roster, but Berkely underlined that they were a part of the team, and made sure they were on the sidelines at Crew Stadium – another move that helped cement the Badin soccer family.

A police escort, sirens blaring, took the Rams out of town. "That police escort was so cool," Hessling said. "We were having so much fun. It was just a ton of nerves and excitement all the way up."

"We were so excited by the charter bus ride, the hotel, the dinner, being on the road by ourselves," Malia Berkely said. "It was exciting. It was a new experience for us."

"When we went to the Olive Garden for dinner, we sang Christmas carols on the bus," Kate Bach recalled, "because that's what was on the radio."

Brian Pendergest had arranged for a special guest to talk to the Rams after dinner – Kristina Anderson, a standout on the 2005 state champions and one of the premier players in Badin girls soccer annals. She was working on a graduate degree at Ohio State, and was happy to come share some thoughts with the girls.

"When I met Kristina that night," Shelby Lamping laughed, "she said, 'I've heard about you!'" as Lamping had been favorably compared to the talented Anderson.

"She showed us her state championship ring," Adams said. "We all said, 'We want one of those!'"

"It didn't seem real until Kristina Anderson's talk," Amy Seither said. "That really got us. Until then we were living in denial. We were trying to act like it was just another game, even though it wasn't."

It was a 12 noon game on Friday ... though the girls could have probably played at 12 midnight the night before for all that anybody could really sleep.

"I couldn't sleep – we just kept talking," Lamping said. "We were playing in the state championship tomorrow!"

"I got on Twitter and everybody was on," Riley said. "I thought, 'Is this real, am I really playing at state?' It didn't really hit me."

"We probably didn't get much sleep that night," Malia Berkely said. "But that was just another obstacle we had to overcome."

After breakfast, it was time to head to Columbus Crew Stadium.

For the OHSAA to arrange to play the state championship games there – three girls games on Friday, three boys games on Saturday – was a major deal. Crew Stadium is the home of men's professional soccer, and both the U.S. National men's and women's teams seem to play there annually. It is a top-shelf soccer facility.

"We were in the tunnel to go to the lockerroom," Todd Berkely said, "and the girls wanted to go directly to the field. In hindsight, that was probably a mistake. We should have gone to the lockerroom to calm down. But the girls went straight to the field."

"When we walked onto the field, that's when it really hit you," Riley said. "It was like, 'Wow!' OK, we've made it to this awesome place!"

"We're at Crew Stadium and I said, 'We're seriously going to play here!' That was nerve-wracking," Annika Pater said. "I said to myself, 'Today is going to be a good day.'"

Kristina Anderson had pointed out that Crew Stadium "was really big," Holly Reed said, "so the four captains decided that we would say, no matter what, that the stadium wasn't as big as we thought it would be. We were a very young team, so we wanted to try to help the girls with their nerves. We wanted them to think, 'whatever,' that it's the same people and the same game."

The Rams had left none of their pre-game superstitions back in Hamilton. They even had a crowded "dance party" in the shower in the lockerroom … and had to be careful not to fall on their heads in their cleats, because there was water everywhere.

When the Rams had finished dancing, they looked over … and there was Renee Balconi, their pre-season trainer, in the lockerroom to wish them well. They were thrilled to see her.

"That was such a nice surprise," Pater said. "We all ran over to hug her. I totally wiped out wearing my cleats on the floor. We were all laughing and having a good time."

Balconi had bracelets for all the girls that said, 'Wear your confidence.' They each put one on their cleats. The Rams were also wearing a blue ribbon on their cleats in honor of the late Erin Golden and cancer's "Kick for a Cure."

Balconi pointed out to the girls that she usually just enjoyed watching the games without a rooting interest. But today, she told them, she was rooting for Badin.

"She just told us to have fun," Riley said. "She said there are so many people who are glad you made it this far."

Pater had a brown box with a voodoo doll made of yarn.

"It's the weirdest thing," she said. "But on the back of the box, it says it's a good voodoo doll. So I'd hit everyone on the head with the doll. I'm going to pass it on when I leave."

Michelle Hessling noted that one of the songs she would listen to before the game was from High School Musical 3 ... with the lyric, "16 minutes left to leave your mark."

"I just thought ... this was my last time to leave my mark," she said.

"You're just trying to look at it as another game, but it's hard to do because you know it's probably the most important game you've ever played in in your life," Pater said. "You're nervous, but nervousness is a good thing. If you're not nervous, you don't care. You just can't be so nervous that you're freaked out."

Shelby Lamping was trying just that – not to freak out. Not very successfully.

"I always lockered next to Madi Kah, and we were freaking out, holding each other's legs," she said. "Sometimes we'd be goofing around before games, but not at state. We were already dripping sweat and the game hadn't even started. We were so ready for it."

Hessling had been at Crew Stadium with Gabby Geigle to watch the U.S. Women's National team play a week earlier, and Malia Berkely had actually played at the stadium before with her fellow 'Magnificent M's', Madi Kah and Morgan Langhammer.

None of them, of course, had played in an Ohio high school girls soccer state championship game.

"The warm-up at state is just out of this world," Malia Berkely said. "It's the most exciting thing ever. You get to take it all in while everything's still calm. Seeing the stands all fill up gets you ready. You know that all of these famous players have been in your lockerroom. It's all a rush."

On Wednesday, Badin guidance counselor Angie Bucheit had put out a sign-up sheet for a student fan bus to Friday's game. Badin had called off school to give students a chance to go to the game, but there was always the question of whether the students would take the opportunity to attend the state title tilt ... or simply enjoy a three-day weekend.

Bucheit hadn't had great success with pep buses over the past several years, but with the administration's blessing, she thought she would at least make 40 seats available.

By Thursday, the students were signing up ... and signing up ... and signing up. Now Bucheit found herself in scramble mode to make sure the private bus line could provide enough buses ... and that she could find enough faculty to ride them.

By the time Friday morning at 9:30 rolled around, five buses pulled out of the BHS driveway for the two-hour trip to Columbus. Nearly 200 students had climbed aboard. When the Rams kicked off at noon, between the fan buses and students going with families and friends, nearly two-thirds of Badin's 520 students were at Crew Stadium.

Badin Athletic Director Geoff Melzer had to laugh when asked, "Are you sure you're a Division III school?" Bucheit's fan bus effort played a huge part in getting the "12th man" in the stands for the Rams.

"When we looked over in the stands and saw the student turnout, that was just awesome," Kate Bach said.

"The crowd was so cool," Madi Kah said. "It was nice watching them all pile in."

"Our warmups were great – the girls looked really loose," Todd Berkely said, an assessment that was echoed in the Time Warner television booth by commentators Dwight Burgess and Chris Black.

"As a team, that's the way we are – we're loose in warmups," Rachel Riley said. "We have a lot of fun with each other. But once it's game time, we're ready to play."

The Rams may have been loose in warmups ... but nerves took over once the whistle blew.

"What can you expect from someone who's never been there before?" Riley mused. "We were just really nervous once the game started."

"Being there was so incredible," Hessling said. "It's real grass, not the (artificial) turf we'd been playing on. We went out there trying to act like we were playing in any other game. Soccer is soccer. And then the game started ..."

Gates Mills Hawken was a strong team ... ranked No. 3 in the state, having lost just one time (to Shaker Heights Hathaway Brown!), having beaten Division I state semifinalist Rocky River Magnificat in the regular season, and capturing a relatively easy 4-1 verdict over Oak Harbor in the other D-III state semifinal.

The Hawks had their own version of Badin's "Thunder and Lightning" ... senior Katherine Zalar and junior Bianca Medancic, who were out front and racing right from the opening kick.

It was a crisp, kind afternoon, 43 degrees, the sun coming and going, not a bad day for early November. Badin's Todd Berkely had expected the Rams to take about 10 minutes to get adjusted to the situation. He didn't realize it would take the entire first half.

"Our nerves really got to us in the beginning," Malia Berkely said. "It took us forever to calm down and play our game. Hawken was really good and we knew very little about them."

"We came out rough – I think we were still in shock that we were there," Gabby Geigle said. "We had to adjust to the field, the crowd, the situation. We were getting the jitters out and Hawken took advantage of that."

"The size of the field was mind-blowing," Morgan Langhammer said. "It was huge. We underestimated the size. We connected on maybe four passes in the first half. We like to play our outside-mids wide and open up the field, but it was just too wide."

"The field was exhausting," Annika Pater said. "Running up and down – the field was never-ending."

"Early in the game, I didn't know what was going on," Kah said. "We weren't connecting on our passes. I was playing terribly – Coach Berkely had to take me out, I was playing so bad. There was just a lot of pressure."

"We had a game plan, but we had to throw the game plan out the window because the field was so large," Todd Berkely said. "In the first half, you didn't see the same Badin team you'd seen during the season."

Five minutes in, Badin failed on back-to-back efforts to clear the ball from deep in its own zone. Hawken freshman Maggie Canitia got control just above the left corner of the 18, and popped a perfect pass into the box, over the heads of Badin defenders Taylor Smith and Shelby Lamping, arrayed on a diagonal between her and the goal.

Nobody expected to see a scoring opportunity this early in the game … but just like that, there it was.

Bianca Medancic was racing right to left, shadowed by the Rams' Brianna Scowden. Medancic tapped the ball down and made a deft move to her right, facing up against a rapidly reacting Michelle Hessling. Scowden suddenly found herself in an uncharacteristic bad spot, on Medancic's outside shoulder and a half-step behind. Hessling was right on top of the play, though, and Medancic would have little shooting angle.

Splat!

Medancic went down as if she'd just been hit by a cement truck. To Badin players and fans, the referee's whistle must have sounded like an air raid siren. Hessling, who had the ball, pounded it hard to the ground in disgust.

Hawken had been awarded a penalty kick.

"I don't think I fouled her," Scowden said. "She just cut across and I tried to stop her. I might have put an arm on her, but I don't think I fouled her."

Former Badin head coach Keith Harring had pulled together a scouting report on the Hawks, and one thing stood out: They loved to get shoulder-to-shoulder with opponents, and then "flop" as if fouled. It was a time-honored tactic in soccer, "honored" because officials frequently fell for the ruse and blew their whistle.

From the sidelines, Badin coaches were wondering if that wasn't exactly what had just happened.

"The official first told me that the foul was on Gabby Geigle, which didn't make any sense because Gabby wasn't anywhere near the play," Todd Berkely said. "When I found out the foul was on Brianna Scowden, I knew it was a bad call. Bri doesn't foul people."

On the television replay, it's hard to tell. Did Scowden get a hand on Medancic's elbow? Did Medancic's momentum cause her to lose her balance? Did she simply live the scouting report and go down on her own? Or was she, in fact, fouled?

At Crew Stadium, a fan's answer to that question might have depended on which team they were rooting for. The center official gets the last word. He called it a foul.

Up in the TV booth, lead announcer Dwight Burgess was skeptical.

"State championship games often come down to the little things," he told the viewing audience. "In my opinion, a bit of a harsh decision by the referee. It appeared to be incidental contact. Both players were moving inside the box. The man in the middle saw it differently."

Chris Black, the color analyst, tempered Burgess's comments.

"Or sometimes it's just their angle. He must have had a little bit of a different angle than what we saw," Black noted. "There's a little bit in there, where maybe it was a continuation where he thought she'd already gotten fouled a little bit possibly – not that it's possible to be fouled a little bit – but enough that he thought at the end that he had to make the call, that she was denied a scoring opportunity."

Hawken certainly had a scoring opportunity now as head coach Stan Shulman motioned Katherine Zalar, with 24 goals on the season, toward the penalty kick line. She was en route to Miami University, but first she would have a huge day at Crew Stadium.

Zalar knocked it into the lower left side, just past a lunging effort by Badin's Hessling, who guessed right but didn't quite get there in time.

With just 5:40 elapsed in the game, Hawken had a 1-0 lead.

"Zalar put her kick in a perfect spot – it was like surgery," Todd Berkely said. "She was as cool as the other side of the pillow."

"In the first five minutes, the whole world came crashing down," Hessling said. "A penalty kick – what if this is the one thing that keeps us from winning the championship? I don't think Bri fouled her. ... But I knew we could come back from one (goal) down."

"I was really surprised the referee called it so early," Malia Berkely said. "Usually they don't blow their whistle that quickly, they let the overall play develop early in the game. ... After that, we knew we just had to try 10 times harder."

"It was a gift penalty kick – discouraging," Langhammer said. "But we had been coming back in the tournament, so we knew we could do it again."

"We were the Comeback Queens!" Pater said.

Badin was not playing well. Hawken was good, the stakes were high, and the Rams were out of sync. If soccer fans from Mars had dropped in on that first half, they'd have probably wondered what Badin was doing in the D-III state championship game.

Up in the stands though, veteran Badin soccer fans were not overly discouraged.

In the 2007 state championship game, Badin had played another private school from Cleveland ... Shaker Heights Hathaway Brown. That day, it was clear very early that the Rams were simply overmatched. Today, another Cleveland-area private school ... Gates Mills Hawken, just southeast of Cleveland in Geauga County. But on this day, there was no thought that Badin had run into a powerhouse; that a one-goal deficit would soon turn into several.

Hawken was a quality opponent ... but Badin had played a number of equally good opponents over the course of the year. The Rams could lose ... but they could win, too. It's just that now, they'd have to score at least two goals to do it.

Badin was trying to counter, but not very successfully. The Rams needed to get their legs under them and at the same time outrun their nerves. They needed to keep things on an even keel until they could get to the break and make some adjustments.

Rachel Riley chased a ball into the net ... but it was the auxiliary net in back of the endline that no one was really trying to score into, Riley included. Malia Berkely and Madi Kah got off a couple of strong headers in scoring territory, and Todd Berkely called those "a wake-up call for the team. That's when the girls started to realize they could assert themselves."

Hawken, however, had already asserted itself once again on the scoreboard, to the tune of a 2-0 advantage.

"I made the biggest mistake of my life," Hessling lamented.

With just over 17 minutes remaining in the first half, defender Shelby Lamping passed a ball back to Hessling so that the Badin goalkeeper could re-start the action for the Rams.

Hessling sent it back out towards Lamping ... apparently oblivious to the fact that Hawken's Zalar had intersected the space and was coming hard at the Badin keeper. Zalar knocked the ball down on the run and it bounced the other way, past Hessling and back toward the Badin goal.

Hessling tried to beat Zalar back to the ball, but Zalar's momentum was taking her to it much faster than Hessling could react. Zalar put a simple tap on the ball, and it rolled quietly, stunningly, into the Badin net.

There was nothing quiet about the explosion in the Hawken stands. Just like that, the Hawks had a two-goal margin.

"(Zalar) jumped perfectly," Hessling said. "I probably said a couple of curse words. I had my head in my hands. Why of all games did this have to happen in the state championship? It left a little bit of a mark on me."

Hessling and head coach Todd Berkely agreed ... Hessling should have kicked the ball out toward the opposite wing, so that the Rams could change the field with a "V" type of passing exchange. Instead, the Rams were left with a woulda, coulda, shoulda regret.

"Michelle was a little too casual with the ball in that situation," Berkely said. "Zalar was in the right place at the right time. She got a gift, and she knew what to do with that gift. It was a goal from nowhere."

Badin players were admittedly in shock.

"I thought it was my fault, because I was the one who passed it back to Michelle," Lamping said. "I had a bad feeling, I have to admit it. I was getting mad. But I realized this Hawken team deserves to be here just as much as we do."

"It was kind of a sinking feeling when it was 1-0, then 2-0," Madi Kah said. "I thought, 'This can't be happening. We're supposed to win!'"

"When we were down 2-0, it was pretty depressing," Pater said.

"I was irritated," Langhammer said. "It was a long journey to give up two easy goals like that. It was not a good first half – it's still painful to watch on TV."

Hessling recalled that Badin senior co-captain Maggie Adams was in her face after the goal, telling her it was OK, trying to keep her head up.

"And then there was an injury stoppage a few minutes later," Hessling said, "and I was just shouting. I was so mad, so upset, and the adrenaline was flowing. We got in a circle. I was screaming, 'We can do this! We can come back! We've done it before!'

"And then we got back to playing soccer."

2013

Eighteen seconds.

That's how long it took. Eighteen seconds for Badin High School to go from a team well on its way to yet another state championship soccer disappointment to a team that, just that quickly, believed in itself all over again.

Head coach Todd Berkely had preached "believe" all season … but as the clock ticked down inside the 25 minute mark at Columbus Crew Stadium, the Rams were starting to wonder if their title hopes were going to end up as make-believe.

It had been a hard first half for Badin, stunned by two opportunistic goals by Gates Mills Hawken, which led 2-0 at the intermission.

"Going into the lockerroom, we were all down, we were walking super slow, there was no pep in our step," Malia Berkely said. "We had the attitude that we were down and we could lose."

Her father, the head coach, was not going to let that happen if he could do anything about it.

"It was looking pretty bleak at halftime – that second goal was a heartbreaker," assistant coach Jeff Pohlman said. "Being down 2-0 is like being down nine runs in baseball. But Todd Berkely had told the girls all year that 2-0 was the worst lead you can have in soccer.

"So that's the first thing he said when he walked into the lockerroom," Pohlman said. "He looked at the girls and said, 'What's the worst lead in soccer?' and all the girls yelled back, 'Two-to-nothing!'"

Once the team trailing 2-0 scores, it's a one-goal game and all of the momentum is in the hands of the trailing team. Berkely was counting on the Rams to make that recovery.

Badin had stemmed the tide over the final 17 minutes of the first half and started to put together some offense of its own. The Rams hadn't scored, but there were at least two teams on the field at that point.

"It was real quiet in the lockerroom, but it wasn't gloom and doom," Todd Berkely said. "I said that's over and done with and now we're going to get this done. I probably said 5 or 10 times, 'We're going to be OK.' We had come back – but we hadn't come back from 2-0 before."

"It's hard to come back from two goals down, but nobody was really freaking out," Morgan Langhammer said. "We're a competitive team. Nobody had given up. That was kind of the way our team was."

Michelle Hessling was sitting in a locker, sobbing. Berkely knew that he had to get his netminder back in the game; that the Rams could not afford to give up any more goals.

"I said, 'What's wrong?'" Berkely recalled.

"I said, 'I believe in you, and the girls believe in you, and we're going to win this,'" he said.

"I was bawling my eyes out, I was crying so hard," Hessling said. "Coach Berkely asked me, 'What's wrong?' I thought, 'I screwed it up, I ruined it for everybody.' Everything was slipping away because I didn't play a good ball. I was so upset.

"I will never forget Coach Berkely's words. He said, 'They believe in you, and I believe in you.'"

A couple months later, Matt Thompson, the first-year boys head basketball coach at Badin who as a student had started for Badin's first-ever state championship team, the undefeated 1988 Division III boys hoop titlists, asked Hessling to come talk to his team and tell them how she was able to bounce back on this particular afternoon.

"I just said I had to get over myself, to stop yelling at myself from the inside," Hessling said. "The girls weren't yelling at me, the coaches weren't yelling at me. I had to pick up my head and keep playing because otherwise it really would be over. 2-0 is a bad score -- but I couldn't let it get to three."

"Coach Berkely gave us a pep talk," Langhammer said. "We made some adjustments. The midfielders stopped setting up so wide. Once we finally settled down, I don't think there was too much worry. We'd come too far to lose. It wasn't going to happen."

"Coach Berkely said we can't give up now – we've come all of this way, and now we have to finish with a bang," Maggie Adams said. "He stressed that it was possible to come back – we just have to believe in ourselves."

"Our feelings varied at halftime," Kate Bach said. "There was a little bit of nervousness, obviously, but there was also a sense of having hope and believing in ourselves. Coach Berkely had some inspirational words for us, and then we just left it all out on the field."

"Todd Berkely did a great job at halftime," Pohlman said. "Instead of going in and berating the girls and being negative, he reminded them that there are only two teams here, we're one of them, take everything in, enjoy it and go right back at 'em."

The Rams left their troubles in the lockerroom. In the second half, they took the game to the Hawks.

Shelby Lamping, "drained and upset" at halftime, recalled coming back onto the field, and there was Kristina Anderson standing at the railing behind the Badin bench, urging her on. "She just looked at me and said, 'You can do it!' I was scared, but I thought someone would pull through for us."

"We are a comeback team," Bach said. "Everyone on the team played a huge role. Everyone had a big impact."

Malia Berkely enjoyed playing for her father. As a coach, he motivated her as well.

"He said we've been down before and in every situation like this we've come back," she said. "We came out a completely different team. That was huge."

Badin, 14-4-4, was unranked in the state, but it had shown resilience throughout the tournament. The Rams had gone 0-1-2 against Cincinnati Country Day, Fenwick and Madeira in the regular campaign, then beaten all three in the post-season. They'd survived that 1-0 tally over previously unbeaten Sidney Lehman in the regional final, and had been a strong second half team all year.

Langhammer thought the underdog mentality served Badin well.

"We weren't ranked, nobody ever expected much from us," she said. "We were the underdog every time we stepped on the field. People were like, 'Badin's nothing.'"

"There are no more learning moments," Holly Reed said. "You've just got to dig deep, take what you know, and keep going."

Hawken, though, was not going to do anything to encourage the Rams' recovery. They continued to play at a high level, generate the occasional threat, and keep Badin at bay.

"I thought Badin would win the game," former head coach Keith Harring said. "I'm surprised it was as close as it was. Badin knew how to score. They could get goals when they needed to. They were the toughest team on the field. They always played well late. And they were determined – they weren't going to give in."

"I thought this team was good enough to win it all," assistant coach Ken Murrell said. "When we got down by two goals at halftime, I thought we were going to lose. But the girls didn't quit. They just kept playing their game."

It was a rugged, tiring, all-hands-on-deck battle. Twice sophomore defender Taylor Smith had to come out with an injury, but she refused to be sidelined. Injuries sent Langhammer and Gabby Geigle to the bench for a time as well. Madi Kah was hit with a second half yellow-card as both teams mixed it up, drawing what the TV commentators referred to as "professional", i.e. by the book, soccer fouls.

Because of the large field, Berkely had to go unexpectedly deep into his bench – but all the Rams performed well, with junior Emily Henson, sophomore Katie Pohlman and freshman Sabrina Bernardo bringing a solid game to the Crew. Bernardo admitted later that she was so nervous when Berkely told her to get ready to sub in, she warmed up twice as long as she normally would have before going to the line.

"We held it together and just kept playing when most other teams would have fallen apart," Michelle Hessling said. "We just kept playing. That's what impresses me the most. I couldn't be prouder."

The scoreboard, showing Hawken on top 2-0, was the Rams' enemy – but so was the clock as it ticked down inside 25 minutes. The Hawks had played shutout soccer for more than 55 minutes, and were battling hard to make their lead stand up.

Todd Berkely thought he saw some hope, though, as Badin was getting some offense out of its halftime adjustments, and Hawken was playing aggressively on defense. He thought that aggression might give Badin some open looks.

On the field, the players were getting concerned.

"All of us were tired," Geigle said. "We were playing so hard in the second half. We said we hadn't come this far to lose. But there were 25 minutes left, and I thought, crap, we're done. But we never stopped playing."

In the stands, Terry Kah was getting ready to be a supportive parent.

"The turnout at the game, Ram Nation, it was beyond belief," he said. "I was serene and happy, just taking it all in. When we got down 2-0, and here it was midway through the second half, I was preparing myself, mentally, to say what a great accomplishment it had been just to get to state.

"The last 20 minutes were totally surreal," Kah said.

With 20:31 showing on the clock, Gabby Geigle put the ball in play on a throw-in for the Rams, deep in Badin territory. The Hawks had just booted one, a seemingly routine kick among many other routine kicks, from their own zone out of bounds in front of the BHS bench.

Rachel Riley knocked it back to Geigle, and with 20:27 showing, Geigle directed a long ball into the Hawken zone, where Annika Pater was double-teamed.

Geigle's pass had plenty of air under it, and was perfectly on target to Pater, who determinedly split both defenders to get possession of the ball to the left of the box.

At 20:18, Pater sent the ball to her right, where Morgan Langhammer had a pair of defenders close at hand. But Langhammer deftly back-tapped the ball further right, and there was Malia Berkely on the run, with a free look at the goal from 20 yards out.

"Morgan and I made the same run," Berkely said. "I went a little wider and lost my mark. We call that a dummy play. The first player lets the ball go for the second player. Morgan faked it so it would come to me."

"Might this be the moment for Badin?" wondered TV commentator Dwight Burgess. "That's a great set-up touch!"

"I was looking to see where the keeper was," Berkely said. "I knew if I hit it hard toward the left post, I could score."

Easier said than done, of course. Putting a soccer ball where you want it to go, on the run, at game speed, in the state championship game? Hard to execute, even for a nationally-ranked player like Malia Berkely.

"And a good shot," said Burgess. "And it's a goal!!!!"

In a split second, Berkely had called her shot. To the right of the goal from 20 yards out, she had sent a bullet that curved just inside the left post. The clock showed 20:13. It had been exactly 18 seconds since Geigle threw the ball in at the other end.

"One of the best shots I've ever seen," Langhammer said.

"She hit a laser and put a hook on the ball," Todd Berkely said. "It was low and hard – the Hawken keeper ended up on her head!"

"Malia always has good goals," Rachel Riley said. "That one really energized us. I think it surprised Hawken. At halftime I think they thought they had it."

"I saw the setup (from the other end)," said Hessling, "and Malia just hit this sweeping shot and it was awesome! And we still had so much time left. I thought, 'this could be incredible!'"

"The first half was awful, but we never once said 'this is it,'" Amy Seither said. "We were a completely different team in the second half. I never thought we couldn't do it. When Malia scored, it was more a relief than a change of emotion. We took a deep breath and just said 'let's keep going.'"

"When nothing was happening those first few minutes of the second half, I thought, 'oh, no, we *are* going to lose,'" Maggie Adams conceded. "But then Malia scored and Coach Berkely was on the sidelines joking that we got that first goal a lot earlier than he expected."

"When we scored that first goal, the bench went crazy," Jeff Pohlman recalled. "Everyone felt like we were back in it. I heard one girl say, 'We're not going to lose this!' From then on, it was all us."

"We knew we were back in the game," Malia Berkely said, "but we needed one more goal. We just kept telling each other ... one more goal!"

At the same time, the Badin defense had to make sure Hawken didn't punch anything else across because that would have meant the end of any comeback hopes.

Shelby Lamping was everywhere. When scouting services pull individual highlights together to send to colleges, they include numerous clips from numerous games. Today, Lamping needs only one film ... her Division III state championship performance.

She blamed herself for the damaging back pass to Hessling that led to the Hawks' second goal, but she was allowing no damage on her watch for the rest of the day. She was a whirlwind of tenacity and skill.

"The Hawken star (Zalar), she was so fast, you really had to work to keep up with her," Lamping said.

"I headed a few balls out, and the student section started chanting, 'Shel-by Lamp-ing'," she recalled. "All of our fans are chanting my name. That was so cool! Kate Bach looked at me and smiled, 'There you go.'"

"Shelby Lamping is one helluva player," Adams said. "Every game she plays, she gives it her all. She's the reason we got our momentum going on defense."

Brianna Scowden didn't go bury her head in the sand after Hawken's early penalty kick, either. She just calmly went about her defensive business in her typically efficient manner, and when the clock finally hit zeroes for the final time, had never come off the field.

Scowden and Hessling were the only players to go the distance for the Rams.

"I didn't think about that, but it's pretty cool," Scowden said of never being subbed. "I was really upset about the penalty kick. At halftime I was just thinking, 'Please let us come back!'"

As well as the defenders played – Kate Bach, Gabby Geigle, Taylor Smith, Maggie Adams and Amy Seither were also back there working hard to keep Hawken under wraps – Hawken had its opportunities. The Hawks were still ahead 2-1, and they responded – but so did Badin goaltender Michelle Hessling.

"She was a tiger out there," Jeff Pohlman said.

"That ability as a keeper to have a short memory is so important," said Joe Geigle, a two-time All-American as a collegiate goaltender. "Michelle could have been a wreck from then on out (after the second goal). Instead, she was terrific."

"Michelle made some amazing saves," Malia Berkely said. "She was the key player in that game. Without her play, we probably would not have won."

And yet, Badin was still trailing as the clock rolled down inside 10 minutes. Berkely had scored a great goal – Pater's ability to get possession of Geigle's long ball despite being doubled was truly the unsung play of that tally – but the Rams still needed to get another one.

"When it was 2-1, I just knew we were going to score a second goal," Todd Berkely said.

"Malia made that shot and that gave us the momentum," Gabby Geigle said. "We all said, 'Yeah, we can do this.'"

With 7:16 showing, Emily Henson stole a Hawken throw-in at midfield and pushed the ball ahead to Rachel Riley. Riley sent it wide to Malia Berkely, who played it ahead to Sabrina Bernardo in traffic. The fleet-footed Riley, sick with a cold, had been having a tough afternoon.

"It was tiring," she said. "I'm a runner and I'm tired just running on a normal-sized field. This field was huge. I don't think I played well. I don't have regrets, it's just one of those games where you look back and think you could have played better."

The whistle blew. Bernardo, knocked around in the middle of the field, had drawn an obstruction call with 7:00 on the clock. The Rams had a free kick, and Malia Berkely would take it with a three-player

Hawken wall arrayed 10-yards in front of her just outside the box.

She didn't quite catch it cleanly, but hit it hard, so when the ball caromed directly off the Hawken players in front of her, it came right back to her with 6:36 showing.

Berkely shuffled it wide to her left, where Gabby Geigle was lurking just outside the penalty area, with plenty of space and time. Geigle was exhausted – but not so exhausted that her ability and muscle-memory failed her. She lobbed a perfect ball into the 6-yard area, where a wide-eyed Morgan Langhammer was cutting hard from right to left.

"I realized the ball was coming in and I thought, 'Oh, I can get to that one,'" Langhammer said. "I hit it and I was hoping the goalie couldn't get to it."

Hawken keeper Hannah O'Day could not. Langhammer slide-tapped it home, between O'Day and the left post, and just like that, the state championship game was deadlocked at 2-apiece.

"It's so weird to think that I scored in the state game because I'm not a scorer," Langhammer said. "That one just happened to be good timing. It's kind of a blur."

There was pandemonium among the green-clad Badin ranks … and apparently in the press box as well. The Badin junior had put all of her knee issues behind her with a game-tying tally at 6:28 … but the game clock didn't stop until 6:03 remained.

"When Morgan scored, I couldn't even believe it," said Madi Kah, who was trailing the play in the box. "I jumped up, I was so excited. I forgot to even go over and congratulate her. I thought at that point there was no way we were going to lose."

There is a still photo of Kah with a huge grin on her face following the Langhammer goal. Her father quipped that it was the same look she had on when One Direction took the stage in concert.

"Morgan timed her run to the ball perfectly," Todd Berkely said. "I think at that point, the tide had turned in our favor."

"Gabby put the ball across the middle and it was picture-perfect," Hessling said. "I put my arms out and just said, 'Thank you!' I was basking in the moment."

Freshman Sabrina Bernardo had been so close to the play that, from a distance, it was hard to tell exactly who scored. Badin had been swarming to the ball on offense in a determined effort to get the game tied. If Langhammer hadn't, Bernardo was so well placed that she might very well have tied the game herself.

"I didn't know we could do that in 20 minutes," Geigle said of scoring two goals to tie as the clock drained away.

"When we scored those two goals, I was just so excited," Scowden said. "I didn't think it was real."

Langhammer came out of her crowd of teammates, arm raised, calling for a substitution. But there was no way Todd Berkely was going to take her out of the game at this point.

"That burst of energy just totally killed me," Langhammer said with a smile. "It was fun. But I needed water."

Langhammer looked at Riley and said, 'That started with you,' Riley recalled. "That made me feel a lot better, because I wasn't happy with the way I was playing," though she'd been on the field for both Badin goals.

It's a team game, and Badin girls appreciated their teammates at all times.

Terry Kah frequently drives to Cleveland on business, "and every time I would drive by Crew Stadium, I'd dream about one of our girls scoring in the last few minutes to win the state championship game. I didn't realize we'd have to score in the last few minutes just to force overtime."

It was 2-2, and Badin felt like its late-game magic was about to carry the day. The Rams had been playing under stress all afternoon. They had no idea what stress was yet to come.

Watching the action, Badin players prepare for the penalty kick portion of the 2013 state championship game vs. Gates Mills Hawken. From left are junior Kate Bach, senior Maggie Adams, sophomore Malia Berkely and sophomore Gabby Geigle. Goaltender Michelle Hessling, otherwise occupied, was the other kicker in the five-player rotation. Photo by Terri Adams.

Soccer captains for the 2013 Badin High state champions included, from left, seniors Holly Reed, Maggie Adams, Michelle Hessling and Amy Seither. Photo by the author.

In a show of sportsmanship, Badin goaltender Michelle Hessling (left) shakes hands with her Gates Mills Hawken counterpart, Hannah O'Day, following Badin's 2013 state championship win in a penalty kick shootout. Hawken's Bianca Medancic, on the ground, shows the agony of sports. She missed Hawken's final penalty kick. Photo by Terri Adams

Head Coach Todd Berkely enjoys the moment as Hamilton City Council honors the 2013 state champion Rams. Photo by Terri Adams.

2013

Michelle Hessling was standing in no-man's land just outside the goal. She had just made the save of the afternoon during penalty kicks in the 2013 Division III state championship game, and for a few moments observers weren't quite sure what she was doing.

And then it became clear – the Badin senior goaltender had turned around, and now she was going to take a penalty kick of her own.

"The ref was surprised, too," Hessling said of her move to the penalty kick line, 12 yards out from the goal. "I love penalty kicks. How weird does that sound?"

Badin and Gates Mills Hawken were taking penalty kicks to determine who would win the 2013 state title ... a verdict neither team could reach during two 15-minute sudden death overtime periods.

Not that there wasn't plenty of action.

Hawken's Katherine Zalar was creating her own opportunities that kept Hessling and the Badin defenders on their toes throughout. Hawken's Hannah O'Day had to grab a header off of Madi Kah late in the first OT, and could do little as an Annika Pater shot bounced off the crossbar midway through the second OT.

"She cracked that one good," Todd Berkely said of Pater's shot. "That was going to be a game-winner."

Badin had used up plenty of energy to get the game tied, 2-2 through regulation, and it had been a long afternoon as first one and then a second overtime loomed.

Shelby Lamping wasn't having any of it.

"We were over by the water and I grabbed Kate (Bach) and I said, 'You're not tired!'" Lamping said. "And I looked at Annika (Pater) and said the same thing. 'You're not tired!' Annika always reminds me of that."

"I was getting a drink and I must have looked tired," Pater said. "Shelby said, 'You're not tired! You're going to go back out there and we're going to win this game!' That positivity – I was ready to play the rest of the game. We had great chemistry as a team. If we saw someone was down, we'd pick 'em back up."

Hessling punched one ball out early in the second overtime, then had to turn and knock the ball over the goal when the carom off of her first save went right to a Hawken player who quickly turned and fired.

"When she made that double save, that was tremendous," Berkely said. "Those were just back to back tremendous saves. She's a brilliant goalie. I wouldn't take anybody else back there."

Rocky River High, from the west side of Cleveland, was soon to win the Division II state title that afternoon. Their coach walked up to Berkely following the Badin game and called Hessling's performance "the best goaltending I've ever seen."

Hessling recalled a one-on-one kick save she had to make against Zalar.

"I saw the state championship flash before my eyes all over again," she said. "Thinking about it makes me sick to my stomach. If I had guessed wrong by a couple of inches, the game would have been over."

"The overtime was stressful," said Brianna Scowden, who played all 110 minutes of the title tilt. "Michelle definitely came through for us a couple of times."

"We had a few scares in the overtime," Rachel Riley said. "Michelle made some great saves that she'll always remember. If not for her, we lose."

Twice Madi Kah had run past the Badin bench during the overtime and said to head coach Todd Berkely, "I'm not taking a penalty kick!" Berkely – thinking about the fact that Kah goals had won both the district championship and the state semifinals – laughed and said, "OK -- just go win the game!"

It wasn't to be. Neither team could knock one into the nets. Badin, rocked back on its heels by two Hawken goals in the first half, settled in and held the Hawks scoreless for the final 87 minutes – more than the typical length of an 80-minute high school game.

Up in the television booth, commentators Dwight Burgess and Chris Black had an ongoing discussion about the various incarnations of Ohio high school tournament overtimes as the clock ticked away.

At one point, Ohio would play two 10-minute overtimes … but

the initial OT would not be "golden goal," so even though one team scored, the rest of that overtime period would be played out so that the opponent could potentially tie or even win the game!

At another point, there were five-minute overtime periods, with players being pulled off the field at the end of each OT, so that ultimately teams would play at 7-on-7. The thought was that it would be easier to score with fewer players on the field ... but the reality was that the field was too big for seven players, exhausted after a full game, to maneuver.

Burgess recalled just such a game during his senior year in high school, when Centerville played a 25-overtime period game that went so long they had to stop at midnight and come back two days later. That, Burgess noted, was just after the Elks had played a 12-overtime tournament game.

It's a small world, because former Badin head coach Keith Harring knew exactly the game that Burgess was talking about – a 1977 contest against Dayton Carroll in the state quarterfinals when Harring was an assistant boys soccer coach at Centerville!

"We dominated the game," Harring recalled, noting that Burgess was one of the Elks' field players that year. "We outshot Carroll something like 118-25. We played until midnight – my wife was wondering what had happened to me.

"We came back two nights later and won the game," Harring said. "But we were exhausted, and lost in the state semifinals to Roger Bacon."

The final score in the longest game in Ohio high school soccer history? After 204 minutes, Centerville defeated Carroll, 2-1.

The point of the TV conversation was simple – how do you end a soccer game? Two great teams playing, goals hard to come by ... you have to end it somehow.

And yet ... Annika Pater nearly ended it for Badin. In the very last second.

The stadium announcer was counting down from 10 seconds in the second overtime when Pater got the ball about 18 yards out from the left post.

"I heard the crowd counting it down," Pater recalled. "We always ended up winning in overtime. I will never forget that moment. I have relived it so much. How can you not put that in?"

Usually the final seconds involve little action, just a long kick out of harm's way or a harmless dribble. But in this case, Pater had the ball in scoring territory, in a tie game, with a good look at the net.

"Nerves definitely got me there," she conceded. "I was way too excited. I thought, 'This is it! This is it! I can win the game!' And then … *pfffft.*"

Instead of drilling the shot, Pater didn't hit it with any authority. O'Day easily scooped it up just outside the goalline at the horn, and the game would go to penalty kicks.

Pater still takes good-natured ribbing about the shot.

"We were so excited – Annika had this wide-open shot!" Malia Berkely said with a laugh. "And then she hit it like a 4-year-old!"

Pater's effort has been described variously as like a 5th grader, a 12-year-old, a 4-year-old … in other words, she hit it "weakly."

Badin, though, had survived. The Rams had rallied from a 2-0 halftime deficit, were outplaying Hawken as this point, and felt good about their penalty kick chances.

Todd Berkely had been thinking about penalty kicks … not obsessively, but enough so that the players were at least prepared for the moment. In fact, in one of the last practices of the year, the Rams had taken penalty kicks at their Queen of Peace field.

"We had some options. I had written down about seven or eight names," Berkely said. "There's no strategy about it, except just put the ball in the net."

"I hate penalty kicks in the worst way," Jeff Pohlman said. "I say just let 'em play until somebody gives up.

"You just ask the question, who wants to do it, and see whose hands go up," he added. "That's who you want out there. Just because somebody's a scorer, if they don't want to do it, you shouldn't send them out."

"Coach Berkely was smiling, laughing, joking with us, trying to keep us calm," Rachel Riley said. "OK, he said, who wants to take one? He didn't have a set lineup."

While the Rams were understandably nervous about the penalty kicks, they had a good feeling based on the practice session. It had taken place in near darkness, and assistant coach Ken Murrell had actually had to drive his car onto the field and turn on his headlights to add some light to the situation.

"We practiced our penalty kicks in the dark, with the headlights on – that was fun in and of itself," Pater said.

"We were practicing penalty kicks that night, and Michelle had said she wouldn't leave until she stopped one of Coach Berkely's," Gabby Geigle said. "We were all gone by then, but I'm pretty sure she stopped one."

It was an eclectic group lined up to take the kicks for Badin – Malia Berkely, yes, but not the big offensive legs of Kah or Pater or Langhammer or Riley among the first seven shooters for the Rams. They didn't want to shoot, and Berkely wasn't going to force them.

Teams line up five players for the first round, and then need to have five more available for sudden death. Only after 10 players have taken shots can someone be used for a second penalty try.

"Just the fact that we had come back from 2-0 down – that was commendable," Morgan Langhammer said. "But now it was going to be disappointing if we lost on penalty kicks. It was kind of stressful just sitting there watching."

Senior co-captain Maggie Adams would lead off for the Rams, followed by sophomore Malia Berkely, sophomore Gabby Geigle, senior co-captain Michelle Hessling and junior Kate Bach. Junior Brianna Scowden and senior co-captain Amy Seither would be the first two up if it went to sudden death.

"I go back and forth over how penalty kicks are to end a game," said Bach, who had volunteered to go last in the order for Badin. "I wasn't nervous. I love taking penalty kicks. Many people don't like them. I love the adrenaline rush."

The Badin players felt like they had a secret weapon in Michelle Hessling. They were confident of her skills in the net – that she could potentially make a defensive stop. And they loved the fact that she wanted to take a kick herself.

"You have to have confidence to try a penalty kick – I hate them," Kah admitted. "But I thought we were going to win. Michelle was really good at saving them, and really good at taking them. The girls we had kicking were good at making them."

"It was great that Michelle was kicking," Adams said. "She's a goalie, so she knows what to do."

Badin had lost two Division II state championship games on penalty kicks – in 1995, in overtime PKs; and in 2006, when the Rams were the defending state champions. In the stands, Badin soccer fans were hoping the third time would be the charm.

"You're watching and you're thinking, as long as we make ours, we're fine," Bach said. "Of course, you're hoping they'll miss theirs. I had a feeling that Michelle was going to do something that was going to be a game-changer."

Through three rounds of kicks, the PK session was deadlocked at 3-3. Hawken was first up in each round. Senior Katherine Zalar had opened with her third goal of the afternoon, followed by junior

Marley Magruder and senior Mackenzie Lesnick. Magruder was not in the starting lineup for the Hawks, but had easily handled her PK assignment. Badin had countered in stellar fashion with Adams, Berkely and Geigle matching Hawken's effort.

Though Hessling insisted otherwise, it appeared that she had nearly gotten her hand on Lesnick's ball. Badin fans were hoping for even better as Hawken sophomore Dana Fann approached the line in the fourth round.

"It was kind of hard for me, because I was the goalie, but I'd have loved to have been down there with the team, holding hands, being a part of it," Hessling said.

She was channeling her grandfather, Richard Black, who had passed away in September.

"He always said, 'fake left, dive right,'" Hessling recalled. "That was always what was on the tape on my wrist. (Before the first kick), I jumped up and touched the crossbar, made the sign of the cross, and was ready."

Fann took a surprisingly short run-up to the ball, one that drew comment from the TV booth. Before they could say too much, it was over. Fann had kicked the ball directly at Hessling ... whose quick reaction simply knocked the ball up and over the crossbar, no good.

Fann, understandably devastated, went to the ground.

"Malia had said, 'Just one ... just save one kick ... and we'd take care of the rest,'" Hessling said. "I like to try to intimidate a little bit. Sometimes it's hard to keep your balance. So I had almost already started to lunge when she kicked it right at me.

"I knocked it up ... then looked around to see if it was over or had gone in," she continued. "I just started pumping my fists. Seeing everybody screaming really pumped me up."

Hessling, as she had done all year, had made another tremendous save at crunch time. The PK score was still 3-3, but now it was "advantage, Badin" as the Rams kicked in the fourth round. Badin was in a position to win the game with two goals, no matter what Hawken did.

"I sort of zoned out on Hawken's fourth kick," Malia Berkely said, "and then it was like, holy crap, she just saved that! I was standing between Kate (Bach) and Maggie (Adams) and I just squeezed them really hard. You know saving that kick had to give Michelle so much confidence."

Hessling was standing her ground ... and for a few moments, no one quite understood what was happening. Then it became clear –

she was next up. She was going to take the Rams' fourth penalty kick.

"I think the ref thought I was still celebrating, but I was calling for the ball," Hessling said.

"She was so much fun to watch," Joe Geigle said. "For her to take a penalty kick – wow."

Geigle had been the goaltender at Tiffin University in Ohio when the Dragons were in a position to get to nationals his junior year. Like Hessling, he turned around to take a kick in the PK round for his school that day.

"We had a dismal penalty round," he said, cringing at the memory. "I hit one so far wide right it was pitiful. For Michelle to take one in that situation, it really says something about her. And it says something about a coach who is willing to listen to his players (about who wants to take the kicks)."

"When everybody is so tense and nervous, expect the fastball and give 'em the curve – Michelle Hessling," Todd Berkely smiled.

"Penalty kicks were so nerve-wracking," Shelby Lamping said. "But I knew we would get a few stops and make ours. Madi (Kah) and I were just squeezing each other's hands. Michelle lived for PKs. She knows exactly what's going through a goalie's mind."

"I couldn't watch the kicks, I was so nervous," Brianna Scowden said. "But of course, I peeked."

Hessling pounded it into the lower right corner.

"The adrenaline rush (of having stopped the previous kick) probably helped me put my kick in," Hessling said.

"When she made hers, that was pretty awesome," Gabby Geigle said. "I was so happy for her. I felt like she really felt better now. I know she had felt guilty earlier in the game."

A handful of Badin players raced to embrace Hessling ... but they had jumped the gun. They were excited – but the game wasn't over yet. Badin led 4-3 through four rounds of PKs, but Hawken still had another kicker – junior Bianca Medancic.

"Once one player misses for your team, it puts a lot of pressure on the other players," Malia Berkely said. "You could tell their final shooter was a nervous wreck."

Medancic had gotten all of the excitement underway seemingly forever ago, just after noon, when she drew a penalty in the box barely five minutes into the game. Now, if she made her penalty kick, it would be up to Badin's Kate Bach to win it for the Rams.

"The last kicker – I knew if she missed it, we won," Hessling said. "And if she made it, I knew Kate would make hers and we would win.

Like Malia said, just one kick. I had done what I needed to do. That was the last save of my high school career."

"I would have made mine," Kate Bach laughed.

It wasn't necessary. Medancic's kick sailed high and wide right, never close, and the game was over.

Now the Badin players could race to embrace Hessling. *Now* the Rams had won the 2013 Division III Ohio girls soccer state championship.

"That moment of realization," Hessling marveled. "I saw Malia running at me. And Holly (Reed) was right behind her. And I just jumped into them. I was like, 'We did this!'

"I referenced back to Emily Flum's letter. There was some sense of fate because I'd messed up so bad earlier. I got to experience that feeling … the dog pile feeling … and so far, it was the greatest feeling of my life."

2013

Jerry Snodgrass, assistant commissioner of the Ohio High School Athletic Association, had a microphone in one hand ... and the Division III girls soccer state championship trophy in the other.

"One of the (Badin) girls I heard say right after the game was over ... 'Can you believe it? We won state!'

"Believe it Lady Rams!" Snodgrass said.

He was doing a great job putting a nice spin on one of the toughest jobs in prep sports – making a devastated second-place team feel good about things, and making a giddy champion actually pay attention to what he was saying.

"Every girl playing soccer in youth sports," Snodgrass told the crowd at Crew Stadium, "dreams of playing on this last championship day."

On television, commentator Dwight Burgess pointed out that there was "one champion ... but two champion-caliber teams."

Badin had just won the 2013 small school state title over Gates Mills Hawken with a gutty 4-3 decision on penalty kicks. That was the head-to-head duel following a thrilling 2-2 deadlock after 80 minutes of regulation and 30 minutes of sudden death overtime. Interestingly, all four regulation goals were scored at the north end of the field, and all of the penalty kicks were taken at the south end.

"State champions – literally hearing that, I can't process it," Annika Pater said. "I still get butterflies in my stomach that it actually happened. It's like a dream."

"I kept telling myself it was just a normal game," Kate Bach said. "I never realized how it would feel. It's amazing!"

"Winning state is pretty much the coolest thing ever," Madi Kah said. "I still can't really believe it. I still get chills every time I talk about the game."

"Being able to witness the sheer joy of the girls," Terry Kah said. "That's something I will take with me forever."

"The celebration was an awesome sight," assistant coach Jeff Pohlman said. "I was looking into the stands and it was something I'll never forget. I must have looked up there for a couple of minutes, just taking it all in, the excitement of it."

After she climbed out of the dog pile of celebrating teammates, Badin goalkeeper Michelle Hessling walked over to her Hawken counterpart, Hannah O'Day, and shook her hand. They shared the warrior's understanding of what it was like to play in the nets. Between them, Hawken junior Bianca Medancic was still on the ground in the agony of defeat.

It is the proverbial picture worth 1,000 words.

"In hindsight, me messing up made it a better story," Hessling said. "Overall, there is a group of girls I can honestly say are my best friends. We have a bond that no one else does. We have a state championship together. It's incredible to be able to say that."

Coming into the campaign, Hessling had expected this to be her final soccer season. She was headed to Miami University to major in education. But after this year to remember, her enthusiasm for soccer had been totally rejuvenated. The College of Mount St. Joseph in Cincinnati wanted her to come play keeper for them. She was happy to say yes.

"Michelle Hessling – she really collected herself after the first half," Badin Athletic Director Geoff Melzer said. "How many huge plays did she make? Then she offered her hand to the opposing goalie. What sportsmanship.

"The whole game was a reflection of what Todd Berkely brought to the program," Melzer added, of being calm, determined and playing with class.

"The girls never quit," Melzer said. "They did not let adversity get to 'em. They didn't get fazed by anything. … Winning a championship, it all goes back to Todd and the girls. He had a plan, and the girls bought into it."

"The state finals were just amazing," said Todd Berkely's wife, Nicole. "It couldn't have been written any better if it was a movie. The look on Todd's face was complete composure. That kind of surprised me. He didn't seem worried, and I was definitely worried. It's a complete Cinderella story."

"Todd's attitude is just so impressive," Terry Kah said. "Watch any game at any time and even in the most tense situation – any picture of him, he's always smiling."

"I remember looking at the crowd and just thinking, 'wow!'" Todd Berkely said. "Not only was it special, but the whole Badin 'family' thing hit me at that point.

"They handed us the trophy and I looked at the seniors," Berkely added. "I saw the look on their faces. I saw it on the others more than I felt it myself."

If you look at the lower rear base of the state championship trophy in the lobby of Badin High School, just outside Mulcahey Gym, you will find a bunch of marks on it. They're teeth marks. The soccer girls each took turns literally biting the trophy, just to prove to themselves that it was real.

"I honestly feel that Coach Berkely made all the difference," Rachel Riley said. "He stuck with us through some bad losses. He's always pushing us to get better. He made it more realistic as the season went on. We weren't just out there playing soccer – we were playing with a purpose."

"There's not a good enough word to describe the pride," Nicole Berkely said. "Just being 'proud' isn't enough to describe it. For Todd to step in the very first year and take the team to the state championship game and win it – I was crying after the game.

"Todd had a big part in that – to get the girls to accomplish that," she added. "He got them all to participate, and then the whole team got them to where they were. ... When I talk about the game, I still get so emotional I have to stop and compose myself."

"It's awesome – I was never so proud," Joe Geigle said. "It was a remarkable achievement. The team seemed like such a tight-knit group all the way through.

"But," he added with a laugh, "they sure knew how to make it interesting!"

"That was one of the best soccer games I've ever seen," Todd Berkely said afterwards. "To be a part of it was something very special."

Gabby Geigle was thrilled to be a state champion, but she also took a wide-angle view of the outcome.

"Penalty kicks – that stinks for the other team, it really does," she said. "You play this great game and then you're in a shootout. It's great to win it, but it stinks for them."

On television, the commentators pointed out that Hawken had played 110 minutes of soccer – and never trailed. In New York state, color analyst Chris Black noted, in that instance both teams share the championship. No penalty kicks in the prep ranks there.

"We played well enough to win," Hawken coach Stan Shulman told the media after the Hawks finished the year 16-2-5. "But give the credit to the other team. They came back and won it. It's two teams fighting for the state championship. That's how championship games are supposed to be. That's why it was a great game to watch."

Shulman, calm after the setback, had been visibly agitated with his squad during the game. While the Hawks only graduated two seniors, both of whom would play D-I college soccer, Shulman would not be back to guide the veteran squad in 2014. He was removed in April 2014, "philosophical differences" sparking what was obviously not a pleasant episode.

According to the NewsHerald of Willoughby, in suburban Cleveland, "Shulman is well known in area soccer circles, and by his own admission, as demonstrative." The paper quoted him as saying, "You have to push kids if you want a good system to prepare kids for college. We were able to build the program."

Hawken – with a high school price tag of more than $25,000 per student -- did not have a junior varsity or freshman girls soccer team, and athletic director Jim Doyle said, "I'd prefer not to discuss the details of what are differences are, but it's fair to say certain things with how Stan ran his program we didn't agree with."

"The philosophy that I teach the soccer team doesn't fit the philosophy of Hawken," Shulman said. "What Hawken wants was a more casual player type of participation in the program. It's almost like we succeeded too much …"

Shulman had been the head coach for eight seasons, and just two years earlier Hawken had named its tennis facility after his family.

"Certain things are deal-breakers," Doyle said of the disagreement in philosophy. "We have to stand up for those things. It was time to look to what's next."

While Shulman was out at Hawken, Middletown Fenwick head coach Tom McEwan also stepped away, taking the reins at Lakota East High in Butler County. He and co-head coach Kate Lohmeyer had directed the Falcons to the state championship in 2008 and again in 2012 – "a state power that pretty much has their own wing down here at Crew Stadium," Black had said of Fenwick during the telecast -- and they were ready for a new challenge at a Division I school.

It meant that both schools that Badin defeated in the 2013 Final Four would have new head coaches for 2014.

"Winning the state championship is the hardest thing you can ever imagine – you can't really imagine it," Todd Berkely said. "You're so focused on the next game that you have no time to enjoy the previous win.

"You don't have time – because if you do, you're shortchanging the girls on the possibilities of what might be," he said after the Rams wrapped up a 15-4-4 state title campaign.

Courtney Gray knew exactly what the possibilities were. She'd played for the state champs in 2005, had earned runner-up medals in 2006 and 2007, and now was enjoying the fact that her cousin, senior co-captain Maggie Adams, was wearing her No. 12 and chasing a title of her own.

"I knew their strength, I knew their depth, I knew their hearts, I knew their bond," Gray said, because she'd lived it herself. "I believed they could make it to the end. I believed they could be the state champions."

It was Gray who helped arrange for members of the 2005 state championship team to send letters of encouragement to the 2013 Rams.

"I felt so honored that someone like Maggie had No. 12 on her back," Gray said. "It was a proud, memorable moment sending off those letters from my teammates to hers."

Gray was as close to a part of it as she could be. The night before the 2013 title game, she and her prep soccer teammate Jessica Hammond were on the Internet searching for anything and everything they could find about Gates Mills Hawken.

"We ended the night watching the video of our 2005 state championship game," she said. "We may have been just as nervous and lost just as much sleep as Maggie and her teammates did that night."

The next day, teammate Ashley Crossley joined them for the trip north to Crew Stadium.

"We were in a state of disbelief, excitement and nervousness all at the same time," Gray said. "It felt so strange to be making the trip not just for us, but for another team of Badin girls soccer. We were extremely excited for the girls because we remembered our experience and all of the fun we had.

"Of course, we were nervous for them, just as we were nervous when we were in their shoes a few years back. But I never felt so secure and confident looking over this team of talented women as I did with two of my teammates and best friends at my side.

"During the game, we screamed, we laughed, we strategized, we questioned and we cried," Gray said. "Tears of joy – for the well-deserved state championship title. It was such a sweet moment knowing these girls had accomplished what I believed they could. Unforgettable – simply unforgettable."

"There's so much you have to go through to get there – that's what makes it so exciting and yet so hard," Malia Berkely said. "It doesn't really hit you, but you know that it's happened. You know you're going to have this forever.

"The fact that you get to share it with these girls makes it that much better," she added. "You do it for the seniors. We loved our seniors. Going into Michelle's arms, embracing my best friend. It's something we'll share together forever. I love that about it."

"We worked hard, and our hard work paid off," Hessling said, thinking back on assistant coach Ken Murrell's thoughts about "luck" playing a role in the tournament. "We did get a little bit of luck at the right time. Certain goals, certain plays are lucky.

"But I don't think either of our goals in the state finals were lucky," she added. "Hawken is a great team, and I don't want to take anything away from them. But neither of their goals were very well earned. Our goals – we earned them fair and square."

According to Annika Pater, the Badin girls all understood it was a shared success.

"That was a big thing that helped us keep our heads about us," she said. "A lot of people were getting interviewed (by the media), but their accomplishments were our accomplishments. No one got a big head. No one tried to take all the glory for themselves."

The girls got their gold medals at Crew Stadium, posed for pictures, then mostly slept on the bus ride home, while a movie about the 1980 U.S. men's Olympic hockey title, "Miracle", played in the background. A big celebration awaited them at Alley's on the River, a pleasant local watering hole at Columbia Bowling Lanes in Hamilton that was owned by a Badin family.

Once the police escort picked them up as they rolled down Route 129, sirens blaring once again, horns honking all around them, now the girls were wide awake, shouting and cheering.

"State champions – I'm not sure it hit me until we got back to school," Brianna Scowden said. "But it's such a great feeling. I'm very proud of that."

"It was so cold after the game, but I didn't care," Gabby Geigle said. "We were all in line to get our medals. I don't even remember it. I was too stoked, I guess. I didn't know how to react. I just know the crowd was awesome."

"The medal ceremony – it didn't seem real," Amy Seither said. "But then we finally got our state championship rings – that was amazing. I wear it every day. It's a reminder.

"It doesn't end – being a state champion, we know it's never going to end," she said. "We can say it for the rest of our lives. The ring is a conversation starter. Yeah, I really did that – and it's a shame it's over."

The next night, Saturday evening, Badin played its first-ever home playoff football game, defeating Mariemont, 37-13, at Virgil Schwarm Stadium. At halftime, the girls were recognized for their state soccer title – and given a thunderous ovation.

They walked out to the field, together, holding hands. They turned, and bowed ... together. It had truly been a team triumph. (Todd Berkely and his daughter, Malia, could be forgiven for their absence. They were on a previously arranged recruiting visit – to UCLA!)

On their lockers, the girls had signs with team goals – the last goal, of course, was winning the state championship.

"I walked into school and got to put a check mark on the sign," Pater said. "We had accomplished what we wanted to get done. That last check mark – that was special."

"It doesn't seem real – it's crazy," Adams said. "You think about the state game, about the road to the state game, and then you look at your ring and you think, wow, what's this?"

"There's a million stories that we talk about all the time," Holly Reed said. "It doesn't feel real – it feels different. And then you look at your ring, and you realize it really happened."

While the girls were honored repeatedly – by the school, by Hamilton City Council, by local members of the Ohio State Legislature, when the championship rings arrived during the school's annual Spirit Week in early 2014, the girls declined the opportunity to be recognized at halftime of a basketball game. They accepted their rings as a team, privately, in St. Basil's Chapel at Badin High.

"They just wanted to do it quietly among themselves," said Geoff Melzer, who was impressed by the girls' attitude. "They had had a great season, a championship season, but they were ready to move on, to try to get ready for the next season."

He thought that was indicative of why the Badin girls soccer program was so good – celebrate success, but don't rest on it. Prepare to achieve some more.

"It's exciting – we'll carry 2013 with us for the rest of our lives," Rachel Riley said. "But it's behind us now. It doesn't matter for the 2014 season."

But, as parent Shawn Pater pointed out, the state championship soccer girls will be known "forever."

"When I'm in public with my (state championship) soccer shirt on, people ask me about it," Shelby Lamping said. "I was in Florida with my family, and somebody congratulated me. It's crazy – people know who you are. Winning the title was just so cool."

"Everywhere I go, people will see my Badin soccer shirt or something, and they will talk to me, congratulate me," echoed Gabby Geigle. "That's the greatest feeling ever – getting recognition from people. They tell you what a great job you did, and you don't even know them.

"Having a state title is a dream for every team – the fact that we have it is pretty cool," she added. "When we got our rings, it was like, yeah! That's when it sunk in."

"Winning the title makes everything we did worth it," Michelle Hessling said. "The level of commitment – to our team, to ourselves, to each other. We gave up a lot to be where we were. We started conditioning at the beginning of June.

"You'd say to someone, 'Do you want to hang out?' and then you'd realize, 'Oh, wait, I have soccer.' It was all worth it."

"I really wasn't sure if it was the right move – a dad coaching his daughter," Todd Berkely conceded in looking back on the year. "When I finally got a copy of the championship game and sat down and watched it, my wife asked me if it was worth it, all the late nights, the scrambling, all of it.

"I just said, hell yes, it was worth it."

Afterword

It's hard to win a state championship – any state championship. Very hard. Badin High School is well regarded to have an outstanding athletic program, and the girls' soccer state title of 2013 represented the seventh team state crown in the school's 48-year history.

I am mindful of the remark that Kim McKnight – whose daughter, Megan, was a standout athlete at Badin – pointed to following Badin's 1998 girls' basketball state title: "You'll meet thousands of people who played high school sports," he recalled a friend telling Megan, "but you'll go through life and you won't be able to count on both hands the number of people you meet who played high school sports and won a state championship. It's an elite group. Not many won all the marbles."

In fact, Badin athletes know full well just how tough it is to win "all the marbles." While the Rams have those seven team championships in various sports to their credit, they have also played and lost in the state finals 15 times – 15 times! -- and had to settle for the runner-up trophy.

It's a reminder that just because you advance to that final game is no guarantee that you will take home the gold. But it should also serve as a reminder that reaching the state championship game is a tremendous accomplishment in and of itself. As time goes on, the athletes, the families and the followers of those second place teams should appreciate that success.

Why did the Badin girls' soccer team win the championship in 2013?

They had a lot of talent, certainly; they played together, and they were very well coached. Todd Berkely, without a doubt, was just what the doctor ordered for the Rams. He brought a positive vibe to the program, and his mantra of "believe" meshed well with the girls' high expectations.

One thing, too, about Badin High School athletes is that they care about being successful. Winning means something to them. Perhaps that is the whole concept of "having heart." Badin athletes generally do not play "half-heartedly." Certainly this team never went out and went through the motions. They were a determined bunch.

Berkely also instilled in them the ability not to panic. He was calm, so the team played calmly. When the Rams were behind – and they trailed in the district finals, the state semifinals and the state finals – they were patient and resilient. They just kept battling – battling in a sport where scoring is always at a premium.

That scoring deficit is no doubt why America – World Cup aside -- is not particularly hooked on soccer as a spectator sport. In baseball, someone might jack one out of the park on any given pitch. In football, somebody might score a touchdown on any given snap. In basketball, points come at a fast and furious pace. In soccer, just getting a scoring opportunity takes time. And then, putting the ball in the back of the net is a herculean task. It's no wonder soccer announcers go bonkers every time someone manages to do it.

The Badin girls of 2013, though, could put the ball in the back of the net. They didn't score in bunches, but you always felt that someone, somehow, some way, could find a way to, as Berkely always put it, "slot one" into the goal. That's one reason why the concern, though high, was not absolutely dire when the Rams trailed 2-0 at the half of the state title tilt. Badin had numerous scoring threats, and as long as Gates Mills Hawken didn't score again, it was still a game. Badin's defense made sure that Hawken did not, in fact, score again.

I asked the senior captains why Badin had won the title. Their answers are a tribute to the Badin family.

"This season was different from the start," said Maggie Adams. "It seemed like in other years there was drama that ruined the team, but that didn't happen for this team. We all got along. We were not only a team, but more of a family, a group of sisters.

"We trusted each other, on and off the field," she added. "We had a lot of stars who knew they were good, but they didn't look down on teammates who weren't as good as they were. We all loved being together and we had so much fun doing what we did and that's why we played so well together.

"That's what I will miss most – the team. I spent every day with those girls in the fall and I wouldn't change that for the world," Adams said. "I was truly blessed to have these girls in my life. I would do anything for any one of them … that's why we succeeded … not as a team, but as a family."

"We were successful because we didn't have any drama," echoed senior Michelle Hessling. "The upper classmen did a good job of separating personal issues from our play on the field.

"I also think we had heart," she added. "We just honestly never gave up. We persevered and came back multiple times. We had a ton of skill but heart is something you can't teach. That's just instilled in a person – and we had a group of girls that had heart and wanted to win."

"We wanted it, and we believed we could do it," said Amy Seither. "We were proud of ourselves and confident in what we could achieve and we didn't let anyone tear us down. We had so much momentum going right from the very beginning that we were unstoppable, no matter what."

"There was little or no drama between any of the girls," said Holly Reed. "The previous three seasons were filled with drama that took our attention away from getting better in soccer. This year was very different in that respect. It was understood that whether you were a freshman or a senior, you are still a human being that deserves respect. You don't have to like everyone on the team, you just have to play with them.

"We had many talks on the hill by Queen of Peace to get rid of the drama. No coaches were involved and it was senior-led, so everyone had a chance to say what was needed to be said. I think this is what created the family environment with our team. The talks opened some of the girls' eyes to what their teammates were feeling and how they felt about one another. The team achieved a sense of unity through these talks," she said.

After the Rams recovered from that 2-0 halftime deficit in the state championship game, Reed was asked by an observer why she felt the Rams had worked so hard to come back. She was slightly taken aback by the question.

"I remember saying simply, 'We're Badin'," she recalled. "It dawned on me that people don't understand how girls who are so close can also be a successful soccer team. We're a family and you don't give up on family.

"When we were running the Ram Run, it was easy to push through for your teammates," Reed noted. "When you can't breathe and your throat is scratchy because you're so dehydrated and you're pretty sure that if you make one more run your legs will actually fall off, you suck it up and make the run anyway because that's what your team, your family, needs.

"One of the quotes that I read before every game said, 'The smiles, the tears and the joys on my teammates' faces are my championships.' I remember this quote because after Hawken missed that last penalty kick, my first thought was how happy my teammates were, not how pretty that trophy was going to look in the glass case outside Mulcahey Gym. We won a state championship because we didn't care about the fame that came along with it. All we cared about was giving the girl to the right and left of us what she deserved: our best."

(With those substantive thoughts, it's no wonder that Reed was a member of National Honor Society and received the Brown University book award for excellence in English.)

I was standing in the lobby of Badin's Mulcahey Gym in January of 2014 when Annika Pater looked at me with a big grin and said, "You wrote a book about the Badin girls basketball team winning the state title. You should write one about the girls soccer team, too."

I smiled and walked away, thinking, 'there's no way I'm going to do that.' I had just put out a book in December 2013 ("Notes for a Book", a serious compilation of fact, fiction and commentary that speaks to the larger world around us. Someone asked me why I wrote it and I said, "Well, we're not getting any younger." He said, "Oh, kind of a bucket list thing …" and I thought, yeah, I had never looked at it that way but I guess that's exactly what it was) and the fact is that it's hard to write a book – even if you love writing, as I do. It's not as hard, I suppose, as winning a state championship, but it's hard nonetheless.

But Annika's challenge kept nagging at me. Winning a high school state championship, after all, is a darn good story. The Badin girls soccer program had been strong for two decades, so there was plenty of compelling material. I knew I would get a lot of cooperation from the girls and from everyone involved in the program.

Much of the fun of a project like this, of course, is pulling all of the information together … contacting young women, coaches, parents who you enjoyed watching and befriending over all the years and getting their thoughts about the games they played, the fun they had, and the bonds they established.

I appreciate the intersection of writing and sports, and here was the opportunity to book-end that Badin girls basketball book with a feel-good story about some more can-do BHS female athletes worthy of attention. When you think of it that way, it becomes the proverbial no-brainer. Thanks for the suggestion, Annika.

Self-publishing and print-on-demand has certainly made these projects much more feasible if you are willing to put in the time and effort. When I wrote "Good Tears" about the Badin girls basketball program and its 1998 state championship, that was a two-year project at a time when print-on-demand was just in its infancy. You had to order the inventory up front.

So, the good news is that there are some 1,200 copies of the 320-page book floating around Southwest Ohio. The bad news is that there are still some 900 copies of the book in my spare bedroom. (It's crowded in there!) I still remember the representative at the printer, C.J. Krehbiel Co. in Cincinnati, cautioning me to gauge my audience effectively, because I didn't want to be left with many boxes of books in my basement.

Well, so be it. "Good Tears" was one of the most enjoyable and rewarding things I have done in my life. Add this book, "The Family", to that list.

The Badin girls soccer program has dealt with two high-profile tragedies that show just how strong the family connection is.

In August of 2006, Megan Filipek was killed in a jet ski accident on Kentucky's Lake Cumberland. Filly, as she was known, would have been a fifth-year senior at Miami University who, as people said, "never met a stranger." She was a talented starter on the 2000 state runner-up team, and a popular member of the Class of 2002. Her boyfriend, fellow Badin grad Greg Vaughn, from the Class of 2003, also perished in the accident. All he'd done that previous May was run the Badin after-prom as if he'd been doing it all of his life.

Filipek's parents, Tom and Beth, have stood tall with their resilience. They help oversee a Filly Fly golf outing each summer in Fairfield that raises money for the Fairfield Parks and Recreation Activity Trust Fund in memory of Megan. And there is a Megan Filipek scholarship fund at Badin High School. Over the years, the teams of Steve Tabar held a 3 v 3 alumni benefit soccer game to raise money for the fund. Sarah Graf, an assistant coach with Tabar and a close friend of Filipek's, helped make that happen.

"Megan Filipek and I lived together in college," said Steph Streit, Badin's goalkeeper on the 2000 squad. "She was my best friend, although I'll be the first to admit that I was not hers. She was loved by everyone who met her, and she was constantly surrounded by great people.

"She and I spent plenty of nights reminiscing about our Badin soccer days. We'd always come back to a 0-0 tie we played against Seton, a great save I made in the last two minutes, and the fact that she spent the entire game on the field, never leaving the side of their striker who was one of the top scorers in the league. She never came out of the game. It was a spectacular thing, really. I can't think of my Badin soccer days without thinking about Filly."

When Filipek would have turned 30 in 2014, her friends from the BHS soccer family still remembered her with birthday wishes on Facebook.

Erin Golden, who starred for three straight state finalists from 2005-2007, is another member of the soccer family who passed on far too soon. The 2008 graduate was diagnosed with a rare brain cancer in early 2012, and passed away in March of 2013.

"Feisty" was the ongoing description of Erin by her coaches and teammates … she was "The Little Redhead That Could." Badin High School hosted the funeral and subsequent reception, and the vast turnout was a powerful tribute to the lives Erin had touched.

"Fearless" was the word Erin used to describe her battle with cancer, and her personable parents, Ann and Marty, have backed an ongoing "Fighting for Golden" campaign that benefits brain cancer research.

Erin and her close friend, Courtney Gray, would come into our office nearly every day because Courtney's mother, Patti, was our administrative assistant. They were always smiling.

"Erin was a great motivator, a great leader," Gray said of Erin. "She was like the Energizer Bunny when it came to soccer. … My dad always said to her, 'No. 1 in our program, No. 1 in our hearts.' We always used to giggle at that. Now it brings tears to my eyes."

The Golden family has the state championship soccer ball from the 2005 game. It has been passed around – with love -- over the years.

Emily Flum, who scored the winning goal in the 2-1 overtime win over Doylestown Chippewa that afternoon, was given the game ball – and then immediately handed it to team captain Heather Rains.

JournalNews sports writer Jay Morrison captured the episode:

"Because she's like my big sister and she's my best friend on the team," Flum said in a broken voice when asked why she gave away something so special.

"This meant so much to me," Rains added while choking back tears. *"I don't know why she did it. She's just so nice to me.*

"I'm gonna have her sign it, and then frame it. Can you frame a soccer ball?"

You can if you're a state champion. You can do anything you want.

But while Rains – now the married Heather Smith – admits to having a few framed soccer balls around, she no longer has the state ball. She gave that to the Filipek family after Megan's tragic accident. But the Filipeks don't have it either – after Erin Golden's death, they gave it to the Golden family.

"Yes, we have the state ball now," Kim Golden, Erin's younger sister, nodded. "The Filipeks gave it to us. They sent it with a letter and said that since Erin played in the game, we should have it. It was very kind of them."

It was the Badin soccer family dynamic at work.

I recall one sunny afternoon in the late-1990s when Xavier University was playing the University of Dayton in the Atlantic-10 tournament, and Stacey (XU) and Shannon (UD) Kuhl were on opposite sides. In fact, at one point the two were tracking each other up and down the field.

I pointed that out in a JournalNews newspaper column, and wondered in print what they might have been saying to each other. A few days later I got a nice note from Stacey, who said, in essence, 'Wouldn't you like to know? Well, that will have to remain between sisters!' I could hear her laughing as she wrote it.

Here's my favorite Shannon Kuhl story: One Friday night in November 2003, she helped lead UD to a 2-0 win over Xavier in the semifinals of the A-10 tournament at the University of Richmond. On Saturday, she was in Hamilton to be a bridesmaid in the wedding of her former Badin teammate, Aimee Hurst. On Sunday, she was back in Virginia, leading Dayton into the NCAA tournament with a 3-0 A-10 championship verdict over host Richmond. And, oh by the way, she was named the Most Outstanding Player of the A-10 event! Kuhl – aka "Kuhlio" ... a tremendous (and always modest) talent!

These same Kuhl sisters – Stacey Kuhl Rhodis '96 and Shannon Kuhl Niemann '99 -- were in attendance at the Badin title match in November 2013.

"We still talk fondly about high school soccer," Stacey said. "With five of our children – ages 3 months to 8 years – surrounding us, they finally watched intently as the penalty kicks started. And Emma, my 8-year-old, asked me why I was crying. It was before Badin won. And I just said, 'Because I remember.'

"Our stomachs were in knots the entire game. But it was the PKs that opened up the tears," Stacey said. "Until then, I was able to separate myself and be the 'coach' who was watching several of the girls I coached create their own magic. We were so very excited for them, and we appreciated being a supporter for their win."

One Saturday afternoon in November 2005, I missed Megan McKnight's wedding to Brett Mahle. I got there for the reception, and Megan graciously said I had a good excuse ... since, after all, that was the day Badin won the Division II girls soccer state championship!

Megan had a rather spectacular athletic career. She was a key member of three Badin state finalists in soccer, was second-team all-Ohio as the point guard on the BHS squad that won the 1998 D-II state basketball championship, then was an All-American soccer player at the University of Dayton.

In fact, the very last time she swung her foot in earnest, she scored a goal for the Flyers in the final minute of a 3-1 loss at UCLA in the third round of the 2001 NCAA tournament. Megan played with skill and class and has been inducted into the athletic Hall of Fame at both Badin and UD. (I had the distinct pleasure of introducing her into the Badin HOF.)

"Having lost three straight – ouch! -- state soccer titles while at Badin," McKnight said, "I quickly understood how bad it hurts to lose. When I finally had the opportunity to be a part of a big win (in basketball), the lesson was really identified when you knew what it took to be a gracious winner. I was fortunate to go on to experience many big wins in the following years, so that was certainly a lesson that came in handy."

From the Mahle home in Louisville, she added, "To those who are lucky enough to wear the Badin gear in the years to come, I wish you the best. Enjoy these four years, enjoy the sport, the competition and the friendships. Celebrate the wins and learn from the losses. It is a privilege to have the opportunity – and the memories will last a lifetime."

While Title IX legislation had started women's sports along the road to becoming a household interest in the mid-1970s by insisting on program equity in the college ranks, former Badin girls soccer coach Katy Brennan pointed to Brandi Chastain and the U.S. World Cup women as a phenomenon that certainly piqued the soccer interest at BHS and beyond.

Chastain hit the winning penalty kick to beat China in the Rose Bowl in Los Angeles in July of 1999 ... and women's soccer was all the buzz. Chastain, interestingly, had missed a PK against China four months earlier, and had been originally marked down as the 6th kicker in the U.S. rotation in that World Cup final. At the last moment, head coach Tony DiCicco moved her up to the No. 5 spot. Of such things are headlines (and iconic photos) made.

Looking at the nearly two decades contained in this book, I note that I have witnessed 15 of the 19 Badin season finales, including six of the eight state title tilts, and plenty of great games in between. I missed the 1995 and 2000 state championship games, and the season-enders in 1999 and 2002.

The bottom line is, I have seen a lot of terrific soccer played by the Badin girls soccer family. But more importantly, I have seen a lot of terrific effort put in by quality young people who acquit themselves well and are a credit to that effort.

After thousands of words in this book, it's hard to sum up that effort. Certainly congratulations are in order to the 2013 state champions ... and to all of those over the years who have made the Badin girls soccer program – coaches, players, supportive parents and more -- one to be reckoned with, and proud of. The hope is, obviously, that you had as much fun being involved in Badin soccer as so many of us have had rooting you on.

Senior co-captain Holly Reed – en route to the University of Akron -- said something that effectively encapsulates the Good, the Bad and the Ugly of trying to get to the mountain top, and finally getting there. Concussions may have kept Holly on the sidelines as a senior, but they didn't undermine her ability to observe and be a part of what was happening all around her:

"This season was crazy with all the ups and downs. If we didn't have each other, we all probably would've given up a long time ago. We pushed each other and relied on one another for the reassurance that we were not the worst soccer players in the world ... we were just having a bad day at practice."

And when Annika Pater – yes, the same Annika Pater who had suggested I write this book – created an award-winning short video in the summer of 2014, she pointed out that the Rams' girls soccer success could be summarized in a trio of key points:

"Hard work pays off."

"Teamwork is a must."

"Life is better when you share it with family."

Addendum

The author smiles alongside former Badin great Ashley Mahoney '12 in the midst of the 2013 state championship game at Columbus Crew Stadium. Photo by Terri Adams.

Badin High School
"Home of Champions"
(results from 1966 to 2014)

Team state championships:
1988 – Boys' Basketball, Division III
Badin 68, Zoarville Tuscarawas Valley 63

1990 – Football, Division III
Badin 16, Richfield Revere 6

1991 – Baseball, Division III
Badin 2, Coldwater 1

1996 – Baseball, Division II
Badin 7, Tallmadge 5

1998 – Girls' Basketball, Division II
Badin 50, Dover 31

2005 – Girls' Soccer, Division II
Badin 2, Doylestown Chippewa 1 (ot)

2013 – Girls' Soccer, Division III
Badin 3, Gates Mills Hawken 2 (penalty kick shootout)

Individual state championships:
1969 – Boys golf (D-1), Jim Urso '70, medalist
1981 – Swimming (D-1), Chris Rigling '81
2000 – Girls tennis doubles (D-II), Nancy Wiegand '01 and Kylee Wiegand '04
2003 – Girls tennis doubles (D-II), Kylee Wiegand '04 and Jessica Flannery '06

State runner-up finishes:
Baseball – 1975, 1984, 2005, 2008 and 2009
Football – 1978 and 1980
Girls' basketball – 2000 and 2004
Girls' soccer – 1995, 1996, 1997, 2000, 2006 and 2007

Badin High School
Girls Soccer
2013 Division III State Champions

Head coach: Todd Berkely
Assistant coaches: Ken Murrell and Jeff Pohlman

State program roster:
Seniors – Maggie Adams, Michelle Hessling, Holly Reed, Amy Seither
Juniors – Kate Bach, Emily Henson, Madi Kah, Morgan Langhammer, Annika Pater, Brianna Scowden
Sophomores – Malia Berkely, Lydia Braun, Gabby Geigle, Ali Kalberer, Shelby Lamping, Katie Pohlman, Rachel Riley, Taylor Smith
Freshmen – Sabrina Bernardo, Lindsey Brinck, Samantha Lehker, Nicole Visse

Regular season: 8-4-4
Trenton Edgewood W, 3-1
Cincinnati Christian W, 7-0
McNicholas L, 2-0
Hamilton W, 2-1
Kettering Alter L, 3-1
Northwest W, 10-0
Dayton Chaminade Julienne W, 3-1
Roger Bacon W, 6-0
Mother of Mercy W, 3-1
Dayton Carroll T, 1-1
Madeira T, 1-1
St. Ursula Academy L, 5-1
Middletown Fenwick T, 1-1
Cincinnati Country Day L, 2-1
Purcell Marian W, 5-0
Mariemont T, 2-2

The tournament:
Sectional
Yellow Springs W, 10-0
Xenia Christian W, 7-1
District
Madeira W, 2-1 (ot)
Regionals
Cincinnati Country Day W, 3-1
Sidney Lehman W, 1-0
State Semifinals
Middletown Fenwick W, 2-1 (ot)
State Finals
Gates Mills Hawken W, 3-2 (so)
(4-3 in penalty kick shootout)

Letter from Emily Flum '08
To the 2013 Badin High girls soccer team

2013 Badin Girls Soccer Team,

I want to write you this letter to wish you the best of luck in this tournament. I can remember how exciting this time of the season was for me. It just seems like yesterday that I was playing for Badin and getting pumped up for the tournament games. As a team, we would always play with 110% and with all of our hearts. It was important to us to play for a reason and have a goal in mind. Our goal was to make it to state. So for you girls I want you to make a goal of yours to play with a 110% and with all your heart each and every game in order to make it to state. Play for Columbus. One of the best feelings in the world was walking onto the Columbus Crew field for the state game knowing that you've accomplished something beautiful.

I share such an awesome bond with the girls that I played soccer with throughout my Badin days. It's a bond that is unable to be described and that's what helped us to play with chemistry and allowed us to make it to state 3 of the 4 years I was playing at Badin. Each and every one of you has something special that you bring to the table and it's important for you all to recognize those things and bring those out on the field. I believe in you girls!

Now I'm going to give you a quick run through of our 2005 state game: I was a sophomore going into the state game in 2005. We had a wonderful team that year, we worked well together and we all left everything out on the field by giving everything we had each and every game. Walking out onto the field that day in November, I was very intimidated by the stadium and the thought of playing and starting in the 2005 state game. I remember thinking to myself, "Is this team good? Are we going to be able to win? Are they going to put up a good fight?" ... then I remember looking around during warm-ups and saw how good of friends and teammates I was surrounded by and knew we could pull out a win.

During the first half, we dominated the game. We had 3 times as many shots on goal as the other team. Unfortunately, we just couldn't seem to find the back of the net. We were giving all we had and never gave up. We encouraged each other that we can do this and we will do this. The first half ended in a tie 0-0. Even though this didn't make us feel good going into the second half without scoring, we continued to encourage one another.

During half time, our coaches reassured us that we dominated the first have but just need to find the back of the net because we had so many opportunities in the first half. They went through things that we could improve on and the weaknesses of the other team. We as a team knew during halftime that we deserved this game and we were the better team; we just had to prove it. So we walked onto the field for the second half knowing we had something to prove.

During the second half, we had so many opportunities on the net. We had the ball on our side of the field 85% of this half. We had multiple free kicks during this half. Towards the middle of the second half a player on the other team broke past our strong defensive line and scored their first goal, making the score 1-0 them. Shortly after, on a free kick, Megan Reimer finds the back of the net and scores our first goal of the game making it a tied game. This is exactly what we needed to give us even more confidence in our abilities to win that game. Even though we continued to dominate, we were unable to score again before the second half was over, which ended the half in a tie.

Before overtime started, my coach came up to me and said "I'm going to put you in as an outside right midfielder during overtime; I just have a good feeling about it." So I started overtime in that position, and even though I never played that position for Badin before, I gave 110% and never gave up. We again dominated in overtime.

We were about 10 minutes or so into overtime when Abby Milillo gets the ball in the center field, and if you know anything about Abby you better watch out! I see her making her way up the centerfield towards the goal, I'm on the right side of the field making my way to the goal with her. She spots me open on the outside closing in on the goal. She crosses the ball right in front of the goalie and towards me. It was slow motion for me running towards the ball and realizing the goalie is closing in on the ball as well. So I lit some fire under my rear and ran as fast as I could. I beat the goalie to the ball and tapped it into the back of the net. Before I realized I had scored the winning goal of the 2005 state game I was on the bottom of a dog pile.

The feeling that we all felt when that ball hit the back of the net is indescribable. It was one of the best feelings in the world. And I want you ALL to feel the way we felt that November day!

I want you ALL to believe in yourselves and know that if you give 110% and play with all your heart you can make it far in the tournament. Just remember, Play for Columbus. I wish you guys the BEST of luck! Remember who and what you are playing for girls!

I will be cheering and praying for you girls the whole way through.

Emily

Pre-game thoughts
Read by senior co-captain Holly Reed
Before every game in 2013

You lace up your cleats, strap on your shin guards, put on your jersey and walk out onto that field, and once you do nothing else matters. It doesn't matter if you failed a test, didn't get the guy or stepped in crap on the way there. Your world is right there between those sidelines for the next 90 minutes and no matter how hard it hurts to run down the field in the last 30 seconds, no matter how sore you are the next day, your passion for the game never fades away.

Somewhere behind the athlete you've become, the hours of practice, the coaches who pushed you, and the teammates who believed in you and the fans that cheered you on is that little girl who fell in love with the game and never looked back. Do it for her.

The goals, the glory and the championships are nice, but the smiles, the tears, and the joy on my teammate's faces are my championships.

People don't play sports because it's fun. Ask any athlete, most of them hate it, but they couldn't imagine their life without it. It's part of them, the love/hate relationship. It's what they live for. They live for the practices, the parties, cheers, long bus rides, invitationals, countless pairs of different types of shoes, water, Gatorade, & coaches you hate but appreciate. They live for the way it feels when they beat the other team, and knowing those two extra sprints they ran in practice were worth it. They live for the way they become a family with their team, they live for the countless songs they sing in their head while training all those hours. They live for the competition, they live for the friends, the practices, the memories, the pain, it's who they are. It's who we are. We are athletes.

I kind of had a bad day. Some people weren't nice to me and some things didn't go my way and I let that get to me. Tonight none of that matters. All the people who like me, all the people who don't, just everyone that watches me, they're all going to know how good I am because tonight I'm going to play and tonight we're going to win.

State Championship Coverage
The JournalNews
Following are the eight lead articles from the state championship soccer games played by Badin High School. Courtesy of the JournalNews, Hamilton, Ohio.

Badin 3, Gates Mils Hawken 2 (penalty kick shootout)
November 2013

By Greg Billing

COLUMBUS -- No state ranking. No league title. No problem.

The Badin Rams girls soccer team played the underdog role perfectly on a crisp Friday afternoon at Columbus Crew Stadium. The Rams overcame early jitters that led to a daunting deficit, then outlasted Gates Mills Hawken to win the Division III state championship 3-2 in a shootout. Badin won the shootout 4-3 for its second state title and first since 2005.

Perhaps no player felt the wild swing of emotion more than Badin keeper Michelle Hessling. The Rams, already down 1-0 on a Katherine Zalar penalty kick after six minutes, went down 2-0 in the 23rd minute. Hessling received a back pass with Zalar charging. She tried to clear the ball but Zalar got a piece of it and deflected a slow roller into the net as a helpless Hessling lay on the ground watching.

"One thing as a goalkeeper is you learn to have a short memory. It can be catastrophic as it was," Hessling said of the miscue. "I just had to keep my head up, keep playing. I couldn't shut down. At halftime, (coach) told me they believe in you and I believe in you."

As short as her memory was in the first half, Hessling will long remember the second.

Sophomore Malia Berkely's 25-yarder with a vicious curve eluded Hawken keeper Hannah O'Day midway through the second half.

Later, junior Morgan Langhammer received a pass in front of the keeper's box and beat O'Day with a touch to the left with 6:27 to play.

After a scoreless 30 minutes of golden goal overtime -- including three game-saving stops by Hessling -- the title game went to the five vs. five shootout. Badin's Maggie Adams, Berkely and Gabby Geigle matched Hawken's shooters for the 3-3 tie.

Hessling then made a pair of memories. In goal she deflected

Dana Fann's shot over the crossbar. On offense she delivered a shot past O'Day, who also played a stellar game, for the 4-3 lead. Hawken missed its next shot, setting off Badin's celebration.

"He asked me if I wanted to (kick)," Hessling said of coach Todd Berkely. "It's my senior year. I said if you feel comfortable with me, of course. I put it in."

And, just as important, she kept Fann's shot out. So which was better, the game-deciding goal or game-deciding deflection?

"The deflection," Hessling said. "First off, I'm a goalie. I don't get to score much so the kick was fun. All the odds are against the keeper in a PK shootout. When you get a save, you feel like Superman."

In the first half the ball seemed like Badin's Kryptonite. Hawken, making its first title game appearance in two trips to state, outshot Badin 4-3 in the first half but benefited from the Rams' mistakes. Badin outshot Hawken 7-4 in the second half and 15-13 overall.

"To get the pregame jitters out took a little longer," coach Berkely said. "I figured it would take 10 minutes. It took a half. We made mistakes but the mistakes didn't get us down. ... We looked around (at halftime) and said we're OK. There was no panic. There was just resolve."

Badin which has six state runner-up finishes in girls soccer, didn't receive votes in the final coaches state poll and finished second in the Greater Catholic League Central Division. Hawken, which won its division of the Chagrin Valley Conference, finished third in the state poll.

But they finished behind Badin on Friday.

Shaker Heights Hathaway Brown 2, Badin 0
November 2007

By Rick Cassano
COLUMBUS -- On another day, perhaps the Badin High School girls' soccer squad could have produced a different result.

On Saturday, however, the better team won. And it wasn't the Rams.

Shaker Heights Hathaway Brown tallied a goal in each half and simply outplayed Badin in the Division II state title game, celebrating a 2-0 triumph at Crew Stadium.

"They were just a fast team, and they were moving," Rams coach Keith Harring said. "It was like that first shot as a boxer. It kind of startled us. Then we didn't get our game going, and I think it was caused by them. It was because of their tough play."

Merrill Bachouros and Lani Smith provided the goals for the Blazers (20-3-1), who are 2-for-2 in the state finals -- they also snagged the championship in 2004.

Badin, playing in its third consecutive title contest, saw its 12-game winning streak come to an end and finished 17-6-1.

"I don't think we came out flat," Rams junior goalkeeper Megan Woodrey said. "I just think they came out wanting to kill us. We didn't win a lot of the 50-50 balls. I think that's what hurt us in the first half."

Hathaway Brown's fire right out of the gate was typical. Blazers coach Dennis Weyn said he's seen it all year long.

Keyed by Smith at striker and Alex Dayneka in the midfield, Hathaway Brown played strong, fast soccer.

"I think our strength of the season is the way we've been coming out at the beginning of the matches," Weyn said. "They're very focused. They're told, 'We've got to take it to this team right away' and they've responded to that extremely well. Today, again, we started dominating immediately."

Harring had special praise for Smith and Dayneka.

"Those two were the best players," he said. "We just couldn't handle them. They were just dynamite. They were just flying.

"We didn't play our normal game," Harring continued. "We gave them an awful lot of space. Then we were doing things we haven't done -- stabbing at the ball here, stabbing at the ball there. We were just on our heels."

Bachouros scored with 22:38 remaining in the first half, taking a pass from Smith and booting the ball past Woodrey.

The Rams showed more offensive thrust in the second half, but they managed few quality shots. And then Smith got loose for a breakaway goal with 11:35 left.

"The first goal, it was pretty much a two-on-one with (sweeper) Christina (Walsh) and Christina had to pressure the ball," Woodrey said. "Then the girl pretty much just cut the ball and passed it. It was one-on-one with me and the girl, and she got the better half.

"The second goal ... my defense could only do so much," she added. "It comes down to me."

Weyn said he was never worried in the second half, even as he watched Badin's increased offensive effort.

"When it's 1-0, of course the other team is going to take some more chances," Weyn said. "I knew eventually what was going to happen. If they started pushing forward a little bit more, we were going to get breakaway chances."

Ellie Shorey earned the shutout in goal for Hathaway Brown with three saves. Woodrey and Emily Andes combined for seven saves for Badin.

Parma Heights Holy Name 1, Badin 0 (penalty kick shootout) *November 2006*

By Rick Cassano

COLUMBUS -- The soccer gods didn't smile on Badin High's girls squad Saturday at Crew Stadium.

Sometimes, BHS coach Keith Harring knows, that just happens.

His defending state champions dominated a good portion of the Division II state title game against Parma Heights Holy Name, but couldn't find the back of the net in 110 minutes of regulation and overtime, then suffered an agonizing shootout defeat.

The Green Wave outpointed the Rams 5-3 in penalty kicks, quelling Badin's bid for another state title.

"I hate PKs," said Harring, whose team finished 15-3-4. "It's not fair to Lindsey Donges. It's not fair to Jenny Rosen. It's not fair to anybody. We really controlled the game."

It was Donges who hit the post on Badin's fourth penalty kick, leaving Holy Name with a 4-3 advantage. Jessica Bound then delivered the clinching shot past Rosen on the fifth kick of the first rotation.

"It's disappointing to end like that," Rosen said quietly after a two-save performance in goal. "We had a lot of opportunities. I thought we would finish one. It's very frustrating."

Kristina Anderson, Sammi Burton and Janie Jeffcoat converted the first three penalty kicks for the Rams. Lynnea Pappas, Tara O'Toole, Michelle Mooren and Emily Balodis scored for Holy Name (18-3-2).

Winning goalie Becky Williams collected seven saves as the Green Wave celebrated its first state championship.

"I woke up at 4 o'clock this morning and wrote down who was going to take PKs," said Holy Name coach Brian Michelson, smiling. "It's tough to end a game like that, but somebody has to win. I thought both teams were deserving of a championship."

Badin had several outstanding opportunities to score in what was an extremely physical affair. Two shots hit the post, including Lindsey Smith's boot with 2:36 left in regulation.

"We had a couple chances where my heart just sank because I thought we had a goal," BHS junior striker Abby Milillo said. "Everything happens for a reason, I guess."

Rosen said she didn't feel comfortable heading into the shootout, and the senior admitted she was a little tentative.

"I started to get nervous toward the end of the second overtime," Rosen said. "It was my last game in high school and the state championship. I was confident, but a little nervous."

"The outcome is nothing on Jenny," Harring said. "She got us here by beating Alter on PKs in the district finals. You can't keep putting your goalie in that situation."

Badin 2, Doylestown Chippewa 1 (ot)
November 2005

By Jay Morrison

COLUMBUS -- Badin High soccer players Abby Milillo and Emily Flum found themselves out of position when the Division II state final went to overtime Saturday afternoon at Columbus Crew Stadium.

Moments later, Milillo, Flum and every other girl on the team were all in the same position -- in a massive, shrieking pile in front of the goal.

Flum, a sophomore defender playing up at midfield, scored a goal 4 minutes and 40 seconds into the first sudden-death overtime period to lift the Rams to a 2-1 victory against Doylestown Chippewa and hand Badin its first soccer state championship in school history after four previous trips to the title game.

"Abby (Milillo) took a shot, and it went off somebody and came to me, so I just shot it," Flum said of the game-winning play that was started by Milillo. "I didn't really know what happened until (Heather Rains) jumped on me. Then I just started crying."

The goal capped an 18-3-2 season in which the Rams finished right where they started -- ranked No. 1 in Ohio.

"This feels tremendous," Badin coach Keith Harring said. "I saw these girls go wire-to-wire. They started the year ranked No. 1 in the state, and not too many teams who do that go on to win it all."

The Rams outplayed previously unbeaten Chippewa (21-1-1) from the outset, outshooting the Lady Chipps 9-1 in the first half and 16-4 for the game.

But that didn't stop Badin from falling behind when Chippewa senior Chrissy Summers intercepted a Megan Reimer throw-in and started a run down the left sideline that ended with Natalie Villers chipping a shot over the head of Badin goalkeeper Jenny Rosen for a 1-0 lead with 33:29 left in the game.

"We knew that wasn't it," said Chippewa coach Ruth Coney, the Division II Ohio Coach of the Year. "We knew it would take at least two goals. A soccer game is never over at 1-0. Never."

Badin senior Kellie Beadle, relegated to a cheerleading role the last two games while battling illness, screamed the same "it's not over" message to her teammates from the sideline.

Then, just six minutes later, Reimer proved both Beadle and Coney prophetic when she scored on a rebound off a long free kick by Kristina Anderson, tying the game at 1-1.

"It bounced off the (Chippewa keeper Samantha Hoffman), and I was there on the backside," Reimer said. "I felt like the goal they scored was my fault, so that felt really good."

Led by the attack of Sammi Burton and Rains, Badin -- which took 10 corner kicks in the game to none for the Lady Chipps -- continued to control play and pepper Hoffman with shots over the final 27 minutes of regulation, but to no avail.

Then while the teams were taking their mandatory 5-minute break before the start of the first overtime period, Milillo approached Harring with an idea.

"I had been playing midfield the whole game, so I asked him to put me up front," Milillo said. "I knew if he put me up there, I could get something started, and I did."

Milillo drove into the box and pushed the ball to Rains, who kicked it back to her. Milillo tried to end the game herself, but her shot was deflected by a Chippewa defender, sending the ball right to a charging Flum, who blasted it into the goal from 7 yards away.

"We've got kids who can make those runs, and that's what she did," Harring said of Flum. "I saw it hit to her, and I knew it was going in."

And when it did, the Badin sideline and half of the Crew Stadium crowd of 1,910 erupted.

But lost in the middle of the raucous celebration was a gesture that epitomizes what this Badin team is all about.

Having just lived every soccer player's dream of scoring the game-winning goal in a state championship game, Flum accepted the game ball and then, without hesitating, handed it to Rains – Badin's leading scorer and one of only three seniors on the team.

"Because she's like my big sister and she's my best friend on the team," Flum said in a broken voice when asked why she gave away something so special.

"This meant so much to me," Rains added while choking back tears. "I don't know why she did it. She's just so nice to me."

"I'm gonna have her sign it, and then frame it. Can you frame a soccer ball?"

You can if you're a state champion. You can do anything you want.

Cuyahoga Falls Walsh Jesuit 4, Badin 1
November 2000

By Jay Morrison

COLUMBUS -- For the second consecutive game, the Badin High girls soccer team decided things early.

This time, however, that decision was not as favorable.

Cuyahoga Falls Walsh Jesuit needed just 191 seconds to score its first goal, and the Warriors added another one 26 seconds later to coast to a 4-1 victory Saturday in the Division II state championship game at Columbus Crew Stadium.

"That was a heartbreaker," Badin coach Katy Brennan said of the two early goals. "I think in the first half we were kind of back on our heels. I think we were just caught off guard by the speed and the talent they had."

All that speed and talent led to a dominating 18-3 shot advantage for the Warriors in the first half, and 25-7 for the game.

"That was probably the toughest team I've ever played against," Badin keeper Steph Streit said. "It was just constant bombarding against our entire defense."

Doing most of that bombardment was striker Kristen Weiss. The All-Ohio junior assisted Katie Schwager for the first goal of the game, then a few seconds later broke free of Badin defender Sarah Graf and sprinted down the field for a breakaway goal.

"I knew (Graf) was playing really tight on me so I just turned real quick, and then there was nobody else there," said Weiss, who finished with the one goal and two assists, giving her 41 goals and 39 assists for the year. "We scored 1:01 into the game in the state semis (a 3-0 victory against Bexley), but that was the closest span we've had between two different goals."

Those two quick goals came on the Warriors' first two shots of the game and served as the perfect remedy for big game butterflies.

"That was huge," said Walsh coach Dino McIntyre, whose team capped an unbeaten season at 21-0-1. "We were a little bit nervous, of course, because this is our first time here, and we score like that, and it calms us down.

"Not to mention what it does to the other team. I mean, you're in the final, you're all pumped up, and then right away you're going uphill. It changes the whole game."

The irony, of course, is that the Rams did the exact same thing in Wednesday's 11-1 semifinal victory against Enon Greenon. The only difference is that the Badin players bowed their backs and fought through the early disappointment and never let it get as ugly as 11-1.

"They were a little frustrated, but they still played the game," Brennan said. "That's the best thing about these girls. Even if they're frustrated or down, they still continue to play all the way to the last second."

And it was that stick-to-it attitude that enabled the Rams to finally punch one in with 4:58 left in the game.

Jenny Rigling passed the ball into the box where Walsh's Kelci Lanich tried a slide kick to clear the ball only to knock it right to Badin's Ann Menke, who blasted it into the goal.

"We had nothing to lose at that point. We were just going out there and playing our hearts out," Menke said.

The goal was the Rams' first in four state championship games, and it kept Walsh from setting a state record for largest margin of victory in a state championship game. The four goals the Warriors scored tied the state record for most in a title game.

"The whole team is very talented, you can't take that away from them because obviously they're state champions," Brennan said. "They played very well."

As devastating as the two goals were, it was the third goal that pretty much spelled the end for the Rams.

The Rams had settled down after the 26-second span that produced two goals, taking a couple of solid shots themselves. But then Schwager stole the ball from Megan Filipek and launched a shot from 30 yards out that was too high for Streit to stop.

"What a pretty goal," Brennan said. "You've got to respect a team like that. Their shots are always on goal, and they're hard hit. They're just very, very talented.

"But that's all right. We've got next year. We're only losing five, and granted they're a great five players, but you know what? I'm looking forward to being back here next year."

The five graduating seniors for the Rams, who finished the season 12-6-4, include Menke, Rigling, Jill Broermann, Heather Schappacher and Angela Vilkoski.

Columbus St. Francis DeSales 2, Badin 0
November 1997

By John Boyle

DUBLIN -- The pain never seems to stop for the Badin High girls soccer team.

It only seems to grow more acute with each passing year.

For the third straight season, the Rams advanced to the Division II state finals only to be turned away.

The culprit Saturday was the team that started Badin's state final misery in 1995 -- Columbus St. Francis DeSales.

The top-ranked Stallions scored a pair of second-half goals to break a scoreless halftime tie and posted a 2-0 victory over Badin at Dublin Scioto High School.

"There's so much emotion that runs through you, you're not sure what to do," said Badin's Megan McKnight, who closed out her career along with fellow seniors Jenny Fiehrer, Emily Gersbach, Lisa Sutton and Aimee Hurst. "This was our one goal and we played hard."

"Three years in a row, I don't have a lot to say," Badin coach Craig Manahan said. "They're a great team ... and we're a great team. It was a great final. What else can you say? We didn't finish our chances and they did. That's the game."

Badin's best chance came with 14:38 remaining in the first half. The Rams were awarded a penalty kick after junior Shannon Kuhl was tripped inside the penalty box. Kuhl corralled a cross from junior Amy Allen and was thwarted by Stallion goalkeeper Mindy Hammond, who came off the goal line to challenge the play.

Kuhl was dumped as she tried to knock home the rebound and was awarded the penalty kick.

But Hammond, who came into the game with 19 shutouts, came up big for DeSales, diving to her right to stop Kuhl's low shot.

"I didn't want the game to end like that," Hammond said. "Letting them get a PK and us losing on one opportunity like that. Luckily, I got a piece of it and we got it cleared out of the box."

"Certainly that changed the momentum," said DeSales coach Erik Ekis, whose team completed a perfect 23-0 season. "And they were on us a bit in the first half."

The Rams didn't seem fazed by the missed opportunity and kept the offensive pressure on as they did for most of the first half.

"They were definitely the best team we've faced all season," said Hammond, who recently committed to play basketball at UC. "I really feel for that team. They've been here three years in a row and haven't been able to get it done."

BHS' first-half momentum ended less than three minutes after intermission when Danielle Slupski's header beat Hurst high to the far post.

Slupski then gave DeSales some insurance with 25:20 remaining when she hit a laser from 25 yards out that found the top corner of the net.

"They came out a lot harder in the second half," McKnight said. "We kind of got back on our heels in the first couple of minutes. We still played hard after they scored but they just had two great shots."

"Aimee played so hard," McKnight added. "She did a great job all year but those were just two awesomely placed shots."

Hurst recorded eight saves for the Rams, who finished 18-2-3.

"What can you say about Badin?" Ekis asked. "It's an unbelievable program with a great coach. They've had some bad luck and I feel for them. But I just don't think there was any denying our team this year."

"When you get back here three years in a row, that's quite an accomplishment," McKnight said. "Most teams can't do that. When you get this far and you know you've played hard, that's all you can ask for."

Chagrin Falls 1, Badin 0
November 1996

By Rich Bevensee

DUBLIN -- This time, the Badin High girls couldn't put their feelings into words. The pain was twice as severe.

For the second time in as many years, the Ram girls soccer team fell one goal short of its dreams in the state championship game.

Outshot, outhustled and outplayed, No. 2 Chagrin Falls capitalized on its only scoring opportunity in the first half and scavenged a 1-0 victory in the Division II state finals Saturday at Dublin Scioto High.

"It happened again," said Ram keeper Aimee Hurst, allowing snow flurries to dot her cheeks, already wet from tears. "I think everybody played with all their heart. We just didn't get it done."

"The hardest thing to do is walk away," said Gina Andriacco, playing her final game for the green-and-white. "After the game, we just sat there and cried. Then we saw them cheering, and we cried again, because that was supposed to be us celebrating."

Badin lost to Columbus St. Francis DeSales in the 1995 final, 1-0 in a sudden-death shootout. The '96 Rams allowed just eight goals the entire season, three in postseason, and closed their campaign 15-3-3.

"It's not easy. I don't even know what to say about it," said junior Megan McKnight.

"That should have been us celebrating," said sophomore Emily Giuliano. "We were on their half so much."

Chagrin Falls, at 22-1-2, becomes only the third champion from northern Ohio in the 12-year history of the girls state tournament. The Tigers lost to DeSales in last year's state semifinals.

"I've been on the other side of these games, so maybe it was my turn to be on this end," said sixth-year Tiger coach Pam Malone. "I think coming so close last year made it easier to go further this year."

The Rams outshot the Tigers 10-1 in the first half and had several close calls with Chagrin Falls junior and 1995 All-Ohio keeper Katie Carson, but couldn't extract a single payoff.

"What can you say? We dominated for 38 minutes, they had one shot in the first half, they scored and we didn't," said Badin coach Craig Manahan.

"I'm feeling frustration, disappointment," he added. "We were the better team here today. To work this hard and come up with second place again, it's hard."

Three minutes into the match, junior fullback Lisa Sutton's header off an Andriacco corner kick was soft enough for Carson to grab.

McKnight gave the Rams their best shot with 23 minutes left in the half. Her direct kick from the left side clipped the left post, then the right one, before the Tigers cleared it.

At the 8:01 mark, Andriacco ripped a laser that narrowly missed the crossbar.

"We had a lot of chances today," Andriacco said. "Our corner kicks, our crosses, our passes back to the 18 ... We had a lot of chances, but we didn't do what we needed to win."

The Tigers were so busy clearing the ball from their defensive end, they went 21 minutes without challenging the Rams' fullbacks.

"Our defense did a good job, except for that one breakdown," Hurst said.

That breakdown came with 1 minute and 33 seconds left in the half. All-Ohio midfielder Jenny Lankford drove up the field and flicked a pass to Jenny Freshman on her right.

Freshman wasted no time in chipping a pass to the left goalpost, where Trish Kruse was waiting for the easy score, her 21st of the year. Hurst was left in no-man's land.

"It was a nice shot. I give them credit," Hurst said. "I feel bad for the seniors. I feel like I let them down."

"It was probably to our advantage that we didn't play in our field a lot," Malone said. "I think it caught their goalie off-guard."

Manahan echoed that sentiment. "We needed to be prepared for when they do have a chance," he said. "We weren't ready for them to come down the field and score. We were in shock."

The four Badin seniors -- Andriacco, Erin Chafin, Erin Kraft and Sarah Vilkoski -- were left with a lasting impression that will be tough to shed. Chagrin Falls faces beaming, orange-and-black bedecked cars honking. Badin fans longing for yet another chance.

Said Andriacco, "I'll remember all the friends I had, how hard we all worked, and how hard it was to end the season that way."

Columbus St. Francis DeSales 1, Badin 0 (penalty kick shootout)
November 1995

By Rich Bevensee

WESTERVILLE -- The season had to come to an end, somehow, some way ...

The Badin High girls soccer team constructed a dream season, and it took 100 minutes of soccer and then some for Columbus DeSales to wake up the Rams.

Stallion goalkeeper Mindy Hammond scored on a sudden death penalty kick, then dove to deflect Erin Kraft's bullet, and the first-ever

Division II state championship belonged to DeSales, 1-0, Monday at Westerville South High.

"When it comes to shootouts, it comes to luck," said Badin coach Craig Manahan. "When it comes to sudden death, it doesn't give us as a chance to show our skills."

The defeat ends a 16-6-1 campaign that no Ram soccer fan could have expected. Badin had just one senior, Stacey Kuhl, listed seven freshmen on the roster and had a first-year head coach.

That's where the Rams had their followers fooled. Manahan was an assistant last year, and had been around the game of soccer since he was a youth. Five of the Rams played together on a summer club team, the FOSC Fox.

That unlikely combination brought Badin its first district and regional championships.

"We got this far, but I wanted to push it to the limit," Kuhl said. "This was our whole life. Over the past three weeks I haven't thought about anything but soccer. It'll be hard to change."

Kuhl gave Badin a second life when she beat Hammond on the fifth and final penalty kick of the first round.

That sent the contest into a sudden-death shootout, where each team sends one player to shoot, and the combination of one miss and one conversion ends the game.

Hammond, who strikes an intimidating presence at 6-foot-1, sent a rocket into the left corner of Badin's net.

Hammond then took her accustomed spot in front of the goal and barely deflected Erin Kraft's shot with her fingertips to end the match.

"I thought it was going in, but it bounced out luckily," Hammond said of Kraft's shot. "We lost the district final last year (to Westerville North) in a shootout. No way could we go through that again."

"It's an awesome feeling," said DeSales coach Molly Barrett, whose club closes at 20-1-2. "I can't believe we're at this point. We owe much of it to Mindy. We think that she's the No. 1 goalie in Ohio. Now maybe more people will think so."

"She made some great saves," Manahan said. "She made saves that I didn't think she would make."

Melissa Fox, who led the Stallions with 26 goals this season, led off the penalty kick session with a laser into the right corner. Kuhl's freshman sister, Shannon, responded in kind to the left.

DeSales' Elise Berry and Badin's Megan McKnight then traded goals before Sarah Walker provided the Stallions with a 3-2 edge. Hammond made a diving save of a Lisa Sutton shot, but Julie Miceli hit the crossbar, giving Badin another chance to even the score.

The Rams' Sarah Vilkoski and the Stallions Julie Fox each had their shots blocked, setting up Stacey Kuhl's temporary heroics.

"I just tried to guess which way to go, then hoped for the best," said Badin goalie Aimee Hurst, unscored upon in the tournament until Monday. "I couldn't have changed anything.

"No one thought we'd be here," she added. "I didn't think we'd be here. It's a good feeling to be here, but now it's not so good. We'll come back next year and we'll win it."

DeSales dominated regulation with constant pressure on Hurst, but could not convert despite several opportunities.

Fox ripped a left-footer that caromed off the left post 15 minutes into the first half. That was the closest DeSales would come to beating Hurst until sudden death, where players line up and take aim from just 12 yards away.

"Badin kept us frustrated," Barrett said. "We had to keep telling the kids there will be some good to come out of this. As young as Badin was, we just didn't think they'd make us wait that long."

"It's OK that this is my last game," Stacey Kuhl said, "because this is the farthest we could have gotten."

Badin High School
Girls Soccer
2007 Division II State Runner-up

Head coach: Keith Harring
Assistant coaches: Mary Burns, Rick Keyes, Ken Murrell,
Stephanie Ratliff, Brian Smallwood, Mark Stewart

State program roster:
Seniors – Emily Andes, Ashley Crossley, Emily Flum, Erin
Golden, Courtney Gray, Jessica Hammond, Emily Leisge, Tori
Mathews, Megan Reimer, Kaitlyn Spradling, Asheton Whitaker
Juniors – Christina Walsh, Megan Woodrey
Sophomores – Carley Breetz, Chelsea Eschenbach, Sammy
Koerner, Jackie Lamb, Katie Maus Michelle Seither
Freshmen – Allie Crossley, Abby Stapf, Janea Van Natta

Regular season: 10-5-1
Wins: Dayton Chaminade-Julienne, Middletown Fenwick,
Madeira, McNicholas, Mariemont, Mother of Mercy, Purcell
Marian, Roger Bacon, Ross and Talawanda.
Losses: Indian Hill, Kettering Alter, Mount Notre Dame, St.
Ursula and Ursuline Academy.
Ties: Dayton Carroll

The tournament:
Sectional
New Lebanon Dixie W, 8-0
Germantown Valley View W, 4-0
Middletown Fenwick W, 3-2 (so)
District
Cincinnati Hills Christian Academy W, 1-0
Regionals
Columbus Bexley W, 1-0
Coshocton W, 5-0
State Semifinals
Madeira W, 2-1
State Finals
Shaker Heights Hathaway Brown L, 2-0

Badin High School
Girls Soccer
2006 Division II State Runner-up

Head coach: Keith Harring
Assistant coaches: Alisha Burns, Mary Burns, Brian Smallwood

State program roster:
Seniors – Kristina Anderson, Sammi Burton, Amanda Hessling, Janie Jeffcoat, Emily Lawall, Ashley Roberto, Jenny Rosen, Lindsey Smith
Juniors – Emily Andes, Emily Flum, Erin Golden, Courtney Gray, Jessica Hammond, Emily Leisge, Tori Mathews, Abby Milillo, Megan Reimer, Kaitlyn Spradling, Asheton Whitaker
Sophomores – Lindsey Donges, Christina Walsh, Megan Woodrey
Freshmen – None

Regular season: 9-2-4
Wins: Dayton Carroll, Kettering Alter, Madeira, Mariemont, McNicholas, Mount Notre Dame, Purcell Marian, Roger Bacon and Ross.
Losses: Mother of Mercy and St. Ursula.
Ties: Dayton Chaminade-Julienne, Middletown Fenwick, Indian Hill and Ursuline Academy.

The tournament:
Sectional
Eaton W, 4-0
Monroe Lemon Monroe W, 4-1
District
Kettering Alter W, 2-1 (so)
Regionals
Cincinnati Hills Christian Academy W, 5-0
Cincinnati Seven Hills W, 3-0
State Semifinals
Bexley, W, 1-0 (ot)
State Finals
Parma Heights Holy Name L, 1-0 (so)
(5-3 penalty kick shootout)

Badin High School
Girls Soccer
2005 Division II State Champions

Head coach: Keith Harring
Assistant coaches: Alisha Burns, Mary Burns, Brian Smallwood

State program roster:
Seniors – Kellie Beadle, Kelsey Fontaine, Heather Rains
Juniors – Kristina Anderson, Sammi Burton, Janie Jeffcoat,
Emily Lawall, Ashley Roberto, Jenny Rosen, Lindsey Smith,
Sophomores – Emily Andes, Emily Flum, Erin Golden,
Courtney Gray, Jessica Hammond, Emily Leisge, Tori Mathews,
Abby Milillo, Megan Reimer, Kaitlyn Spradling
Freshmen – Lindsey Donges, Megan Woodrey

Regular season: 11-3-2
Wins: Middletown Fenwick, Indian Hill, Mariemont, McAuley,
McNicholas, Mother of Mercy, Purcell Marian, Roger Bacon,
Ross, Summit Country Day and Talawanda.
Losses: Kettering Alter, Seton and St. Ursula.
Ties: Mount Notre Dame and Ursuline Academy.

The tournament:
Sectional
Dayton Northridge W, 11-0
Germantown Valley View W, 2-0
District
Kettering Alter W, 1-0 (ot)
Regionals
Madeira W, 5-1
Springfield Northwestern W, 2-1
State Semifinals
Columbus Bexley W, 5-1
State Finals
Doylestown Chippewa W, 2-1 (ot)

Badin High School
Girls Soccer
2000 Division II State Runner-up

Head coach: Katy Brennan
Assistant coaches: Erin Alexander, Rick Keyes

State program roster:
Seniors – Jill Broermann, Ann Menke, Jenny Rigling, Heather
Schappacher, Angela Vilkoski
Juniors – Megan Collins, Megan Filipek, Sarah Graf, Amanda
Margello, Reba Sedlacek, Steph Streit, Ashley Timmer
Sophomores – Stacy Beadle, Alicia Bruewer, Steph Caudill,
Lauren Gersbach, Jenny Hessling, Annie Hinkel, Linze Thieken
Freshmen: None

Regular season: 6-5-4
Wins: Hamilton, McNicholas, Mount Notre Dame, Purcell
Marian, Talawanda and Wyoming.
Losses: Kettering Alter, McAuley, Mother of Mercy, Roger Bacon
and Seton.
Ties: Indian Hill, St. Ursula, Summit Country Day and Ursuline
Academy.

The tournament:
Sectional
Peebles W, 7-0
Summit Country Day W, 6-0
District
Mariemont W, 4-1
Regionals
Bellbrook W, 2-0
Indian Hill W, 3-1
State Semifinals
Springfield Greenon W, 11-1
State Finals
Cuyahoga Falls Walsh Jesuit L, 4-1

Badin High School
Girls Soccer
1997 Division II State Runner-up

Head coach: Craig Manahan
Assistant coaches: Jill Carter, Steve Wolf

State program roster:
Seniors – Jenny Fiehrer, Emily Gersbach, Aimee Hurst, Megan McKnight, Lisa Sutton
Juniors – Amy Allen, Sarah Gaynor, Emily Giuliano, Christina Hinkel, Shannon Kuhl, Shannon Roberto, Lisa Vilkoski
Sophomores – Suzanne Dietz, Kerri Fiehrer, Brianne Giesting, Julie Rais, Amber Rue, Caitlin Wolf
Freshmen – Angela Vilkoski

Regular season: 12-1-3
Wins: Middletown Fenwick, Hamilton, Indian Hill, Kettering Alter, Lakota East, McNicholas, Mother of Mercy, Mount Notre Dame, Purcell Marian Roger Bacon, Springfield Greenon and Ursuline Academy.
Losses: McAuley.
Ties: Seton, St. Ursula and Summit Country Day.

The tournament:
Sectional
St. Bernard W, 8-0
Cincinnati Seven Hills W, 4-0
District
Cincinnati Roger Bacon W, 3-0
Regionals
Summit Country Day W, 2-0
Cincinnati McNicholas W, 3-1
State Semifinals
Kettering Alter W, 2-0
State Finals
Columbus DeSales L, 2-0

Badin High School
Girls Soccer
1996 Division II State Runner-up

Head coach: Craig Manahan
Assistant coach: Jill Carter

State program roster:
Seniors – Gina Andriacco, Erin Chafin, Erin Kraft, Sarah Vilkoski
Juniors – Jenny Fiehrer, Emily Gersbach, Aimee Hurst, Megan McKnight, Lisa Sutton
Sophomores – Amy Allen, Sarah Gaynor, Emily Giuliano, Christina Hinkel, Shannon Kuhl, Shannon Roberto, Lisa Vilkoski
Freshmen – Lindsay Andriacco, Kerri Fiehrer

Regular season: 10-2-3
Wins: Edgewood, Finneytown, Hamilton, Indian Hill, McNicholas, Mother of Mercy, Mount Notre Dame, Purcell Marian, Roger Bacon and Springfield Greenon.
Losses: McAuley and St. Ursula.
Ties: Middletown Fenwick, Seton and Ursuline Academy.

The tournament:
Sectional
Finneytown W, 10-1
District
Cincinnati Roger Bacon W, 3-0
Regionals
Indian Hill W, 3-1
Mariemont W, 3-0
State Semifinals
Bellbrook W, 4-0
State Finals
Chagrin Falls L, 1-0

Badin High School
Girls Soccer
1995 Division II State Runner-up

Head coach: Craig Manahan
Assistant coach: Jill Carter

State program roster:
Senior – Stacey Kuhl
Juniors – Erin Chafin, Erin Kraft, Sarah Vilkoski
Sophomores – Emily Gersbach, Aimee Hurst, Megan McKnight, Lisa Sutton
Freshmen – Amy Allen, Sarah Gaynor, Emily Giuliano, Christina Hinkel, Shannon Kuhl, Shannon Roberto, Lisa Vilkoski

Regular season: 10-5-1
Wins: Colerain, Edgewood, Finneytown, Hamilton, McNicholas, Mount Notre Dame, Purcell Marian, Roger Bacon, Talawanda and Wyoming.
Losses: Middletown Fenwick, McAuley, Mercy, Seton and St. Ursula.
Ties: Ursuline Academy.

The tournament:
Sectional
Hamilton Ross W, 5-0
Finneytown W, 3-0
District
Cincinnati Roger Bacon W, 2-0
Regionals
Kings Mills Kings W, 1-0
Clermont Northeastern W, 1-0
State Semifinals
Kettering Alter W, 2-0
State Finals
Columbus DeSales L, 1-0 (so)
(1-0 in sudden death penalty kick shootout)

Badin Girls Soccer, 1995-2013

1995
Record: 16-6-1
Head coach: Craig Manahan
Outcome: Lost the Division II state championship game to Columbus St. Francis DeSales on penalty kicks after a scoreless tie in regulation

1996:
Record: 15-3-3
Head coach: Craig Manahan
Outcome: Lost the Division II state championship game to Chagrin Falls, 1-0

1997
Record: 18-2-3
Head coach: Craig Manahan
Outcome: Lost the Division II state championship game to Columbus St. Francis DeSales, 2-0

1998
Record: 12-4-4
Head coach: Craig Manahan
Outcome: Lost the Division II district championship game to Roger Bacon, 2-1

1999
Record: 8-6-4
Head coach: Dan Cullen
Outcome: Lost the Division II district semifinal game to Wyoming, 3-0

2000
Record: 12-6-4
Head coach: Katy Brennan
Outcome: Lost the Division II state championship game to Cuyahoga Falls Walsh Jesuit, 4-1

2001
Record: 6-9-3
Head coach: Katy Brennan
Outcome: Lost the Division II district semifinal game to Indian Hill, 1-0

2002
Record: 8-9-2
Head coach: Keith Harring
Outcome: Lost the Division II district final game to Wyoming, 2-1

2003
Record: 8-8-3
Head coach: Keith Harring
Outcome: Lost the Division II district semifinal game to Fenwick, 3-1

2004
Record: 12-3-3
Head coach: Keith Harring
Outcome: Lost the Division II district championship game to Kettering Alter on penalty kicks

2005
Record: 18-3-2
Head coach: Keith Harring
Outcome: Won the Division II state championship, 2-1 over Doylestown Chippewa in overtime

2006
Record: 15-3-4
Head coach: Keith Harring
Outcome: Lost the Division II state championship game to Parma Heights Holy Name on penalty kicks after a scoreless tie in regulation

2007
Record: 17-6-1
Head coach: Keith Harring
Outcome: Lost the Division II state championship game to Shaker Heights Hathaway Brown, 2-0

2008
Record: 12-6-4
Head coach: Keith Harring
Outcome: Lost the Division II regional championship game to Madeira, 1-0

2009
Record: 11-5-4
Head coach: Keith Harring
Outcome: Lost the Division II regional semifinal game to Wyoming, 1-0

2010
Record: 10-8-3
Head coach: Steve Tabar
Outcome: Lost the Division II regional semifinal game to Indian Hill, 1-0

2011
Record: 7-10-2
Head coach: Steve Tabar
Outcome: Lost the Division III district championship game to Summit Country Day, 1-0

2012
Record: 13-3-3
Head coach: Steve Tabar
Outcome: Lost the Division III district championship game to Troy Christian, 2-1

2013
Record: 15-4-4
Head coach: Todd Berkely
Outcome: Won the Division III state championship game over Gates Mills Hawken on penalty kicks after a 2-2 tie in regulation.

Division I girls' soccer players from Badin High School

Kristina Anderson '07 – Ball State University
Megan Collins '02 – Morehead State University
Sydnee Fields '10 – Xavier University
Lauren Gersbach '03 – Butler University
Emily Giuliano '99 – North Carolina/Charlotte
Kim Golden '12 – Morehead State University
Sarah Graf '02 – Morehead State University
Bekah Hamblin '94 – Michigan State University
Shannon Kuhl '99 – University of Dayton
Stacey Kuhl '96 – Xavier University
Ashley Mahoney '12 – Kent State University
Lauren Mathews '12 – Miami University
Bridget McKnight '05 – Eastern Kentucky University
Megan McKnight '98 – University of Dayton
Abby Milillo '08 – Ball State University
Heather Rains '06 – University of Akron
Megan Reimer '08 – Gardner Webb University
Ashley Roberto '07 – North Carolina/Charlotte
Shannon Roberto '99 – North Carolina/Charlotte
Jenny Rosen '07 – Xavier University
Reba Sedlacek '02 – University of Dayton
Caitlin Wolf '00 – University of Dayton/Miami U.

Commitments as of 9/1/14
Malia Berkely '16 -- Florida State University
Madi Kah '15 -- Ohio University
Morgan Langhammer '15 -- University of Evansville
Annika Pater '15 -- Eastern Kentucky University

Acknowledgements

Thank you very much to the following people who offered input to this project, either by in-person interview, phone interview, or by e-mail. It would not have been possible without your assistance.

Maggie Adams '14
Kristina Anderson '07
Kate Bach '15
Malia Berkely '16
Nicole Berkely (parent)
Todd Berkely (coach)
Katy Brennan '93 (coach)
Sammi Burton '07
Megan Collins '02
Lindsey Donges '09
Emily Flum '08
Gabby Geigle '16
Joe Geigle (parent)
Kim Golden '12
Sarah Graf '02
Courtney Gray '08
Keith Harring (coach)
Michelle Hessling '14
Joe Hurst '71 (parent)
Madi Kah '15
Terry Kah (parent)
Sally Kocher (AD)
Shannon Kuhl Niemann '99
Stacey Kuhl Rhodis '96
Shelby Lamping '16

Morgan Langhammer '15
Craig Manahan (coach)
Ashley Mahoney '12
Lauren Mathews '12
Megan McKnight Mahle '98
Geoff Melzer '87 (AD)
Abby Milillo '08
Steve Milillo '73 (parent)
Ken Murrell (coach)
Annika Pater '15
Jeff Pohlman '77 (coach)
Dan Purcell (coach)
Heather Rains Smith '06
Holly Reed '14
Rachel Riley '16
Reba Sedlacek Thompson '02
Brianna Scowden '15
Amy Seither '14
Brian Smallwood (coach)
Lindsey Smith '07
Taylor Smith '16
Steph Streit '02
Steve Tabar (coach)
Angela Vilkoski Breetz '01

About the Author

Dirk Q. Allen is the director of admissions and media relations at Stephen T. Badin High School, the co-ed Catholic high school in Hamilton, Ohio. A native of Lakewood, Ohio, in suburban Cleveland, Allen is a graduate of Princeton High School in Cincinnati and Brown University in Providence, R.I. He was an award-winning journalist for more than two decades, including extended service as the sports editor, opinion page editor and managing editor of the JournalNews in Hamilton. In 2013, Allen received the Media Service Award from the Southwest District Board of the Ohio High School Athletic Association. He was also honored by the Greater Cincinnati/ Northern Kentucky Women's Sports Association for "demonstrating a commitment to educating the community about the benefits of sports for young girls and women, and for assisting in the advancement of girls' athletics." He lives in Oxford, Ohio.

Also by Dirk Q. Allen

"Notes for a Book" (published in 2013)
A powerful combination of fact, fiction and commentary that is simply hard to put down! In six compelling chapters, Allen displays a deft touch and sharp focus on the world around us. Readers will be making their own mental notes about the things that matter most. It's an eclectic mix of thought-provoking material that delivers a clear-eyed view of life as we know it.

192 pages
ISBN # 978-1-4575-2387-8
Dog Ear Publishing, Indianapolis, Ind.
Available via dirkqallen.com and amazon.com in print and e-book format

"Good Tears"
"Badin High Girls Basketball -- 10 years to a title"
Published in 2000, this book chronicles the decade-long march to the Ohio Division II girls' basketball championship by the dedicated Badin High School girls program. A tale of trauma, tragedy and finally triumph, "Good Tears" tells the story of a determined group of student-athletes who battled to the 1998 state title, an afternoon in March 1998 when the Badin girls' basketball team finally learned what it was like to shed "good tears."

320 pages, including photos and statistics
ISBN # 0-615-11595-0
C.J. Krehbiel Co., Cincinnati, Ohio

Front row from left: Holly Reed, Brianna Scowden, Ali Kalberer, Shelby Lamping, Annika Pater, Kate Bach, Madi Kah, Michelle Hessling, Taylor Smith, Katie Pohlman, Amy Seither, Emily Henson and Nicole Visse.

Top row from left: Lindsey Brinck, Sam Lehker, Sabrina Bernardo, Maggie Adams, Lydia Braun, Morgan Langhammer, Rachel Riley, Jessica Stein, Morgan Deitschel, Gaby Ems, Maddie Smith, assistant coach Jeff Pohlman and assistant coach Ken Murrell.

Not on hand for the halftime recognition were head coach Todd Berkely and his daughter, sophomore Malia Berkely, who'd taken the red-eye Friday night for a college visit to UCLA!

Members of the Badin High School girls state championship soccer team hold hands as they walk onto the football field to be recognized on Saturday, Nov. 9, 2013, the night after they won the Ohio Division III state title, 3-2 in a penalty kick shootout over Gates Mills Hawken at Columbus Crew Stadium. Photos by Terri Adams.

9 781457 533655